ALL IN

ALL IN

Memoirs of the Freshworks Founder

GIRISH MATHRUBOOTHAM
WITH PANKAJ MISHRA

HARPER BUSINESS
An Imprint of HarperCollins *Publishers*

First published in India by Harper Business 2025
An imprint of HarperCollins *Publishers*
HarperCollins *Publishers* India, Cyber City, Building 10-A, Gurugram,
Haryana – 122002, India
www.harpercollins.co.in

2 4 6 8 10 9 7 5 3 1

P-ISBN: 978-93-6989-747-6
E-ISBN: 978-93-6989-458-1

Typeset in 11.5/15.5 Garamond Premier Pro at
HarperCollins *Publishers* India

Printed and bound at
Replika Press Pvt. Ltd.

MIX
Paper | Supporting responsible forestry
FSC
www.fsc.org
FSC™ C016779

This book is produced from independently certified FSC® paper to ensure responsible forest management.

HarperCollins Publishers, Macken House, 39/40 Mayor Street Upper, Dublin 1, D01 C9W8, Ireland

In loving memory of my appa, R Mathrubootham

'The Man in the Arena'

It is not the critic who counts;
not the man who points out how the strong man stumbles
or where the doer of deeds could have done them better.
The credit belongs to the man who is actually in the arena,
whose face is marred by dust and sweat and blood;
who strives valiantly; who errs, and who comes short again and again,
because there is no effort without error and shortcoming;
but who does actually strive to do the deeds;
who knows the great enthusiasms, the great devotions;
who spends himself in a worthy cause;
who at the best knows in the end the triumph of high achievement,
and who at the worst, if he fails, at least fails while daring greatly,
so that his place shall never be with those cold and timid souls who neither
know victory nor defeat.

Theodore Roosevelt,
'Citizenship in a Republic',
address at the Sorbonne in Paris, France, 23 April 1910

Contents

SECTION 1

BAMBARAM

The Spin of Grit, Falls and Rise

Chapter 1

I can still feel the raw string between my fingers, its tautness growing with my excitement as I wound it carefully around the cone of the bambaram.

There was something magical about those evenings in Trichy when the world slowed down after the day's bustle. Monkeys swung from tree branches along our street, their chatter blending with the distant hum of vehicles, a sound like the drone of bees. The soft October breeze carried with it a soothing stillness, and it was just me and my bambaram—what the spinning top is called in Tamil.

Mine wasn't one of those glossy, plastic toys you see on Amazon nowadays. It was rough-hewn, carved from wood, with a nail jutting out of its conical end—a simple, unpolished toy that held the magic of a hundred perfect moments.

I checked the cord again, fingers brushing the smoothened edge of the nail poking out of the coiled string. It was ready. So was I.

With a quick flick of my wrist, the bambaram was off—hitting the ground with a satisfying thud, springing to life with a whizz. I'd watch it whirl, fast and steady, kicking up faint spirals of dust. In that moment, nothing else mattered. No noise, no worries—just the little top spinning on the ground, holding my complete attention.

I was an eager, chubby, dark-skinned boy. At home, they called me 'Srikanth'. I attended Campion Anglo-Indian Higher Secondary School, one of the best schools in Trichy, run by the Montfort Brothers. We wore neat uniforms—blue shorts, a white shirt, a tie, a belt and polished black shoes. But the moment I got home, I'd shed that uniform like shedding another identity, transforming from 'Girish' at school to the familiar 'Srikanth' within the walls of home.

Mornings in Trichy began in the cool, pre-dawn quiet, as the first light traced the outlines of coconut leaves and weathered brick walls. I'd roll off the floor beside my father, folding my mat and tucking it away with practiced care.

The red oxide floor was cool and smooth underfoot—no fancy tiles or marble, just burnished red, polished by time and countless footsteps. Looking back now, the simplicity of that ritual—rolling up our mats in the quiet of a waking house—felt like the only life we ever needed.

Saturdays came with their own charm. I'd pull on my NCC army uniform, the stiff fabric making me stand a little taller, imagining myself as a proud cadet. Two hours of drills and marching left me ravenous. The two small pooris and masala served after parade practice barely sated me, so I'd head straight to Mumtaz Cafe. There, a steaming plate of appam and egg korma awaited—a simple but delicious meal after a morning of pretending to be a soldier.

—

I was always surrounded by friends—restless, eager and constantly moving from one game to the next. Football, cricket, chess—anything that promised excitement was fair game. Plans were often half-formed, but that never stopped us. I was always ready to dive in, fuelled by the sheer thrill of the moment.

Outside of school, my wardrobe was simple: shorts, a half-sleeved shirt and sometimes just an inner vest on lazy afternoons. My shirts were always stitched, never store-bought, with hems that didn't always sit perfectly but felt comfortable and familiar. There was a kind of freedom in that outfit—it let me climb trees, kick a ball, or roam the neighbourhood with ease.

Our home was a patchwork of old and new. The older section, with its red-tiled roof, had weathered gracefully over the years, while the newer, two-story concrete wing was added after my parents' marriage. The house sprawled across more than two grounds (about 5,400 sq. ft.), shaded by eight towering coconut trees and five mango trees, along with scattered papaya, guava and neem trees.

Behind the house was our little farm. A shed housed three cows and two buffaloes, their presence a constant rhythm in our lives. Fresh cow dung was pressed into cakes and dried against the wall, later used as fuel for the kitchen. There was no geyser; hot water came from firewood burning under a tin shed in the backyard. Winters meant heating water in a brass pot and mixing it with cold water in a bucket for a warm bath. Summers, however, were for wild joy—I turned the outdoor water tank into my personal swimming pool, splashing about with glee to everyone's dismay.

A gate led to a shaded porch at the front of our house, a quiet space that came alive with daily rituals. In the summer, we draped the porch with a pandal made of dried coconut leaves to keep the heat at bay. Every morning, my father sat there with his newspaper and coffee, reading each page meticulously, as if it held secrets of the world. I'd join him sometimes, watching as he folded the sheets with precision, the crackle of the paper punctuating the stillness.

On mornings when the air was particularly still, the occasional bark of a distant dog would echo faintly through the neighbourhood. Once my father finished reading, the porch transformed into our cricket pitch. The folded newspaper was set aside, and I'd grab my bat, swinging for sixes that soared over the gate and into the front yard.

Our street, Ramarao Agraharam, was a narrow stretch lined with houses as different as the people who lived there. Across from our home stood the Raju Estates bungalow—a sprawling property with manicured lawns and imposing wrought-iron gates. It exuded an air of elegance that felt worlds apart from the simplicity of our own house.

It was more than just a grand property—it was the home of my friend, Rajesh Raju.

His family owned the first television I ever saw, and that TV became a magnet for half the neighbourhood. We'd gather in their polished, comfortable living room, Rajesh's family seated on soft sofas with a swing by the window. A few of us kids would perch on the staircase, craning our necks for a glimpse as Doordarshan flickered to life, feeling like we'd stumbled into a little slice of magic. Returning to my home afterward was always a jarring contrast. We had simple folding chairs made of plastic and steel, besides a wooden armchair that had seen better days. But there was a sense of comfort in the familiarity, in the no-frills warmth of our space.

Next door lived Dr Kannan and his family. Their car was a spectacle in itself: a sleek, dark-green Mitsubishi Lancer, rare and commanding, almost mythical in our neighbourhood. It glided down the street like royalty, gleaming under the sun, and heads turned instinctively as it passed. Nobody said, 'There goes Dr Kannan.' Instead, they said, 'There goes Dr Kannan's car!'

There was something about that car—a symbol of power and ambition—that stirred questions inside me.

What would people say when they saw me coming? Would they know my name? Would I have an identity at all?

Then there was Sukesh's family. They had stacks of *Phantom, Tintin* and *Asterix* comics piled high, enough to fill entire afternoons with adventure and laughter. Those comic books offered me an escape, a doorway into worlds filled with larger-than-life heroes and wild journeys, vicarious thrills that left me breathless.

—

Once in a while, something came along to break the pattern, to add colour and sound.

Diwali was our explosion of colour, the one day that shattered the monotony. My father and I would buy crackers by the dozen weeks in advance, mapping out a meticulous schedule for the night before the festival and Diwali morning itself. By dawn, the preparations began. My grandmother would ready us with an oil bath, her warm hands pressing heated oil onto our skin in a soothing, ritualistic embrace.

Once bathed and dressed, we started with the grandest display: the garland bombs. Long strings of explosions tore through the morning silence, leaving echoes that lingered in the air. My uncle, ever the adventurer, would bring us onion bombs from his travels—small but powerful crackers that we'd hurl to the ground, each one bursting into a loud cloud of smoke. By the end of the morning, the street looked like a battlefield of red paper and charred casings, the smell of sulphur hanging in the air. It felt monumental, a day that vibrated with life.

And then, as always, the quiet returned. The rhythms of daily life reclaimed their place, but those small rituals—grounded and familiar—kept me tethered.

Our home was surrounded by coconut trees, their neat rows giving the space a serene, grove-like charm. Beyond the trees lay our small farm, where our buffaloes and cows lived. Every weekend, my father and I would walk out to bathe them, a task that turned into something more. We'd lather them with Lifebuoy soap, a simple but tender ritual. It was our way of showing love, an unspoken bond that held its own significance in our grounded world.

The mango trees in our backyard were my personal treasure. I'd devour those mangoes with abandon, sinking my teeth into their juicy flesh, unbothered by the mess. It was pure, unpolished joy—the kind that defines childhood.

Papayas, on the other hand, were the neighbourhood monkeys' delight. They treated our papaya tree as their personal buffet, feasting with reckless glee. None of us complained much; papayas were never popular in our family.

Life, though, has its way of bringing things full circle. These days, with diabetes reshaping my diet, papayas have become a staple. Once dismissed, they're now a daily companion—a reminder of how time softens and reshapes our relationships with the world around us.

—

My father was like a banyan tree—steady, serene and quietly sheltering everyone under his care. He never commanded a room, preferring instead to observe from the sidelines with a calm, grounding presence that made you feel safe.

He wasn't tall or lean, just of average height with a slight potbelly that he never seemed to mind. His thick-framed spectacles, perched squarely on his nose, lent him a look that was both serious and gentle. His wardrobe was simple and predictable: neatly pressed Raymond trousers paired with checked shirts in big square patterns, alternating between light and dark. At home, he'd trade those shirts for a dhoti and a sleeved baniyan, lounging on the porch in the evenings, content to catch any passing breeze.

On sweltering nights, we'd roll out our mats and sleep under the stars, my father beside me, his presence a comforting constant against the vast, open sky.

He was soft-spoken, never one to raise his voice, yet discipline was his domain. His 'no' was unyielding in tone but rarely final. I learned quickly that persistence usually turned it into a 'yes'. It was a game my sons now play with me, carrying on the tradition.

I can still hear him from downstairs: 'Srikanth! Come down immediately.'

I'd groan, abandon whatever I was doing, and trek down to find him waiting in the hall. 'Switch off the bedroom lights,' he'd say.

'You know, you could've just switched them off yourself,' I'd reply, half exasperated, half amused.

'You have to get into the habit of switching off the lights when leaving the room,' he'd say firmly. To him, every flick of a switch, every rupee saved, mattered. These small lessons, ingrained in his everyday actions, were his way of teaching me the value of the little things.

Among his siblings, my father commanded quiet respect. They leaned on his steady authority for decisions, even though he never demanded it. He was, without question, the head of the family. His younger brother, Ganesan, brought humour to the household, with original jokes and witty remarks that kept everyone laughing.

When Ganesan married, his wife—my Chitthi—joined our bustling home, and soon after, Aunt Seetha and her husband moved into the side portion my father had built. Ganesan worked at Nerolac Paints, fifteen steps from home, and he'd joke about the 'terrible traffic' and demand someone 'drop him home' after work! My father's amused chuckles at these antics made their camaraderie a bright spot in our busy household.

In his own quiet way, my father provided for everyone. No complaints, no fanfare—just a calm sense of duty. He was the quiet heart of our home, making sure everything kept moving, even if we hardly noticed it.

He was strict but never harsh, teaching us not through words but through his steady, unwavering example. His lessons were simple but profound, shaping us in ways we only came to appreciate much later.

Mom was a whirlwind—a burst of energy that filled every corner of our home. Bold and unstoppable, she was a force in constant motion. Even our daily routines seemed to carry her momentum.

I can still feel the sharp tug of her comb through my hair, followed by a quick smack on the head if I flinched. I'd sit there, hands clenched, staring at the floor, holding my breath so I wouldn't disrupt her rhythm. It's funny, the things that stick.

She loved to travel—the thrill of being somewhere new, somewhere different. I think she picked it up from movies, her escape into a world of possibilities. But life didn't match the dreams she had stitched together from those films. My father didn't have the means or the time to indulge them, and so she carried on, fiercely independent, making friends wherever she went, never waiting for anyone.

Then everything shifted. One day, she was there, vibrant and unstoppable; the next, she was gone. I was seven when my parents divorced, and my mother left. The house felt quieter, heavier, as if her absence had drained something essential from the walls. I didn't have the words to describe what I felt, but I knew something had been taken from me.

In her absence, my father became everything. He was the pillar holding up the sky, the one everyone leaned on. After my grandfather passed away, he carried not only the responsibility of raising me but also the weight of his siblings' needs. Supporting two brothers and five sisters, he stepped into his father's shoes without complaint. But even his strength came at a cost. It stretched him thin, and maybe, just maybe, that was why my mother left.

—

A quiet bond grew between my father and me—a constant, like the steady pulse of life in our small home on Ramarao Agraharam street. Weekends became our sacred time. Every Saturday, he'd come back from work with garlic khara sev from Balaji Ramana Bakery, its sharp, fried aroma filling the air. We'd sit together, savouring handfuls of crispy sev, and for a while, the world was uncomplicated. Even now, the smell of garlic sev takes me back to those moments.

Sundays had their own charm. Early in the morning, just the two of us would slip out for breakfast. We'd find a small cafe and order idlis or dosas, but it wasn't the food that mattered—it was the ritual, the quiet comfort of being together.

He made the harder parts of school easier too. Biology, with its endless diagrams, was my nemesis. The human ear, with its intricate parts and labels, felt like a puzzle in a foreign language. The only thing I felt confident drawing was an amoeba—it was formless, so I couldn't get it wrong.

But my father, steady as ever, would sit beside me, breaking it down piece by piece. 'The ear has three main parts...' he'd begin, explaining in simple terms and making sure I followed every step. Then he'd make me repeat it back to him until I got it right.

He was teaching me much more than biology. He was training me to think clearly, structure my thoughts and find a pattern in how things connected. Looking back, those lessons were more than just schoolwork—they were the building blocks of storytelling, the first steps in finding structure and flow.

He had a way of keeping me on track without holding me back. On restless afternoons, when my friends were spinning bambarams on the street or Sachin was at bat on TV, he'd sigh and say, 'All right, go for a while, but then come back and study.' It was a small, unspoken agreement between us—a give-and-take that kept me grounded and moving forward.

In his own, steady way, my father taught me balance: How to pause without losing momentum, how to bend without breaking. Even now, I carry that lesson with me—a quiet strength, woven into the person I've become.

—

I didn't fully understand what it meant to grow up without a mother until much later. As a child, it felt like a hole I couldn't name, an absence that shaped the edges of my world. The lessons I learned—lessons people often uncover through years of therapy or soul-searching—came at a steep price. They stole from me the ability to express emotion, to be vulnerable.

My greatest loss in life wasn't a business deal or a missed opportunity; it was the simple human capacity to show love.

Love, they say, is something you learn from your parents. But that wasn't my experience. For years, I struggled to express affection, even when I desperately wanted to. It felt impossible, as though a crucial piece of me was missing. I've come a long way since then, but getting here took time, effort and more reflection than I care to admit.

Beyond my father, my aunts and uncles—especially Aunt Seetha—stepped in to help ease the pain of my mother's absence. Aunt Seetha tried to fill the gaps in her own way: warm meals, gentle reassurances and an unwavering presence. She softened the edges of my mother's absence.

Still, something inside me never quite settled. Her care was a balm, not a cure, for the void I carried.

But life can shift when you least expect it, pulling you into a new reality without warning.

One evening, when I was twelve, I came home from school in my usual whirlwind—dropping my bag, yanking off my tie and flinging my belt onto a chair as I made a beeline for the kitchen. But something stopped me cold. A woman I'd never seen before stood at the stove, stirring something in a pan. She moved like she belonged there, but to me, she was a stranger.

I froze in the doorway, staring. Who was she? Why was she here? Without a word, I turned and sprinted to my grandmother, breathless.

'Who's that in the kitchen?'

'Oh,' she replied, hardly looking up, 'she's here to help with cooking and the household chores.'

Her nonchalance calmed me, and I shrugged it off as just another addition to the day. But in reality, she was already part of our family—married to my father just days earlier. I just hadn't known. The truth would come later, dropped in a conversation with Aunt Seetha. But back then, she was simply the cook to me.

Over the next few months, the woman settled into her role, moving through the house quietly, preparing meals and handling chores. I noticed her, of course, but brushed it aside—she was just a helper, nothing more.

Then one day, everything changed.

I was standing at the front door, waiting for my father. It was supposed to be our usual monthly movie outing, a ritual I always looked forward to. But the minutes ticked by, and he didn't come out. I paced, glancing back at his door, wondering what was keeping him.

Finally, the door opened—but it wasn't my father. It was her. She was dressed and ready to leave. My heart sank as my father stepped out behind her. He wasn't waiting for me; he was waiting for her.

A sharp ache shot through my chest. What was going on? Why were they leaving together? What did this mean?

We all went to see the movie together—*Agni Nakshatram*—but the questions lingered, gnawing at me.

The next day, Aunt Seetha pulled me aside. Her voice was gentle, but her words hit me like a punch to the gut.

'She's not just here to help with cooking,' she began. 'Your father married her. She's your stepmother. We didn't tell you before...We thought it might be too much for you to understand.'

I stood there, stunned. My mind raced, but no answers came. Why hadn't anyone told me? Why did I have to find out like this? All I knew was that everything had changed.

I couldn't accept it. I didn't want a new mother. The very idea felt painful, like a betrayal. My father had moved on without me, and that woman—how could I possibly see her as part of my life?

I couldn't. I didn't.

From that moment on, every interaction with her became a battle. I didn't want her in my life, and she made no effort to fill the void. Her presence felt like an intruder's, and the anger inside me only grew. The fragile sense of control I clung to was slipping through my fingers, and I couldn't stop it.

Rebellion was my escape. I fought back against this new reality, pushing away my father, her, and anyone who reminded me of how powerless I was.

It wasn't just that I had lost control; it was the betrayal of decisions made without me, choices that had upended my world and left me with no say.

The delicate balance I'd tried to build, the one that had held me together, shattered like glass. I was left spinning in a storm of anger and confusion, unsure of where I fit or what I could hold on to.

In my mind, rebellion felt like reclaiming my life. But in reality, all it left me with was a hollow ache—a reminder that pushing people away didn't fill the void. It only made it deeper.

—

My stepmom was a small woman, barely five feet tall, but her presence filled the room like a storm cloud. She'd grown up in a rural village, never went to college and spoke with a bluntness that could cut through steel. Arguments seemed to be her natural language, and she sparred with everyone—me, my father's sisters, even my father. Whenever tempers flared, she'd wield my mother's absence like a weapon, her scathing remarks cutting through me. It was a reminder of what I'd lost and of the gap she could never fill.

Every morning, like clockwork, a plate of rice, dal and vegetables waited for me at 7:25 sharp. But there was no one to eat it with. I'd sit alone at the table, the house quiet except for the clink of my spoon. Those meals, solitary and mechanical, left a mark. Even now, eating alone brings back those memories, the silence as heavy as the food.

At night, it was the same. I'd come home to an empty dining room, my plate waiting while everyone else had already finished. She was prickly, but she made sure I was fed—at least at first. But as things between her and my father deteriorated, some days she just wouldn't cook anything at all. The fights would leave the house in a heavy silence, pressing down, hollowing out my stomach.

She could be ruthless in arguments. At first, I fought back, but I quickly realized that engaging with her only made things worse. Her anger was relentless, feeding on my words like fuel. So I stopped. I learned the power of restraint, of staying calm and holding my ground. When I kept quiet, her anger would swell, but it felt like I had won. Those moments taught me a lesson I carry to this day: the silent strength of choosing not to react.

The worst moments weren't the big fights but the small humiliations. Once, I asked my dad for ₹20 to watch a movie with friends. Instead of handing it to me, he left the money hidden on a shelf, as if it was something forbidden I had to sneak away with. It felt humiliating, as if my small request for happiness was something shameful.

Even for little things like pocket money, the constant struggle wore me down. My father was trying to avoid conflict with her, but it left me feeling like I had to beg for what should have been freely given. The fights over small things taught me something, though—they sharpened my instincts and honed my ability to choose my battles.

It was like the bambaram, the spinning top from my childhood: the harder you try to control it, the more it wobbles and falls. But if you let it spin freely, it finds its balance. So, I began to distance myself—not just from the conflicts at home, but from anything that threatened to unsteady me.

I promised myself, 'I'm not going to give the remote control of my happiness to anyone.' And I meant it.

Chapter 2

LOOKING back, life in Trichy was a patchwork of routines and small comforts, stitched together with moments of fleeting joy. Yet beneath its warmth ran deep fractures—a mother's absence, a stepmom whose presence was as sharp as it was unyielding, and silences that seemed to linger longer than they should.

Amid the quiet complexities of home, school became my sanctuary—a world with its own structure, rules and rhythms. At Campion Higher Secondary, where I studied from UKG to Class 10, I found order and even escape.

The library became my refuge. In Enid Blyton's adventures and Hardy Boys' mysteries, I discovered stability and adventure. Later, Sidney Sheldon, Jeffrey Archer and Arthur Hailey opened up more intricate worlds, places where chaos had reason and endings made sense. Those books were more than stories—they were lifelines to a reality I could control, where I could freely enter and leave.

Sports became another outlet. I wasn't the fastest or the strongest, but chess stuck with me in a way no other game did. Its quiet intensity mirrored something inside me. Even today, I start my mornings with a chess puzzle—a small ritual that keeps me sharp.

Cricket, though, was a fever. The whole country lived and breathed it, and Trichy was no exception. Our neighbourhood had its own 'field,' a patch of dirt and gravel that transformed into a stadium when we stepped onto it. We didn't have proper gear—just stumps fashioned from sticks and a rubber ball—but it didn't matter. In those moments, we were cricketers, competing in our own 'street leagues' that felt as intense as any international match.

Outside school, I took Hindi lessons at the Dakshina Bharat Hindi Prachar Sabha. Between Class 6 and 11, I progressed from Prathmik to Visharad Uttarardh, just one semester shy of earning the equivalent of a bachelor's degree in Hindi literature. Even today, it amuses me how my North Indian friends unconsciously assume I don't understand Hindi. They'll speak freely around me, only to apologize and translate when they remember I'm from Chennai.

Those lessons gave me more than language. They introduced me to Babu, a classmate in whose home I would continue the studies. His mother, an exceptional cook, would prepare a delectable chicken starter during our study sessions. My first bite was a revelation—the rich, savoury flavours an entirely new world for a TamBram vegetarian boy like me. It was a moment of crossing a threshold, one that would shape my relationship with food forever.

Those school days were filled with simple pleasures. Right outside the gates, street vendors lined up with trays of candy, Pepsi Colas and Paneer Sodas. Pocket money was scarce, but occasionally, my grandmother would slip me some change. Thanks to her generosity, I could join my friends in savouring those small, cherished luxuries.

Looking back, those small pleasures—the library books, the cricket matches and the candy outside the gates—were fragments of a childhood that, despite its complexities, taught me resilience, curiosity and the joy of discovery. They were the rhythms that steadied me, shaping who I would become.

—

Leaving Campion after Class 10 felt like trading a starched uniform for something looser, freer. I switched to ER High School—Edayatru Mangalam Rangasamy Iyer Higher Secondary School—shedding prestige for a place where rules bent more easily, and routines started with the sun, not the clock. Campion kicked off at 8 a.m. sharp; ER didn't start until 10, and on Amavasya, the 'no-moon' days, classes pushed back to 10.50 a.m. That kind of freedom was hard to ignore.

At Campion, life moved in orderly rows. ER, in contrast, was wild and unpredictable. It was my first taste of a world beyond discipline. Most of my friends were there, and I convinced my father that the switch would be better for my marks—and my sanity.

ER felt more like college than school. The uniform was khaki pants and white shirts, but I often stashed a casual T-shirt in my bag for quick swaps. My uncle would drop me off in the morning, and I'd head straight to the tea shop with friends. Class or a film? Most times, movies won.

We watched everything, from Rajinikanth blockbusters to obscure dramas. Without YouTube or reviews, I became the film critic of our group, the one deciding which films were worth the ticket.

The thrill of rebellion seeped into everything. I tried alcohol for the first time, smoked my first cigarette and wandered the grounds like a free agent. By 10.30 a.m., just after the first period, the canteen would tempt us with the smell of fresh bondas and bajji. Heart pounding, we'd sneak out to beat the crowd, snagging a few before the trays emptied. It felt like rebellion but tasted like freedom.

Even in the chaos, there were pockets of discipline. Chemistry had been my Everest until Professor Thyagarajan took me under his wing. He agreed to tutor me and my friend Ashok, but only if we arrived at his door by 6 a.m. Every morning, we'd wait outside by 5.50, the street still quiet. He made organic chemistry come alive, and by the end, I scored 184 out of 200. It was a reminder that the right teacher can make the impossible seem achievable.

Classes at ER were packed to the brim. In computer science, 115 students crammed into one room. The Biology Tamil section had 165 kids, forcing us to clamber over desks just to find a seat. It was a zoo, but it was *our* zoo. In the back rows, we'd tear into our lunch hours before the break, the smell of tamarind rice giving us away. Teachers would mutter sarcastic remarks but that was it.

Life at ER was much more than academics—it was life in raw form. Attendance was optional for some of us; a quick 'Yes, Sir!' in the right tone was enough to dodge scrutiny.

Video games were a world of their own. At Super Bazaar in Trichy, I'd step into that dimly lit arcade, where the air buzzed with the static hum of machines and the flicker of neon screens. With his relentless jumps and frantic dashes, Mario was more than just a game; he was a tiny hero fighting his way through impossible odds. Contra felt like a battlefield—each level demanding precision and nerves as I guided my character through waves of enemies. Each coin I dropped felt like a passport to another world, a brief reprieve from reality.

Sometimes, though, my rebellion crossed a line. My uncle suspected me of using drugs, though I'd never touched them. One evening, he confronted me, his face mixed with fear and accusation. Anger flared, and I shouted back. That's when he raised his belt, striking me hard. Without thinking, I grabbed a bottle and threw it at him. It shattered against the wall, missing him by inches. He stared, shocked, and then said quietly, 'Do whatever you want with your life,' before walking away. It wasn't hate—I understand that now. It was fear, the worry of a guardian trying to steer a young, restless kid in the right direction—tough love in its bluntest form. Anger, maybe, but no hate.

Freedom became an obsession after that. Once, after an argument at home, I left and stayed at a friend's house for three days without telling anyone. The thrill of disappearing, of living on my own terms, was intoxicating—but short-lived. By the third day, a relative tracked me down, his face a mix of relief and disbelief. My runaway attempt was over.

Looking back, my time at ER wasn't about academic excellence or conventional discipline. It was about learning to navigate chaos, finding freedom's limits, and understanding the balance between rebellion and responsibility. It was a life of routines and rebellion, a mix of order and disorder that shaped me, one hard-earned lesson at a time.

Chapter 3

THE year 1992 was supposed to be the one when my plans came together. Fresh from my Class 12 exams, engineering was my future, meticulously mapped out. But instead of unfolding as I had envisioned it, the year turned into a series of unexpected setbacks—each one chipping away at the confidence I had worked so hard to build.

My vacation was planned: A trip to Chennai, where I would stay with my aunt and cousins and enrol in an entrance coaching class. But Chennai had other plans for me. Instead of attending coaching sessions, I found myself swept up in the vibrant energy of the city. My cousins introduced me to a new world of English music—Michael Jackson, Madonna, MLTR, Pink Floyd—and our days were spent immersed in chess, Monopoly and the magic of *Qayamat Se Qayamat Tak*. The film, already three years into its run, cast a spell over us, its songs and story making the outside world fade away.

During those weeks, studies became an afterthought. My entrance exam score reflected that: 32.9 out of 50. It wasn't disastrous, but it wasn't stellar either—especially in the fiercely competitive engineering entrance arena. Still, I clung to the belief that my Class 12 marks, combined with my entrance score, would secure me a spot in a Tier 2 college.

Then came the blow I hadn't anticipated. A conflict between the Central and Tamil Nadu education boards changed the rules overnight: only entrance exam scores would count for admissions. My Class 12 performance, my ace in the hole, was now meaningless.

One lazy morning in Chennai, I was savouring a rich filter coffee from my aunt and flipping through *The Hindu* when my uncle pulled up a chair beside me. A man of few words and towering expectations, he rarely spoke to me directly, but when he did, his words carried weight.

'What's your plan for life?' he asked, his tone sharp and probing.

I folded the newspaper, meeting his gaze with as much confidence as I could muster. 'I will finish engineering and go to the US for my master's,' I replied firmly.

His laugh wasn't just dismissive—it was cutting, laced with disdain. 'With marks like yours? You're only good enough to pull a rickshaw, not go to the US.' His words hit like a slap, the sting lingering as I walked away. Tears burned at the corners of my eyes, but I blinked them back, vowing silently to prove him wrong—not for his approval, but for myself.

When my engineering dreams crumbled, I found myself enrolling in a BSc in chemistry at St Joseph's College. It felt like settling for something lesser—not just for me, but for my father, whose disappointment hung in the air like an unspoken accusation.

His disapproval was not just about my academic path. It was the company I kept, the friends who seemed more like distractions than inspirations—the kind he feared would derail me completely. One evening, he pulled me aside, his voice firm but calm.

'If I could get you into engineering,' he asked, 'would you take it?'

'Yes, Appa,' I said without hesitation.

This wasn't about the coveted IITs or the NIT in our hometown—those were out of reach. Even Tier 2 and Tier 3 colleges seemed unattainable on merit alone. But my father wasn't ready to give up. Determined, he took me to Shanmugha College of Engineering (now SASTRA University) to inquire about a management quota seat.

They were willing to offer one, but at a price: ₹75,000 in capitation fee—an amount my father didn't have.

Unfazed, Appa reached out to his younger brother for support. My uncle didn't mince words: 'Don't waste it on him. Don't wade into the river riding a sand horse.' These were his exact words, clearly advising my dad that I was not worth betting on. And considering where I was in life at that point, maybe he was right.

But my father wasn't ready to let go. Turning to another uncle, Swaminathan—known in the family for his financial savvy—he made his case. Uncle Swaminathan, with his characteristic calm, listened and then acted. He broke some fixed deposits and extended a loan, enabling me to secure a place in the Electrical and Electronics programme at SASTRA.

The money from Uncle Swaminathan had given me a second chance. A chance my father fought for when others had written me off. That seat at SASTRA wasn't just an admission—it was the start of a journey I would have to prove was worth every rupee.

My first day at college felt surreal. Sitting in a lecture hall teeming with students and listening to professors drone on, I reflected on the winding path that had brought me here. My father had placed his hopes on me, and there was no turning back. This was my second chance.

Hostel life in the first year was an odd mix of freedom and longing. Sharing a sprawling, noisy room with nine others taught me resilience, but it also underscored how much I missed the comforts of home. Privacy was a luxury we rarely enjoyed, and every interaction was a lesson in coexistence. My roommates ranged from the generous to the cutthroat, those always on the verge of conflict and others simply trying to get through each day. It felt like survival training—a safe zone where resilience was built without real consequences.

Meals were another challenge. Once or twice a week, we endured kanji, a porridge that tested our patience. On other days, uthappam came in giant steel drums delivered on squeaky tricycles. Arrive early, and you'd get a warm piece. Arrive late, and you'd be left with something cold, limp and barely edible. We carried our own plates and tumblers, washed them ourselves and learned to appreciate the gritty camaraderie that came with self-reliance.

In other moments, the hostel became a place of unexpected lessons. I often hung out with a group of mechanical engineering students, our conversations drifting from classes to movies to obscure topics. Over time, I noticed a strange phenomenon: The more I was around, the less they seemed to notice me. Then there was Jayakannan, a quiet guy from Erode who rarely joined us. But when he did, everyone paid attention. It was a lesson in boundaries and overexposure—realizations I would carry with me for years.

Most of my hostel friends managed with ₹600 to ₹1,000 a month in pocket money. Appa, cautious as ever, devised a plan to avoid spoiling me. He told the hostel warden, 'I don't want to give him cash. His meals are covered in the mess, but he needs essentials like toothpaste, soap and notebooks. I'll leave money with you. When he asks, buy what he needs, but don't hand him cash.'

It was practical, but it left me cash-strapped. Necessity sparked my entrepreneurial streak. Back then, at SASTRA, in the middle of 200 acres, running out of essentials meant a long trek or a borrowed moped to town. I pitched an idea to my friends: 'Tell me what you need—cosmetics, groceries, books. I'll make a list, give it to the warden, and he'll buy it. I'll bring it to your room for cash.' The warden became my personal delivery service, my personal Zepto (or Blinkit), and soon, I had found a way to collect my pocket money in cash.

One weekend, just before my birthday, I went home to Trichy with plans for a celebration—a movie and a few beers with friends. Hoping for an extra ₹500, I asked Appa. He refused outright. Frustrated, I decided not to return to the hostel immediately. Instead, I announced I'd stay home until he relented.

SASTRA's hostel rules were strict. Missing the warden's rounds meant trouble. My friends covered for me, saying I was showering or napping. It worked for a few days until the warden caught on. My rebellion unravelled, and I was suspended, requiring my father to come and explain things to the college.

The principal was firm but willing to listen. After hearing my case, he asked me to write an apology letter. Thanks to my schooling at Campion, my strong English skills came to the rescue. When the principal read my letter, he paused, amused. 'Your writing,' he said, 'is as elegant as that of King

Henry VI!' My English professor, who had lent me novels, nodded along, more entertained than upset by my mischief. That day, I learned how words and a bit of charm could sway situations.

But there was a twist. Just as Appa arrived, a polytechnic teacher, viewing himself as a moral guardian, walked in. 'Your son is a chain-smoker,' he declared. 'I've seen it myself.' 'No, Sir. I quit smoking months ago,' I protested. 'Shut up, man! The stain on your teeth says it all,' he thundered.

My father's response was calm and unwavering: 'Those stains are from Pan Parag, Sir, not cigarettes.' The teacher, taken aback, had no choice but to let it go. Appa's humour and firm belief in me were a reminder that he had my back when it mattered most.

Chess remained my anchor throughout college. The chessboard taught me lessons beyond strategy: Anticipate, respect your opponent, stay focused and keep emotions in check.

Exams were another arena for proving myself. My approach was unconventional but surprisingly effective. I relied on my photographic memory and visual recall, often seeing pages of textbooks turn in my mind as I wrote my answers. This gift, combined with a straightforward strategy, shaped my study style. I typically began preparing just 48 hours before an exam. I'd gather a study group, teach them the material and break down complex concepts. Teaching didn't just help my peers—it cemented my understanding, making even intricate ideas memorable.

That instinct to guide and coach has stayed with me, shaping my leadership style in ways I didn't realize at the time. Watching those under my wing take steps forward, even if it meant moving on to new roles, has become one of my greatest joys.

Looking back, the game stacked against me in 1992 transformed into a journey of resilience, adaptability and relentless determination. From the streets of Trichy to the halls of SASTRA, every twist and turn taught me invaluable lessons that continue to guide me today.

—

My gut has always been my compass, leading me into the unknown with a mix of curiosity and conviction. In 1995, that compass pointed me towards an adventure I couldn't resist—the Air Force Short Service Commission recruitment test.

A senior at SASTRA had just cleared the exam, and his story sparked something in me. Feeling inspired, my friend Ravi Raman rallied me and a few others to join him in applying to it. The government even covered our train tickets to Mysore for the written exam—it felt like a college tour sponsored by the government.

The train journey to Mysore was an adventure. Laughter echoed through the compartments as we joked about the physical tests, imagined ourselves in uniforms, and soaked in the thrill of what lay ahead. Excited and nervous, we were a band of adventurers eager to embrace whatever awaited us.

The excitement, however, dimmed after the written test. When the results were announced, I stood alone as the only one who had passed. Elation and solitude washed over me in equal measure. I was thrilled to advance but keenly aware of the isolation that came with it. My friends, who had shared the journey's excitement, now faced a premature return home. That evening, they planned a party in Mysore—a night of camaraderie and shared memories. I wanted to join them, but moving to the next round meant staying back. As they packed their bags, I realized that stepping forward sometimes means leaving behind moments that can never be reclaimed.

Advancing to the next phase—a rigorous physical training round—I felt a renewed surge of energy. Before I left for Mysore, Appa had warned me about the physical demands. I brushed off his concerns, fuelled by youthful confidence and vivid daydreams of becoming an Air Force engineer.

Then came the tiger leap test. The challenge was simple but daunting: Climb a ladder to a ten-foot platform, leap across a four-foot gap and grab the swaying rope. Standing atop the platform, I watched as others hesitated, looking down and retreating. My pulse quickened, but I refused to let fear hold me back. Fixing my gaze on the rope, I took a deep breath and leaped.

For one exhilarating moment, my hands grasped the rope. Triumph surged through me—until I felt myself slipping. The rough fibres burned my palms, and instinctively, I let go of the rope. Time seemed to slow as I plummeted, the world blurring until I hit the ground with a thud, landing flat on my back. Pain shot through me, radiating from my spine as I lay there, staring up at the sky.

That fall was more than physical—it was a wake-up call. It taught me the weight of overconfidence and the importance of preparation. Yet, even in failure, it reaffirmed my belief in the power of boldness. Vulnerability and courage often walk hand in hand, and it's in those moments that we truly find ourselves.

The ache from that fall lingered, a constant reminder of the risks I had taken. Two years later, when the pain flared and led to surgery, it was a final lesson in listening to advice and respecting my limits. But even as I recovered, I knew one thing for sure: I wouldn't stop following my gut—it was how I found the courage to leap, even when the landing wasn't guaranteed.

—

At 20, in my third year of engineering, I boarded a bus to Coimbatore with a slip of paper and a heart full of unanswered questions. For years, my mother's absence had been a silent wound, a void I filled with fragments of imagination. That day, I decided to confront the ghost of her memory.

The address had been unearthed by my Aunt Seetha, whose determination handed me the key to a locked room in my heart. Holding that slip of paper, I felt the weight of a decision I could no longer ignore. I had to see her, to confront the emptiness she had left behind.

The five-hour bus ride with my aunt from Trichy to Coimbatore felt like a journey through my own fears. The miles dragged on, each one tightening the knot in my chest. My thoughts spiralled into a mix of hope and dread. Would my mother welcome me with open arms? What if she didn't? I gripped the seat before me, palms slick with sweat, and couldn't help but feel like Karna from the Mahabharata—abandoned, cursed by fate, seeking a mother who might not want to be found.

Arriving in Madukkarai, a suburb of Coimbatore, I stepped off the bus into a world that felt both familiar and alien. My legs felt heavy as I approached the modest white bungalow, its fresh coat of paint gleaming in the morning sun. A purple TVS Scooty rested on the porch, a splash of colour against the stark walls. My maternal grandfather opened the door, his expression calm, as if he had been expecting this moment for years.

We settled into a small room, the silence thick with unspoken words. Then she entered—the woman who had once cradled me, whose face I had tried to reconstruct from faded memories and old photographs. I searched her features for something familiar—a shared smile, the curve of her eyes—but her gaze was distant, her eyes reflecting a stranger's indifference.

Aunt Seetha spoke to her in hushed tones, words I strained to hear. I clung to the hope that she might ask about me, about my life, about the mundane details that mothers cherish. Instead, her words pierced through me: 'Why has he come now? What does he want?'

The ground beneath me seemed to dissolve. I had come seeking answers, forgiveness, perhaps even love. But the mother I had imagined all these years existed only in my mind. The reality was a woman who saw me not as her son, but as an unwelcome visitor. The boy inside me, who had longed for her affection, stood alone in that room, his hopes shattered.

The bus ride back to Trichy was a blur. The vibrant landscapes outside faded into obscurity as the weight of rejection settled deep within me. It's strange how we chase certain things, believing they'll bring closure. But some voids can't be filled, and some wounds remain tender no matter how much time passes.

In the years that followed, I pieced together fragments of her story. She had always been a dreamer, longing for a life of travel and freedom—a spirit that couldn't be confined. My father, ever grounded and loyal, was tethered by duty and family, a steady anchor she perhaps found stifling. Her departure wasn't a rejection of me, but a pursuit of something she felt she couldn't live without.

Understanding this didn't erase the pain, but it brought a semblance of closure. I accepted that some questions remain unanswered and some relationships never mend. The scars of that day remain—a testament to a chapter that shaped who I am.

Sometimes, the past lingers not to haunt us but to remind us of the resilience we've cultivated along the way. While some wounds may never fully heal, they become part of our story—a story of endurance, understanding and the complexities of the human heart.

The days after finishing engineering felt heavy, like I was carrying an invisible burden. Back in Trichy, where life should have felt familiar, I felt like a stranger in my own skin—lost in a sea of expectations that weren't my own.

There was no job waiting for me, no clear path to follow. Yet, the world around me moved at full speed, as if mocking my standstill. Conversations with family, neighbours and distant relatives became unbearable. Their well-meaning questions—'What's next?'—felt like a chorus of doubt I couldn't escape. I had no answer, only the growing realization that staying here meant drowning in the weight of those expectations.

The only solution I could see was to leave. Escape to a place big enough to disappear in, somewhere like Chennai, where I could breathe, think and figure out my next step without the constant hum of judgement in my ear.

One of my favourite places in Trichy was the Ayyappan temple in Cantonment, near Campion school. It wasn't like the ancient temples that dotted India with their sprawling complexes and centuries of history. This one was simple, serene and egalitarian. There were no VIP queues, no hundi for offerings—just the quiet promise of equality before God. Even the wealthiest visitors sometimes stood as caretakers for the chappals left at the entrance, seeing it as a service to the divine.

Inside the temple, a red letterbox caught my eye. The words painted on its lid—'Letters to God'—felt like a call. Every week, priests would remove the letters, placing them at God's feet. I'd seen the letterbox many times before, but that day, it felt different. It felt like the box was daring me to speak my truth.

I tore a scrap of paper from my notebook, my hand trembling as I gripped the pen and poured out my heart:

Dear God,

I've done everything that I could—I have completed my engineering. But I don't have a job, I don't know where I will go or what I will do with my life. I want to get out of home and get out of Trichy. I cannot stay here any longer. I have no idea where I should go. I have too many questions in my mind and no answers. I'm leaving for Chennai because I can't stay here. I don't know what's out there. Ayyappa, you have to show me the way and guide me along. Please create something—anything—for me to go on.

I folded the paper and slipped it into the box, not expecting a miracle but feeling a weight lift from my chest. Admitting my fear and frustration was like uncorking a bottle I had kept sealed for too long. Tears welled up in my eyes, and I let them trickle down freely. That letter was my first real step forward—not because it held answers, but because it held my resolve.

Trichy was behind me now. Chennai lay ahead. And a spark of possibility flickered for the first time, even if I had no idea where it might lead.

SECTION 2

THE FURNACE OF DREAMS

Where Survival Shapes Purpose

Chapter 4

CHENNAI embraced me like a blazing furnace—radiating ambition, desperation and relentless energy. I arrived in the sweltering summer of 1996, carrying little more than a thin wallet and a head full of doubts.

Freshly graduated from college, I had no job lined up, no grand blueprint for the future—just an unspoken urge to escape the suffocating expectations back home. Everyone around me seemed stuck on the same question, playing on an endless loop: 'What's next?' But here, in this sprawling metropolis, I was just another face in the crowd, free to forge my own uncertain path.

As the KPN Travels bus pulled into Guindy, I stepped off, feeling the weight of the day still clinging to me. But all of that seemed to fade with one thought at the forefront—I was about to meet my dear friend, Rajesh Rajasekar. Of course, no one calls him Rajesh. Back in college, he earned the nickname Pattai and, somehow, it's followed him like a loyal shadow ever since. Even now, years later, my sons call him Pattai Uncle, as if it's the most natural thing in the world. There's something about that nickname, a thread connecting all the years and memories, that always brings a grin to my face.

Pattai was a calming presence amidst the whirlwind. He welcomed me into his tiny room at AA Mansions on Lake View Road in West Mambalam, a place that barely qualified as living quarters. The room was a stifling 10x10 box, its walls faded to a dull cream by years of sweat and grime. A creaky single bed with a sagging mattress leaned against one corner, while our scattered belongings fought for space, with the faint smell of damp laundry and tobacco smoke drifting in from the hallway.

Pattai had arrived in Chennai a few months earlier, already entrenched in the grind of city life, but his struggles were no less daunting. Working for an IT company, he earned a paltry ₹1,500 a month under gruelling conditions. Every missed day cost him ₹100, an amount that felt like a deep cut in his already strained finances. He was a survivor in every sense of the word, adapting and enduring without complaint, even as life threw challenge after challenge his way.

Every room in that building pulsed with life, with people racing against time to survive and make something of themselves.

Our neighbour next door drove an auto-rickshaw, weaving through the city's chaos day after day.

Down the hall lived a guy who worked nights at a bar but dreamed of making it big in the film industry. Then there was the eloquent addict with impeccable English—his talent overshadowed by his dependency. He'd inject himself in his room, slipping the needle in as casually as stirring sugar into tea. He stole my calculator to fund his fix once, leaving behind a well-crafted apology. I almost believed him.

Below us, a shopkeeper filled cans with tap water, slapped on labels, and sold them as 'mineral water'. Survival often trumped ethics in this part of the city.

Life in the mansion was a daily negotiation with reality. Mornings began with people queuing up to use a set of shared toilets. Amid the gritty routines, I found myself, like others around me, clinging to whatever dreams we could afford. It was survival in its rawest form, but I was learning to endure in this relentless environment—one small victory at a time.

Appa sent me ₹1,500 each month—barely enough to maintain a strict ₹30-a-day meal plan. Mornings began with the warm comfort of pongal and vada, the crispy edges of the vada perfectly golden and the pongal melting on the tongue, all from a hole-in-the-wall eatery that smelled of sizzling spices and fresh ghee. Lunch at Data Udipi Hotel meant steaming plates of rice, fragrant sambar and the soft clang of stainless-steel plates. Dinner was simpler: two chapatis with curd rice at Kamadhenu Tiffin Centre, the tartness of the curd cutting through the day's exhaustion.

When Pattai ran short, I'd cover for him without hesitation. By the twentieth of each month, I'd anxiously dial home, waiting for my father to refill my dwindling bank account. And when the funds finally arrived, we'd treat ourselves to a shared beer on the terrace, feeling the city's vastness stretching endlessly below us.

Pattai's gift for listening shone brightest during those moments. He would absorb my frustrations and doubts with empathy, offering solace without ever trying to impose solutions. I often marvelled at his patience, his ability to anchor those around him even as he struggled to steady his own ship.

Living with Pattai taught me the value of resilience. He was a man who didn't act until pushed into a corner, but when the time came, his decisions were unwavering and deliberate. He bore the burden of providing for his family back in Trichy—a responsibility that weighed heavily on him. Yet, he remained generous, often covering for me when I fell short, even though his own pockets were nearly empty.

As the days stretched on, it became clear that our situation in Chennai was unsustainable. Pattai confided in me about his growing frustrations—his salary barely covered his expenses and the rigid deductions left him with little room to breathe. He had even approached a friend working at a multinational company, hoping for a small loan to tide him over. But the friend refused, leaving Pattai visibly disheartened. It was a rare moment when his resilience seemed to falter, but even then, he refused to give in to bitterness.

I advised him to return to Trichy, to reassess his options and find a solution that would allow him to return to Chennai on firmer ground. Pattai took my advice to heart, leaving the city with a mix of hope and disappointment. Within weeks, he enrolled at Bitech as a Java trainer, a role that would not only improve his financial situation but also set him on a path towards greater stability.

—

Unlike those with lofty ambitions, my goals were humble. I just needed a steady job to help me find my footing. Every day, I pored over the newspaper, circling classifieds and applying to anything that offered a glimmer of opportunity. Each morning began with that same quiet hope.

When I landed in Chennai, there were no grand dreams. There was only a pressing urgency: I had to do something, become someone. It wasn't about achieving success; it was about surviving.

Finding a job in Chennai felt like navigating a labyrinth of endless bus stops and crowded dormitories, and enduring the blistering sun. The city buzzed with the constant hum of auto-rickshaws, the piercing cries of street vendors and the smell of frying masala vadas wafting from roadside stalls, mingling with the tang of diesel fumes.

As a fresh engineering graduate from a Tier 2 college, I quickly realized that the odds weren't in my favour. Companies weren't lining up to hire us—and the truth was, we weren't job-ready either. The gap between what we learned in college and what employers wanted was glaringly wide.

Chennai, with its bustling streets and relentless pace, had also become a hub for software training institutes. Their colourful billboards and catchy slogans were impossible to miss, promising to bridge that gap by teaching us the latest technologies and programming languages—'job guaranteed' was their constant refrain. For many of us, jobless and desperate, these courses felt like the only lifeline.

Like so many others in my position, I decided to take the plunge. Signing up for one of these courses felt like a leap of faith, a calculated risk that just might pay off. If programming was the ticket to employment, I was determined to learn the skills that would finally open a door for me.

After some frantic research, I zeroed in on SSI's 'Impact CS' programme. Unix, C, C++—the trifecta every employer seemed to want. But the cost was steep: over ₹50,000, a small fortune back then. My dad covered the fee without hesitation, his faith in me speaking louder than words. I felt the weight of that investment like a stone in my chest, an unspoken challenge to make it count.

The training institute was a crowded, buzzing space filled with the clatter of keyboards and the low hum of air conditioning that barely fought off the

Chennai heat. In front of each computer sat a hopeful student like me, eyes fixed on blinking cursors as the sharp smell of fresh markers mingled with the slightly metallic scent of overheated CPUs. It was here that I first heard the rhythm of code—the click, compile, crash and repeat cycle that would soon become second nature.

When the classes began, I encountered something unexpected: I loved programming! What started as a reluctant necessity turned into a passion. Coding felt like building with Legos as a kid, only infinitely more complex and rewarding. With just a programming language and a compiler, you could create anything your mind could dream up. It was exhilarating.

Not everything clicked, though. The course included RDBMS concepts with Oracle—and I hated every second of it. Unlike programming, which offered endless freedom to create, learning Oracle felt rigid—an exercise in memorizing someone else's rules and systems. It was like comparing two career archetypes: A doctor versus an engineer. Doctors immerse themselves in existing knowledge, becoming masters of what already is. Engineers take first principles and imagine something new. I knew, without a doubt, which one I wanted to be.

Programming became my world. C and C++ were tools to craft solutions, to build something out of nothing. I felt alive, completely in my element. This was more than learning syntax or debugging errors. It was about discovering what I could do and who I could become.

And with discovery came a little mischief.

One day, during a Unix shell programming session, inspiration struck: A prank that would test my new-found skills and entertain me for days. I wrote a programme that mimicked the login console. It looked identical—the same blinking cursor, the same prompts. I loaded it onto every terminal in the lab, then waited.

The programme was simple but elegant. Anyone who sat down and hit Enter would see the 'login' prompt reappear endlessly. But if they entered their username and password, my programme quietly logged the details to a file, flashed a 'login failed' message and exited gracefully to the real login screen.

Within an hour, I had nearly everyone's passwords. To my classmates, it was a puzzling glitch; to me, it was a test of ingenuity. The prank wasn't just about having some fun; it was a glimpse of what I could achieve with code—both its power and its potential for misuse. Reflecting now, I recognize the ethical line I flirted with, but, at the time, it was a thrilling experiment.

The course didn't just teach me how to programme; it showed me the kind of person I wanted to be: A builder, a creator, someone who could shape their own path—even if it meant occasionally breaking the rules along the way.

Chapter 5

THE days after graduating from SASTRA in April felt like a ticking clock, each moment amplifying the unspoken expectations from family and friends. At a family event in May, my aunt's casual remark stung more than I let on: 'Don't worry; it's only May. You'll get a job soon.' Her words, meant to reassure, only reminded me of how little time had passed—and how fast it was slipping away. It felt as if a time bomb had started counting down and I was expected to defuse it before anyone noticed my struggle.

The pressure wasn't just external; it clawed at me from within. I was an engineering graduate, but that didn't seem to count for much in Chennai without specialized skills or standout communication. Confidence was another thing I lacked. As I walked through the city's crowded streets or stared at job listings in the classifieds, the challenge of finding a decent job loomed like a mountain I wasn't equipped to climb.

Amid this growing tension, I happened to apply for the MBA programme at the University of Madras, which felt like a glimmer of hope—a lifeline I desperately needed. It was more than acquiring another qualification; it was about finding a way to ease the weight of expectations. If I got in, I'd have something to say to the next person who asked, 'So, what are you doing now?' It would buy me time to regroup, to rebuild my confidence.

When the results came out, my heart sank. I was ranked fifteenth—just three spots shy of the Open Category cut-off. But fate has a way of intervening when you least expect it. Three candidates ahead of me chose other paths and, suddenly, I had my place.

The relief was immense. I wasn't just relieved to have something to do—I was relieved to escape the looming shadow of joblessness and its unspoken judgement. 'I'm doing an MBA' became my armour against questions I didn't want to answer, a way to project progress while I continued to figure things out.

Getting into the MBA programme felt like finally coming up for air after being submerged by the weight of joblessness. The classrooms buzzed with the sound of friendly banter and the murmur of case-study debates, while the faint whiff of chalk dust lingered in the air. Each morning, I walked past towering stacks of books in the placement cell library, their musty pages whispering tales of opportunities waiting to be seized.

To most, the placement cell library was just a forgotten corner of campus—a quiet refuge filled with dusty shelves of business magazines and yesterday's financial newspapers. But to me, it was a portal to a world I longed to be a part of. I would lose track of time flipping through *Business India* and the *Economic Times*, soaking in tales of companies climbing to greatness, markets shifting like tides, and leaders steering the course of industries with vision and daring.

The final pages of those business magazines always held a special allure—snippets about executives switching roles, their career moves dissected like chess strategies. Sometimes, they'd recommend books that shaped their thinking, offering a peek into their world of ideas. Those little notes fuelled my daydreams. I'd imagine my name printed there one day as part of the narrative that others like me would read and aspire to. Back then, it was nothing more than a wild fantasy, a fleeting hope from someone who was, at the time, a complete nobody. But in those dusty pages, I discovered a dream of how things could be.

Another thing that helped was my love for coding—the spark that was lit during the SSI course didn't fade. In 1997, even as my MBA studies consumed my days, I signed up for a Java programming course at the World Wide Web Institute. My schedule became a relentless cycle: Lectures at B-school by day, Java classes at night, and a few stolen hours of sleep in between. It was exhausting, but the sheer joy of building something with code kept me going.

—

By 1997, the injury from my 'tiger leap' during the Air Force recruitment test two years earlier returned with a vengeance. At the time of the fall, it seemed like nothing more than a reckless misstep—a sharp jolt of pain, a bruised ego and a story to laugh about later. But as the years passed, what I dismissed as a minor mishap revealed its true colours.

The ache began quietly, a whisper of discomfort in my lower back. It was easy to ignore at first—after all, who pays attention to an ache at twenty-three? But the whispers grew louder, turning into sharp, relentless stabs of pain that raced down my legs with every step. Walking became an ordeal; my posture bent under the invisible weight. Some days, it was a dull throb, like a drumbeat in the background of my life. On others, it was a sharp, radiating pain that made walking unbearable.

Desperation drove me to try everything. I submitted to traction therapy in Trichy, lying on an inclined bed with weights pulling at my legs in a futile attempt to stretch the pain away. Painkillers became a daily ritual, just enough to scrape through another day. A single misstep—lifting something heavy, twisting too quickly—and the pain would flare back to life, a relentless reminder of my fragility.

At twenty-three, I felt far too young to carry such a burden. The spectre of surgery loomed, terrifying yet tantalizing in its promise of relief. Friends warned me of the risks, their voices tinged with concern and caution. But I had reached my breaking point. I couldn't keep existing like this, trapped in a cycle of agony and fear.

In 1997, I took the plunge. The lumbar laminectomy at Amar Hospital was not the minimally invasive procedure it might be today. It was a full-scale operation, leaving me with a deep incision and twenty-eight stitches running down my back—a scar that felt like both a badge of survival and a reminder of vulnerability. The surgery itself was daunting, but it was the recovery that truly tested my mettle.

For twenty-six days, the hospital room became my world—a crucible of pain and resilience. Movement was agony. Even turning over in bed required bracing myself against the window, gripping it like a lifeline. Every adjustment felt as if I was lying on a tray over open flames. Independence was stripped away; basic acts like relieving myself required a nurse and a bedpan. The doctors had offered me the option to avoid surgery and, instead, manage the pain with medication, but that life would have been very restrictive.

My father stayed by my side, a quiet pillar of strength. He brought food from nearby restaurants and small comforts to break the monotony. My aunts, with their rasam kanji, spoon-fed me when my body refused to cooperate. Their care was both humbling and life-affirming.

Even after I was discharged from the hospital, recovery was slow and stubborn. Six months passed before I could even dream of riding a two-wheeler. My loyal friends took turns ferrying me to college along Beach Road. They filled my days with laughter and my nights with stories, crowding my room with warmth and camaraderie.

—

During those months, the grind of long commutes became unbearable. So, I packed up and moved to Triplicane, closer to college, where life was cheaper and simpler, but undeniably raw. My first stop was Odean Mansion—a name that promised grandeur but delivered very little.

The 'mansion' was little more than a crumbling relic of the past, and my room was a cramped, dimly lit space shared with two others. Shared toilets down the hallway completed the set-up. It wasn't ideal, but for a broke student, it was affordable. That was all that mattered.

—

What Odean Mansion lacked in charm, my roommates, Manivannan and Mustafa, made up for in spirit. Mustafa brought life into that tiny box of a room with his quirky habits. Every morning, like clockwork, he buried himself in the *Economic Times* and *The Hindu.* He didn't just read them—he consumed them with a kind of reverence, dissecting every word and number as if they held the secrets of the universe.

'Did you know this? Did you know that?' he'd fire off excitedly, his enthusiasm filling every corner of the room. Mustafa turned that dingy space into a lively newsroom, where debates on stock prices and global politics competed with the faint hum of ceiling fans.

But my time at Odean Mansion wasn't without its challenges. Having just undergone surgery, climbing the stairs to the first-floor room became a painful ordeal. Every step felt like a mountain and my back was in no condition to take the strain.

I made the move to Malar Mansion, a modest improvement, for one simple reason: I scored a ground-floor room there. The room was tiny, shared with one other person, but it came with an attached toilet—a luxury in the world of student housing.

For a while, it was a welcome reprieve. The ground floor meant no stairs and the attached toilet felt like a five-star upgrade. But life in Malar Mansion was still a tight squeeze and it wasn't long before I sought something better.

That's when I moved to Thomson Mansion. The room was once again on the ground floor, which was non-negotiable for my post-surgery recovery, but it was significantly more spacious.

This move also brought another blessing: Ubab. He moved in with me and quickly became more than just a roommate—he became my lifeline.

Every night, after a gruelling day of classes and commutes, my back pain would flare up, sharp and relentless. Without fail, Ubab would grab the tube of Voveran Gel and gently massage my aching back. He'd stretch my legs and feet like a seasoned physiotherapist, his care easing not just my physical pain but the weight of the day itself.

Looking back, those months felt like a trial by fire—a mix of pain, dependence and unwavering support. It was the crucible that shaped me, teaching me that, sometimes, the hardest battles are the ones that strip you bare, leaving only the bonds of love and resilience to see you through.

The PG hostel for men at the University of Madras wasn't just a hostel—it was a legend among students. Its location was unbeatable: Perched right on Chennai's iconic Marina Beach, with ocean views that would make any real estate agent weep with envy. But what made it truly coveted was the price—₹115 a month for a room and ₹600 for meals. It was beachfront living on a broke student's budget.

When I first applied, I landed on the waitlist, holding onto slim hope. Then, one day, the allotment letter came through. Room Number 14—allotted to me and my friend Mani. I didn't just feel lucky, I felt like I had won the lottery.

—

Room 14 had a direct, unobstructed view of the beach. From my window, I could watch waves crashing onto the shore and gaze out at the endless horizon. Every morning, the salty breeze carried a promise of something new and, every evening, the setting sun painted the sky with colours that seemed just for me.

That room became more than a place to sleep—it was a refuge, a front-row seat to Chennai's coastline and a hub for my friends.

At the centre of it all was an antique wooden chair: With lions carved into the armrests, it belonged more in a royal court than a student's room. It had been passed down through several hands before ending up with me. Somehow, it gave the room an air of importance, as if it had stories of its own to tell.

That chair became the throne of countless nights. Friends would gather, drinks in hand, as we sprawled across the room, pouring our hearts out. Life, ambition, dreams—nothing was off-limits. The conversations were as endless as the view from that window, and, for a few fleeting hours, anything felt possible.

The hostel itself was a chaotic mosaic of students from every discipline—MBA, MA, MPhil—all thrown together in a ramshackle building that somehow functioned. The toilets were creaky and the dining hall perpetually noisy, but none of it mattered. The million-dollar views more than made up for these shortcomings.

Some students gamed the system. They'd enrol in MPhil programmes not for the degree but for the cheap accommodation while they hunted for jobs. I couldn't blame them. With a set-up like this, who wouldn't?

For me, though, the hostel wasn't just a financial hack. It was a classroom all of its own. Every person I met there, every late-night chat and every chaotic dinner in the Mess hall taught me something new.

The hostel was alive with ambition and struggle, camaraderie and solitude. It was a space where dreams were debated over cups of chai, where laughter filled the cracks of old walls and where we learned as much from each other as we did from our courses.

Room 14 wasn't just a room. It was a chapter—a place where the ocean met my ambitions, where friends became philosophers and where life's big questions were tackled with the vigour of young, hopeful minds.

It wasn't just a hostel. It was a front-row seat to life.

—

Manivannan—or simply Mani—was more than just my roommate in the hostel; he was the heart and soul of our little world in Room 14. Hailing from a village near Salem, Mani had studied engineering at Adhiyamaan College in Hosur. But it wasn't his academic credentials that defined him. Mani was the kind of person everyone seemed to know and, more importantly, the kind of person everyone loved.

Mani had a gift —he simply couldn't say no. Whether it was a friend, a junior, a senior or someone from his village, if they found themselves in Chennai, they inevitably ended up at our doorstep. Some needed a place to crash for the night, others sought advice, introductions or even help finding a job. And Mani was always there—listening, offering, connecting. Our room often felt like a revolving door of visitors and Mani was the glue that held it all together, the constant in an ever-changing line-up of faces.

Our parties in Room 14 were legendary. Loud debates, boisterous laughter, and the kind of friendly banter that only comes with shared trust and familiarity filled the air. But like college kids often do, we sometimes crossed the line without realizing it.

During one of our quieter moments, Mani asked to speak to me in private. His face was uncharacteristically serious, his usual cheer subdued. 'Girish,' he started, his voice trembling slightly, 'I love spending time with you. Every day I spend with you, I learn something new, and it's one of the best times of my life.'

I smiled, feeling touched by his words, but then he continued. 'But...' Mani's eyes filled with tears as he went on, 'when you all gang up on me during our evening chats, it hurts. You might think it's all in good fun, but I feel really sad when I'm the one being targeted. It makes me feel small. And especially when it comes from you, it hurts even more.'

Mani's confession hit me like a bolt of lightning. What I had always brushed off as harmless fun suddenly felt cruel when seen from his perspective. Those loud debates, the jabs and the teasing—we thought they were just part of the camaraderie, a kind of college-style ribbing that no one took seriously. But to the person on the receiving end, it wasn't always so light-hearted.

I realized then that even friendly banter can leave scars behind, especially when it becomes a daily routine. It wasn't just about Mani—it was about everyone we laughed at in turn, thinking it was all part of the fun. In my mind, it was never malicious, but Mani's vulnerability showed me how easily good intentions could be overshadowed by thoughtlessness.

That night, something shifted in me. Mani wasn't just a friend; he became my teacher. He taught me the importance of seeing situations from another's perspective, of being mindful of how words and actions can affect those around us.

From that day on, I made a conscious effort to change. The loud arguments and unnecessary jabs gave way to more thoughtful conversations. I started focusing on building relationships, treating people with the respect they deserved and avoiding the kind of 'fun' that came at someone else's expense.

Mani's openness wasn't just an emotional moment; it was a turning point in how I understood friendships and relationships. He taught me that true connection isn't about how much you laugh together but about how much you care for each other's feelings.

Mani was—and still is—a reminder that the best friendships are built not just on shared memories but on mutual respect, trust and the courage to be vulnerable. Room 14 might have been our physical space, but it was Mani who made it a home.

Chapter 6

AFTER my MBA, I found myself standing at a crossroads, the weight of my future resting heavily on my shoulders. I was one of the first in my batch to land a job offer—Cookson Electronics, a storied British firm with nearly 300 years of heritage, had come through with a salary of ₹12,000 a month. By today's standards, that'd translate to about ₹60,000 or $725—a respectable start by any measure. The job was to sell eutectic alloys to industrial manufacturers.

For most, a position at Cookson would've been a dream come true: Stability, prestige and a handsome salary. But as I sat with the offer letter in hand, doubt gnawed at me. I'd been devouring business books and magazines, and one thing was becoming increasingly clear: History didn't guarantee the future. The world was shifting and global trade seemed stuck in a lull. Could I truly see myself building a career selling silver brazing flux to battery manufacturers?

Then there was software—a sunrise industry that brimmed with potential. With my new-found passion for programming, I couldn't shake the feeling that this was where the future lay. I needed to take a leap, even if it meant leaving behind the comfort of a hefty paycheque.

That leap began with the World Wide Web Institute. It was a door to new possibilities. One day, while wandering through their other division, Athene Softech, I stumbled upon something that piqued my interest. They were knee-deep in Java development projects for US clients. Soon after, I sought a meeting with the founder, Mr Vidhya Sagar, and made my pitch: 'Here's why you should hire me.'

It wasn't a planned move and it certainly wasn't a campus placement. But I'd learned that sometimes, the best opportunities don't come knocking—you have to find the door and open it yourself. My impromptu pitch worked. He offered me the job on the spot, with a salary of ₹5,000 a month. It wasn't much, but I had my foot in the door to the software world.

I could hardly contain my excitement as I rushed to tell Aunt Seetha the news. But not everyone shared my enthusiasm. My uncle shook his head in disbelief. 'Why would you throw away the Cookson job? It pays more. This makes no sense!'

For him, it didn't. But for me, it was crystal clear. I wasn't chasing money—I was chasing happiness. I wanted to wake up excited about what I did, not just about the paycheque at the end of the month.

Aunt Seetha, ever practical, had her own advice. 'Keep your expenses under ₹2,000. Send ₹2,000 to your dad every month and save ₹1,000 in a fixed deposit.'

I laughed. '₹5,000 isn't even enough for me to spend! Let me focus on earning more first before thinking about saving.'

And with that, I embarked on a journey about choosing the kind of life I wanted to live—one driven by passion, curiosity and the courage to carve my own path.

—

During my first year of MBA, I made it a point to stay in touch with Ravi Raman, my buddy from SASTRA. Back then, staying connected meant writing letters—those iconic blue Inland letters that carried more than just words; they carried emotions, updates and pieces of life. I told him all about my MBA course, the classes, the buzz and the potential it held. Somewhere in those exchanges, I convinced him to apply. A year later, Ravi became my junior in my MBA programme, a twist in our friendship that neither of us saw coming.

Fast forward to 1998, Ravi came over to my place in Triplicane one day, full of purpose. He had a mission: He wanted to learn Java. It seemed simple enough at first. He asked for recommendations on institutes and I did what any good friend would—I told him to do his homework. 'Talk to the trainers,' I advised. 'Make sure you don't end up with a quack.'

The problem was most skilled Java instructors were already snapped up by IT firms. The ones left weren't worth their hefty fees. A few days later, Ravi was back, visibly frustrated. 'None of these guys are good,' he said, his voice tinged with both determination and exasperation. 'Can *you* teach me Java?'

Teaching a friend didn't seem like a big deal. I loved Java and Ravi was someone I trusted. 'Sure,' I said casually, not thinking much of it.

But Ravi wasn't done. 'I'll pay you,' he added, catching me off guard. 'That way, you'll take it seriously. And so will I.'

I couldn't help but admire his logic. This wasn't about money; it was about commitment. If it felt like a proper arrangement, we'd both be invested. And then came the light-bulb moment. 'Why don't we find a few more students and turn this into a real class?' I suggested. 'We'll all learn better together.'

Ravi's eyes lit up. Within days, he had rounded up five of his friends who were just as eager to learn. Suddenly, my humble bachelor pad in Triplicane became a makeshift classroom. We bought cheap furniture from Saravana Stores, rented three second-hand computers and pieced together a basic set-up. It was far from fancy, but it worked.

And just like that, my first entrepreneurial venture—a Java-training business—literally walked into my life. What started as a favour to a friend became an experience that taught me the power of initiative, community and seizing opportunities, even when they show up in the most unexpected ways.

—

One casual evening in the computer lab at the World Wide Web Institute, a friend approached me, his tone tinged with opportunity. 'My sister works at Polaris Software Lab,' he said. 'They're looking for a Java trainer for their team of C programmers. You're good at Java and I thought you might be interested.'

Here was another suggestion that caught me completely by surprise. Teaching a few friends in my Triplicane pad was one thing. Training seasoned corporate professionals at a company like Polaris? That felt like stepping into an entirely different league. I hesitated, unsure if I was ready for such a challenge. But then a thought crept in: What's the worst that could happen? I had nothing to lose and everything to learn.

So I said yes.

At the time, I had a small batch of students—a handful of friends from four different companies crammed into my living room, learning Java on rented computers. Not much to speak of, but it was a start. When I prepared my profile for Polaris, I crafted it carefully to read: 'Trained employees from Amdocs, Cognizant, etc.' Technically true, even if the 'employees' were my friends who had paid me ₹3,000 each.

The day I walked into Polaris to meet Mr Bharat, their VP, my nerves were firing on all cylinders. He asked me a few technical questions, probing my understanding of Java. Thankfully, I passed his informal test and, before I knew it, they'd decided to bring me on board.

The engagement was for fifteen days, with ₹30,000 on the table—a sum that felt almost mythical at the time. The classes were scheduled from 7 a.m. to 9 a.m., before Polaris' workday began. It was perfect for me, juggling multiple commitments as I was. Their office was a twenty-minute ride from my home and I'd make the commute on my old TVS Champ bike. But the real work began long before the first class.

This was the era of OHP projectors and floppy disks, where every presentation had to be meticulously crafted. Each two-hour session demanded at least ten hours of preparation. I pored over every detail—structuring concepts, pacing lessons and crafting examples that would resonate. My handwriting, however, was a disaster. No one could decipher it, let alone take notes from it. Enter Kamal, my friend's brother who lived with us. With handwriting so neat it could grace wedding invitations, he became my secret weapon.

By midnight, I'd sketch out the content and hand it over to Kamal, who'd burn the midnight oil, carefully transferring it onto OHP sheets. At 5 a.m., I'd review the slides, pack my materials—floppy disks, backups of backups and those precious slides—and head out.

Every morning, as my TVS Champ buzzed down Mount Road, my mind raced with questions. Would the slides work? What if the floppy disk fails? Would I fail? The stakes felt impossibly high. Facing a room full of C programmers eager to learn Java was nothing short of stepping into an arena.

The first day was nerve-wracking. Rows of professionals sat waiting, their expressions neutral but expectant. As I fired up the OHP projector, my heart pounded. But the moment I started explaining the first concept, something inside me shifted. The panic faded and I found my rhythm. Thereafter, for two hours every morning, it was just me, the code and a room full of learners. The training turned out to be a success.

When I went to collect my ₹30,000 fee, I noticed the amount was ₹28,500. For a moment, I was confused. Then I realized—TDS, tax deducted at source. I wasn't complaining. It still felt monumental, especially compared to my monthly salary of ₹5,000. I had just earned six months' pay in two weeks.

That evening, I rounded up my friends to celebrate. We headed to Pizza Hut, a luxury back then. Pizza Hut had just launched in Chennai and most of us had never tasted a pizza in our life. That first bite of pizza was pure indulgence; it was symbolic. It was a taste of progress, of stepping into a world I'd only dreamed about.

The spree didn't stop there. I bought Ray-Ban aviators, a Casio digital diary with 64KB of storage, Levi's jeans, and, of course, more pizza and beer. The money disappeared almost as quickly as it came, but I didn't care. For the first time, I felt that life was a celebration.

Then came the shoes.

At an Adidas store, a pair of gleaming Air Pump sneakers caught my eye. Curious, I asked the salesman about them. His response was laced with condescension: '₹4,500.' His tone said it all—This isn't for you. You can't afford it.

That was all it took. Ten minutes later, I walked out of the store wearing those shoes. It was not about the sneakers anymore. It was about proving a point—to myself and to the world.

Later that day, my aunt spotted them by the door. 'How much?' she asked casually.

'₹4,500,' I replied.

Her gasp was audible. '₹4,500 for a pair of *shoes*?'

For her, it was inconceivable. But for me, it was not about the price tag. It was about the journey—the steps that had brought me here and the conviction to take the next leap, no matter how daunting.

—

The tech job market was on fire and I had thrown my hat in the ring for a position at HCL-Cisco, one of the most coveted names in the industry. Their written test in C programming was gruelling, but a few days later, I received a call letter inviting me for an in-person interview. My heart raced with a mix of excitement and nerves. This was HCL-Cisco Offshore Development Center (ODC)—a gateway to working with a true multinational like Cisco. It was a dream job.

What made it even sweeter was the fact that many of my engineering friends, some from the Computer Science department, had taken the test but didn't clear it. Just passing the written test felt like an accomplishment. But now, I was staring at the real challenge: Proving myself in the interviews. I remember sitting at home, a notebook in hand, carefully writing down answers to every common interview question I could think of. 'Tell me about yourself' stared back at me from the top of the page, a deceptively simple question that could make or break my chances. This was not any ordinary interview; it was *the* opportunity I had been waiting for and I wasn't going to leave anything to chance.

Once I had my answers sketched out, the real work began. I stood in front of the mirror, looking at my own reflection, rehearsing every word. At first, it was awkward, like I was talking to a stranger. But as I repeated the answers, tweaking my tone, refining my pauses and perfecting my delivery, it started to feel real.

As I stood there, running through my lines one more time, I reminded myself that this was my chance to prove what I was capable of. The stakes were high, but so was my resolve. I wasn't just preparing for an interview; I was preparing to take a leap towards the life I wanted.

The interview process was rigorous—three rounds that drilled deep into my knowledge of C and C++, followed by a lighter HR interview that focused on my non-technical interests. I felt I'd done well and was eagerly awaiting the results of the interview. Kavitha, the HR recruiter, approached me and said, 'There's one more meeting. You'll be speaking with Krishna Kumar [KK], our general manager.'

I went to meet KK in his office, feeling equal parts anxious and curious. KK was a man who commanded attention, his presence both charming and authoritative. He got straight to the point. 'Girish, you've cleared all the interviews, but there's one issue,' he said, his tone cryptic. 'That's why I wanted to see you in person.'

I braced myself.

'You'd be the first and only MBA in our team,' he continued. 'Everyone else is an engineer, mostly from the IITs and IISc. Are you sure you'll be able to fit in?'

The question could've thrown me off, but I knew my answer. 'Sir, I want to be a programmer and I'm absolutely sure this won't be a problem,' I replied, my voice steady.

That was it. The meeting ended and, soon after, I was offered a role as a technical staff member with a salary of ₹17,000 a month—a staggering number at the time. HCL-Cisco was the kind of place my friends dreamed of and, now, I was in. Working on cutting-edge networking technologies during the dotcom boom felt like a validation of my decision to bet on a sunrise industry.

To celebrate, we threw a small party at home. Amidst the cheers and congratulations, a friend raised his glass and said, 'Buddy, congratulations! You're now settled for life!'

I laughed and replied, 'Settled? I'm just getting started.'

—

My time at HCL-Cisco was invaluable. It was my first taste of working in a structured, large-scale environment, and I soaked up every bit of it. But even as I adapted to corporate life, the entrepreneurial itch refused to fade.

That unshakable entrepreneurial pull found its first true outlet in Xpert Labs—my inaugural business venture. It started modestly, with Ravi and a handful of students eager to learn Java. We squeezed into my bachelor pad, navigating around rented computers and makeshift desks. The enthusiasm in that room was palpable but space was tight, and it quickly became clear we needed more room to grow.

Ravi suggested hosting the next batch at his place in Vadapalani, where he lived with friends. We converted one of the bedrooms into a classroom—it was large enough for eight students to gather. I commuted there daily, teaching Java in whatever corner we could clear. Despite the humble set-up, word of mouth helped spread my business like wildfire. Demand was building and it was time to think bigger.

The next step was renting a hall in Shenoy Nagar. It felt like a bold move, but the response exceeded my expectations. Twenty-two students signed up for the batch, filling the room with an energy that was both thrilling and humbling. That month, I earned ₹1.1 lakh—a figure that felt like a dream. For the first time, I wasn't just surviving; I was thriving.

With part of that money, I took another step forward. I paid ₹55,000 as a rental advance for the top floor of a bungalow in Anna Nagar. This was a significant milestone. The space felt like a symbol of everything I had worked for. A couple of years ago, I had arrived in Chennai with nothing. Now, I had an office, a growing business and a vision taking shape.

The decision to install an air conditioner in the computer lab felt monumental—part indulgence, part necessity. Growing up in Trichy and then battling Chennai's unrelenting heat, I had never slept in an air-conditioned room. To me, ACs were the domain of luxury hotels and elite homes, not something owned by middle-class families like ours. But this wasn't just about comfort; it was about creating the right environment for the lab—a place where students could focus, undistracted by the oppressive heat.

The first night, as the hum of the AC filled the room and cool air washed over me, I lay awake, overwhelmed by the sheer contrast. More than relief from the heat, it was the feeling of having arrived at a milestone I hadn't even dared to set. For someone who had spent countless sleepless nights swatting at mosquitoes in a stifling room, this was transformative.

The lab quickly became more than a workspace. My cousin and I began sleeping there, rolling out our mats on the tiled floor beneath the blessed coolness of the AC. It wasn't luxury in the traditional sense, but it felt like it. At 5.30 a.m., we'd wake up, fold our makeshift beds and clean the room before the first students arrived. Each morning, as the cool air dissipated into the day's heat, I couldn't help but feel gratitude. The AC wasn't just a machine—it was a symbol of progress, of how far we'd come.

Xpert Labs was a crucible for everything I wanted to learn about entrepreneurship. It taught me how to build something from scratch, inspire others and find opportunities even in the smallest corners. It wasn't perfect, but it was mine—a testament to the resourcefulness and the courage to chase a dream.

Xpert Labs had momentum—sharp marketing, a growing customer base and ambition—but it didn't survive.

—

Over the years, I made more attempts to reach out to my mother and our conversations continued—getting woven into the fabric of our evolving lives. I visited her a few more times, each meeting a quiet reaffirmation of our bond. Then, in 1998, she decided to move from Coimbatore to Chennai to be closer to me.

For a while, I tried living with her, believing it might bring us both a sense of comfort. But as time passed, we realized that while we wanted to stay connected, we also needed our own space. So, we settled on an arrangement—separate homes, but always in touch. And that understanding, that unspoken agreement, has stood the test of time.

—

It was 1998, a whirlwind year when my days were packed to the brim. Mornings were devoted to MBA lectures, evenings to Java classes at the World Wide Web Institute and, somewhere in between, I felt an urge to explore something different. That's when Amway had swept into India with the force of a tidal wave, promising financial independence and dreams wrapped in shiny packaging. Their multilevel marketing model was either genius or folly—depending on whom you asked.

'Don't waste your time,' friends warned me. 'Nobody makes it big with this stuff.' But I wasn't looking for quick wins—I was chasing something far more elusive: Experience.

A curious mix of scepticism and intrigue led me to an Amway event with an invitation from my MBA junior, Arvind. The atmosphere was electric—blaring lights, roaring cheers and stories of underdogs turned millionaires filling the air. For the first time, I saw what belief could do when amplified. Standing in that room, I felt a magnetic pull: If these people could stand tall under the spotlight, why not me?

Arvind introduced me to Yasmin Menon. Yasmin and her husband, Raj Menon, were seasoned pros in the Amway ecosystem. Over cups of coffee, she demystified the mechanics and the achievement levels of the system, breaking it down like a general briefing a soldier. 'Six "downlines" get you Silver. Nine? That's Gold. Climb higher and you'll shine like a star,' she said, her eyes gleaming with conviction.

I was hooked. Selling came naturally to me. In two weeks, I hit Silver, fuelled by my network of friends and acquaintances. Two weeks after that, I stood on an Amway stage, medal in hand, soaking in the applause. The high was indescribable. But then, reality intruded. The pool of willing recruits dried up. Selling soap and shampoo to strangers was draining.

That's when Yasmin shared something transformative. She handed me the idea of the 'dream book'. 'Write down your goals. Visualize them,' she urged me. My dream book became my personal manifesto, filled with cut-outs of luxury cars, sprawling mansions, vintage single malts and even a luxury yacht. But it wasn't only about material things; it was about believing in possibilities.

With Yasmin's mentorship, I shifted my strategy. Instead of selling products, I sold a vision. Amway was my platform, but I was offering something deeper—hope, freedom and the promise of a better life. It wasn't manipulation; it was connection. People weren't just buying soap; they were buying into a dream. And I loved it.

But dreams, no matter how grand, can clash with reality. Downlines faltered, products gathered dust and enthusiasm waned. Slowly, my Amway chapter came to a close and my dream book was tucked away, its pages forgotten. Yet, the lessons it held stayed with me.

Looking back, my journey wasn't about shampoos or silver medals—it was about belief. Belief in myself, in others and in the power of a shared vision. Whether building teams, pitching ideas or mentoring today, one truth remains: People don't follow products—they follow purpose. And that's a lesson I owe, in part, to Amway and Yasmin Menon.

Chapter 7

THE late '90s were electric, a time when India's tech scene was booming. In Bangalore or Chennai, it seemed every engineer was one phone call away from a US visa, poised to tackle the Y2K bug or ride the surging dot-com wave. The joke went that a recruiter could fling a stone into any crowd and hit an engineer who'd be on a flight the following week. It was a seismic movement, one that etched Indian software engineering into the global narrative.

At HCL-Cisco, the migration was in full throttle. Colleagues were disappearing left and right, headed for 'greener pastures' in Silicon Valley. The buzz was contagious. Java, networking and software engineering were the golden tickets, and the world couldn't get enough of Indian tech talent. By early 2000, it was my turn. I'd signed on with Fourth Technologies, a staffing firm in Santa Clara that specialized in placing Indian talent. By June, I was buckling my seatbelt on a flight to the US, leaving Chennai behind with a suitcase, my degrees and an unshakable resolve to make my mark.

The send-off at the airport was pure Indian drama. My family had rented a van, packing it with relatives, cousins and what felt like half the neighbourhood. There was a cake, hastily cut at the terminal as tears mixed with laughter. I was the first in the family to set foot abroad, and the weight of their pride and expectations was palpable.

As the plane taxied down the runway, I looked out the window, feeling a tangle of emotions. Excitement coursed through me, but so did the fear of the unknown. I didn't just want to be part of the exodus; I wanted to define my own story in this sprawling, foreign chapter. Little did I know, the journey ahead would be as challenging as it would be transformative. But, in that moment, with Chennai shrinking into the distance, it felt like I was at the edge of something monumental—a leap not just into the skies, but into possibility itself.

Landing in San Francisco was like stepping into a movie, except I wasn't sure if it was a feel-good flick or an existential drama. Pattai was waiting for me outside the airport in his beige Honda Accord, a car so quintessentially Indian-American it might as well have come with a packet of masala peanuts in the glove box. We exchanged grins, loaded my luggage and hit the 101 freeway.

The first thing that struck me was the scale. The highways stretched out endlessly, flanked by orderly lanes and massive signs that seemed to shout their directions. Everything felt impossibly vast, as though the world here had been built to a different scale. The infrastructure screamed abundance, efficiency and—most of all—possibility. It was intoxicating.

Pattai drove us to Sunnyvale, to a sprawling apartment complex on Fair Oaks Avenue. From the outside, it looked impressive—endless rows of identical doors, neatly aligned corridors and an almost hotel-like anonymity. But when we stepped into the studio apartment, my illusion shattered.

The place was sparse, bordering on bleak. There was no sofa, no dining table, no TV—just a cavernous room doubling as a bedroom, living room and, judging by the faint aroma, sometimes a dining hall. The kitchen had the barest of essentials: A microwave, fridge and an oven, all standard-issue. Four guys already occupied the space, their pillows and comforters strewn across the floor. I was about to become the fifth.

It hit me like a gut punch. Back in Chennai, I had my rolled-up mattress in an air-conditioned room. My friends in the US had painted such a rosy picture over long-distance calls: 'Girish, we're living the dream! Wine every night!' they'd brag. But the reality? The 'wine' was cheap $5 cartons from Albertsons and dinner was usually tamarind rice, eaten off paper plates while crouched on the floor. This wasn't the American Dream. This was survival.

I couldn't accept it. After all the build-up, after years of imagining what life here would be like, I wasn't about to settle for this. Something inside me snapped. The rebel in me stirred. 'This has to change,' I told myself.

We started small. Someone in the building was moving out, and selling their dining table and sofa. We bought them both for a couple of hundred bucks. That first night, we sat around the table, eating proper meals like civilized humans. It felt like a tiny victory.

Next came the entertainment set-up. A pilgrimage to Fry's Electronics ended with us hauling back a big-screen TV and a home-theatre system. It was sleek and modern for the times—the early 2000s —and the sound was glorious. That evening, we dimmed the lights, cranked up the surround sound and immersed ourselves in a movie. For a few hours, our cramped little apartment transformed into a theatre. We felt like kings.

Until the cops showed up.

The neighbours had complained about the noise and two officers knocked on our door, politely but firmly reminding us that studio apartments weren't meant for Dolby-grade soundscapes. It was a humbling moment, but also a wake-up call—literally.

We realized that cramming five people into a studio was not only uncomfortable, it was unsustainable. If we were going to make it here, we needed more space—we needed a real foundation. And so, the search began for a new apartment, one that would give us room to breathe, grow and start building the lives we'd imagined when we first dreamed of America.

The answer came in the form of a townhouse-style apartment complex. Unlike the cramped studios with paper-thin walls, these units were stacked vertically instead of side by side. The best part? No shared walls. The only connections between neighbours were the ceilings and floors, and even those felt solid enough to buffer our soundtracks and subwoofers. It was as close to acoustic freedom as we could get without owning a standalone house.

The moment we stepped inside Heritage Park apartments on E. Washington Ave, we knew this was the upgrade we'd been craving. It was a canvas for the life we wanted to build. Moving in felt like a fresh start. We weren't just leaving behind the cramped studio, we were shedding the survival mode it represented. This was our chance to live unapologetically—to fill our space with sound, laughter and the kind of chaos that comes with chasing dreams in a new country.

—

The next big step in my American adventure was buying a car. Depending on Pattai for daily drops and pick-ups from the Fourth Technologies office in Santa Clara wasn't sustainable, and public transport was a far cry from convenient. Pattai was the only one with a car in our apartment and it was clear I needed wheels of my own. But there was one small hurdle: I needed a driver's license first.

What followed was a crash course in classic Indian-style exam prep. Forget the California Driving Handbook—I went straight for the real deal. Armed with fifteen or twenty old driving test papers, I pored over them, spotting patterns and drilling myself on the most common questions. Within days, I was ready. I cleared the written test on my first attempt, paving the way for my driving test. A couple of practice sessions later, the license was mine.

Now came the real challenge: Buying a car. I had just landed in the US, hadn't started client work and was still, technically, on the bench at Fourth Technologies. My bank balance wasn't exactly screaming 'down-payment ready'. But when you want something badly enough, you find a way. And, as luck would have it, Ubab's shiny new credit card arrived just in time.

'Can you help me with the down payment?' I asked. Ubab, always up for an adventure, didn't hesitate. A few hours later, we were at the Nissan showroom, test-driving a line-up of cars. I had my eye on the Nissan Xterra, a car I'd seen with a friend, but the moment I slid behind the wheel of the Nissan Pathfinder, I was sold. It was big, spacious and felt like a rolling fortress of luxury.

We made the $2,000 down payment on Ubab's card, signed the paperwork and drove off the lot in my brand-new Pathfinder. That weekend, the car's inaugural road trip clocked over 1,000 miles. With its roomy interior and smooth drive, it was freedom on wheels.

Come Monday morning, reality came knocking—or rather, the dealership did. 'Your loan application was rejected,' the voice on the other end of the line informed me. I didn't have a US credit history and, without it, no lender was willing to take the risk. For a moment, my heart sank, but I wasn't about to let this derail me. 'What do you want me to do?' I said, half-joking but fully determined. 'Take the car back? I've already driven it over 1,000 miles!'

After some back-and-forth, the dealership found a solution. Nissan Finance agreed to take on the loan—but at a much higher interest rate. It wasn't ideal, but it was a win. I got to keep the car, though the monthly payments combined with insurance and gas set me back by a hefty $950.

Looking back, it was a financial gamble, a leap of faith made in a moment when I was living fully in the present, unconcerned with tomorrow. The Pathfinder was more than just a car; it was a symbol of independence, of staking a claim in a country where everything felt bigger, brighter and boundless. It was a reckless decision, sure, but one that made me feel alive, steering my own way forward, one mile at a time.

—

We moved into the new apartment at a time when I was still in professional limbo, waiting for a project that felt right. My friends, meanwhile, were all working at a company called Reez—Real Estate Made Easy—and their team was full of Visual Basic programmers. The tech world was shifting fast and Java was the shiny new tool everyone wanted to wield. They didn't just want to learn Java; they *needed* it.

That's how Java Jumpstart was born—right in our living room. The concept was simple but bold: A one-month crash course to transform Visual Basic programmers into Java developers. Back in India, I'd been teaching Java already, so the module was already mapped out in my mind. Execution was just a matter of logistics.

We bought a whiteboard and reconfigured the dining area into a makeshift classroom. The dining chairs were lined up in neat rows, and the whiteboard stood front and centre, ready for scribbled code. My supportive roommates retreated into the bedroom during class hours, turning the rest of the apartment into a quiet zone.

I charged what I had back in India—₹6,000, which translated to about $150. It wasn't much, but it was fair. These were Indians living in the US, paying out of pocket, not corporate trainees with expense accounts. Word spread quickly and, soon enough, the classes filled up. Two batches later, I had earned close to $3,000.

With the money, I started building my version of comfort. The first splurge was a comfortable queen bed with a real mattress—not just some makeshift arrangement. It cost $899, but the sheer joy of a good night's sleep made it worth every penny. Then I indulged in something I'd been eyeing for a while: A Sony Handycam, a sleek, cutting-edge video recorder that felt like the ultimate tech toy at the time.

Java Jumpstart was more than a side hustle; it was a bootstrap operation that turned my living room into a classroom and my vision into reality. It brought in not just money but a renewed sense of purpose.

The two-bedroom apartment was more than just a place to crash—it was our little ecosystem, a chaotic yet harmonious blend of friendship and improvisation. The camaraderie made the tight quarters feel less like a compromise and more like a shared adventure.

Chores were divided with an unspoken ease. Pattai was the self-appointed dishmaster, while Mohan and I did the laundry. Ubab cooked delicious dinners for us every day. Sundays became sacred—three hours of tennis in the morning, our amateur enthusiasm far outweighing our skill. Afterwards, we'd undo all our effort with a pitcher of beer and a pizza feast at Pizza Hut. The ritual was indulgent, predictable and perfect. Evenings, as always, were reserved for movies.

Coconut Hill, a quaint Indian grocery and video rental shop, became our temple of choice. We'd browse its aisles filled with Indian movie VCDs, always hunting for a mix of nostalgia and novelty. Back at the apartment, the VCDs would slide into the VCR, the screen would flicker to life and our home-theatre system would turn our living room into a mini cinema. Weekends often morphed into epic movie marathons—three, four, sometimes five films in a row. On weekdays, dinner was rarely complete without at least one film playing in the background.

More than the movies, it was about the moments in between that we enjoyed the most—the heated debates over the best directors, the collective groans at cheesy dialogues and the laughter that filled the room like background music. The apartment was more than just walls and furniture; it was a stage where we lived out our own story, framed by the glow of a TV screen and the hum of dreams still taking shape.

—

Joining Fourth Technologies felt like a leap forward, but I wasn't about to settle for just any project. 'Bay Area or nothing,' I told them flat out. Mountain View, Milpitas, Sunnyvale—this was my territory. They nodded, assuring me they'd find something, and, a week later, handed me my first assignment: A project in San Francisco. Not exactly my dream location, but I figured I'd give it a shot.

Mornings started with a friend dropping me off at the Sunnyvale Caltrain station. The train ride became an unexpected window into California life. As we stopped at station after station, I'd imagine my eyes as a camera and my brain as a hard disk, capturing every sight. For a guy from Chennai, where the pace of life hummed to a different tune, this journey felt surreal—a mix of quiet observation and the thrill of the unknown.

But the romance wore off quickly. The moment I stepped off the train in San Francisco, the cold hit like an unwelcome slap. I hadn't prepared for this kind of weather, and walking five blocks to the office felt less like a commute and more like a punishment. By the time I arrived—a modest start-up tucked into the second floor of a nondescript building—I was frozen to the core.

The manager greeted me with a fat stack of printed papers—project specifications. No introduction, no context, just a brusque 'Get started', followed by a gesture towards a vacant workstation. It was like being thrown into the deep end of a pool without knowing how to swim. My first day was a blur of confusion and frustration, piecing together fragments of the project with help from a few other consultants who'd already been on it for weeks.

Every hour or so, I'd escape to the street for a smoke, braving the cold just to break the monotony. It was the only part of the day that felt remotely human. Later, I realized the manager wasn't thrilled about these breaks. At $225 an hour, every minute counted. But back then, I didn't understand the economics of body shopping—the billable hours, the transactional nature of consulting. All I knew was that this wasn't the dream I'd signed up for.

A week in, I'd had enough. The long commute, the biting cold, the distant work environment—it wasn't worth it. I called Mike Samy, my sales manager at Fourth Technologies, who had become a good friend. 'Find me something closer to Mountain View,' I told Mike. It was a bold move, but I knew one thing for sure: If I was going to succeed here, it wouldn't be by freezing my way through five-block walks and drowning in isolation.

Mike delivered on his promise and I landed a project at Vertical Networks. Their office was in the heart of Silicon Valley, right next to the legendary Fry's Electronics on Arques Avenue—a spot that felt like the epicentre of tech innovation. Walking through those doors every day, I could sense I was stepping into something that mattered.

Vertical Networks was building a PBX system for enterprises—a sophisticated set-up that allowed a single phone line to support multiple extensions. It was cutting-edge, the kind of technology that felt like a bridge to the future. They were in the middle of transitioning from Java AWT to the newer and more advanced Swing for their user interface components, and that's where I came in. My task was clear: Design and build the new UI elements.

I dove headfirst into the work, surrounded by lines of code and the hum of ambition that seemed to fill every cubicle. Somewhere between debugging and perfecting layouts, a spark ignited. One day, as I worked on creating an admin screen for the PBX system, I felt the pull of something bigger. It was the idea of crafting tools that empowered users, systems that didn't just work but simplified complexity.

At the time, it was just a flicker of a thought—something buried beneath the relentless rhythm of deadlines and deliverables. But that admin screen? It stayed with me, a seed of an idea I didn't yet know I'd carry for years to come. Every product I built later in life had an admin screen that was inspired by this one—intuitive, easy to find, everything in its place, a place for everything.

For now, though, life was a balancing act—coding by day, unwinding with friends by night, and learning to dream in a place where every corner seemed to whisper possibility.

Consulting in the US was in stark contrast to what I'd experienced back home. At HCL-Cisco in India, collaboration was second nature. We'd huddle around desks, brainstorm openly and problem-solve as a team. Here, full-time employees had the keys to the kingdom—access to systems, decision-making power—while consultants like me were hired hands, expected to keep their heads down and deliver. It felt transactional, solitary and alienating.

The cubicle culture didn't help. Everyone had their own little fortress and interruptions were frowned upon. For someone like me, who thrived on connection and collaboration, the isolation was jarring. I couldn't shake the feeling of being an outsider, a cog in a machine I didn't quite belong to. So I decided to quit consulting and pursue full-time employment.

At a bustling job fair, I crossed paths with Khurram Jaffar from eForce, a systems integrator thriving in the dot-com frenzy. He had an eye for potential and, within minutes of our conversation, he made me an offer: $85,000. It was a leap from the $55,000 I was making at Fourth Technologies—a ticket to step out of the shadows and into a real role. No more playing supporting act; this was my chance to take centre stage.

I stepped into a pre-sales and training role, a blend of tech and strategy that felt tailor-made for me. My job was to train teams on platforms like BEA WebLogic and ATG Dynamo, the backbone of the nascent e-commerce revolution. These weren't just tools; they were the infrastructure powering the early internet. Khurram saw my hunger and gave me free rein to maximize vendor training programmes. I became the go-to attendee for sessions with BEA, Novell, ATG and IBM. Every time I returned, I shared what I'd learned, training eForce employees and building the company's technical arsenal.

The exposure was exhilarating. With each session, I dove deeper into cutting-edge tech, sharpening my skills and expanding my horizons.

Confidence came in waves and, soon, I was no longer just the guy who knew Java—I was someone who could bridge technology and business, an enabler in the truest sense.

The good times didn't last long though. By mid-2000, the cracks in the dot-com bubble became impossible to ignore. Projects stalled, funding vanished and the whispers of layoffs grew into an unrelenting roar. It felt like the ground beneath us was crumbling and the boundless optimism that had once defined Silicon Valley evaporated almost overnight.

At eForce, the atmosphere shifted. Once lively with ideas and innovation, the office turned sombre. Projects disappeared as clients tightened their budgets and the dreaded layoff lists started circulating like storm clouds overhead. The weight of uncertainty was suffocating.

The collapse rippled through the industry, sparing no one. I watched friends and colleagues pack up their desks, their ambitions reduced to severance cheques and cardboard boxes. My roommate, Mohan, was among them. Every evening, I'd find him slumped on the couch, a bag of potato chips in hand, staring blankly at the TV as if willing it to show him a way forward. Conversations in our apartment became grim and pragmatic: How long could severance last? Would another opportunity come before savings ran out? How did we keep hope alive when it felt like the world had pressed pause?

I couldn't take it. The negativity was stifling and it bothered me. My mind wandered, tracing paths back to Chennai and the life I might have built had I stayed. The familiar rhythms of home beckoned, but they also sparked something else—a glimmer of possibility.

I started to dream again. Sketching out plans late at night, I envisioned a training business in India. Back home, institutes like SSI and Radiant were booming, churning out tech talent to meet the demands of a rapidly globalizing world. What if I built a franchise model? What if I could extend the reach of these centres to places like Trichy and Coimbatore, creating opportunities not just for students but for myself and others?

I began reaching out to friends in India, testing the waters. Some were intrigued, and a few even agreed to take up franchises. Slowly, a blueprint for something big began to take shape—a network of training centres that could scale across cities, empowering students while offering me a path forward.

But every plan, no matter how detailed, comes with a question: Do you have the courage to act? As the dot-com world collapsed around me, that question loomed larger than ever.

—

On New Year's Eve 2001, Pattai, Ubab and I found ourselves in a cozy Mexican restaurant in the Bay Area, clinking glasses of margaritas as we toasted to a new millennium. The air was alive with celebration, but underneath the surface, I couldn't shake the restlessness brewing inside me. Later that night, we decided to watch *Cast Away*.

Watching Tom Hanks stranded on an island, his only companion a volleyball named Wilson, hit harder than I expected. As he returned home after four years to find his world irrevocably changed—his family had moved on, his life was unrecognizable—I felt the weight of it all. America was my island. The isolation was more than a metaphor; it was my reality.

That night, as the credits rolled and the room fell silent, I made a decision: I was going back.

By March 2001, I was in Chennai once again, my head buzzing with optimism and plans. I opened MindSphere, a training venture, with a small office in Adyar. It was modest, but it was mine—a chance to create something meaningful. Within the first week, we landed a contract with Cognizant worth ₹80,000. It wasn't much, but it felt like a win, a sign that things were falling into place.

But optimism can only carry you so far. The aftershocks of the dot-com bust had travelled across oceans and India's tech job market was frozen solid. The big IT firms halted hiring and the students signing up for Java courses at MindSphere quickly realized their training wouldn't lead to job offers. The excitement faded into a sobering reality.

I tried to hold on, pouring everything I had into teaching. My days blurred together—standing at the whiteboard by day, grabbing street food with my cousin by night and clinging to slivers of hope. Life felt stagnant, and so did MindSphere.

By July, the writing on the wall was undeniable: MindSphere couldn't survive. The market wasn't there and no amount of passion or effort could conjure demand where none existed. Shutting it down felt like swallowing glass. It was the collapse of a dream I'd carried back across the world.

As I locked the MindSphere office for the last time, I carried more than just the weight of failure. I realized the importance of timing. Back in 1998, I'd thrived because I caught a wave—a surging demand for Java programmers and a job market hungry for talent. In 2001, despite being a better teacher with more experience, the wave was gone. Talent, effort and passion made my craft, but I was paddling in still water without the wave.

Life had come full circle in the span of a few months. I had left behind the comforts of the US—the steady paycheque, the dollar salary, the stability my friends envied. I returned to India with a vision and a bet on myself to build something meaningful after the dot-com crash. But, within three months, the dream had unravelled.

At twenty-six, I was unmarried, unemployed and staring down a recession. The safety net I thought I'd built was gone, leaving me with nothing but an empty canvas and a daunting question: What next?

SECTION 3

FOUNDATIONS

Crafting the Launchpad

Chapter 8

BY July, MindSphere was just a memory—a start-up dream snuffed out before it could truly burn. The vision I'd clung to, of building something from scratch, was gone in a blink. With it went the energy that had propelled me forward. I found myself wandering Chennai's bustling streets, not as part of the crowd but as a detached observer watching life pulse on without me.

The days stretched long and empty. I passed time with daytime dance classes and aimless chatter with equally adrift friends, but the void only deepened. I was navigating not just the streets of Chennai but also the creeping sense of futility, the sharp sting of potential slipping away.

The same question haunted me each evening: What am I doing with my life?

'This is just a bend in the road,' I whispered to myself, trying to kindle a spark of optimism. It wasn't the end. Dusting off my résumé, I flipped to *The Hindu's* Opportunities section, the bold ads promising pathways out of my rut. Every Saturday morning, I scanned those pages with the fervour of someone searching for a lifeline, desperate for one listing to open a door.

The first flicker came in the form of Oracle. The ad felt like an invitation to a brighter chapter.

By 6.30 p.m., I was ready, adrenaline coursing as I waited for the Oracle call. When the call came with a request to reschedule, it felt like a minor hiccup. But the next day brought silence. With no name to trace or follow up to pursue, I realized the opportunity had slipped through my fingers. It stung more than I cared to admit—a bitter lesson in preparation and luck.

Still, there was no time for pity. *Forward. Always forward.* It only took one open door, I reminded myself; one break. The classifieds became my compass once again, guiding me towards the next opportunity.

The next lead came in the form of a GE ad: Walk-in interviews at the Taj Coromandel. The Taj—its grandeur had always loomed as a distant symbol of success, something to admire but never touch. Now, it was within my reach for the first time, even if only for a morning.

By 8.45 a.m., I was standing in its shadow, early enough to outpace the growing storm of hopefuls. Inside, the lobby—with its polished marble floors—had been repurposed into an interview hall. Conversations hummed softly from every corner, each charged with ambition and nerves. This was a brush with a future I'd only imagined.

I couldn't help but think of *Jack: Straight from the Gut*, Welch's book, where GE stood as a beacon of innovation and leadership. The thought of being a part of that legacy sent a current of excitement through me. Could this really be the break I had been looking for?

The interview began with routine questions, as predictable as they were unsettling. 'Rate yourself in Java from one to ten,' they asked. I chose a safe seven—enough to imply competence without arrogance. They nodded without betraying a hint of reaction.

Then came the coding challenge. There was no computer, just pen and paper. Each line I wrote was a mental puzzle, visualizing logic and structure. I handed in my work, feeling a flicker of optimism. Maybe, just maybe, this was the moment.

But that spark was quickly extinguished. The response was one of practiced indifference: 'We'll get back to you.'

As I stepped outside, reality struck like a punch to the gut. The line of hopefuls stretched on endlessly—down the marble stairs, across the driveway, spilling into the street. It was less a queue and more a crush of humanity, faces brimming with the same hope I'd carried into the building. It looked more like the premiere of a Rajnikanth movie than a job interview.

I'd been lucky to make it through the doors early, to have my shot without the interminable wait. But luck could only take me so far. It wasn't enough.

Stepping out into the sunlight, I shook off the disappointment. There was no room for despair, no time for second-guessing. The grind wasn't over. *Forward. Always forward.* One door had closed, but somewhere, another was waiting to open. All I had to do was keep looking.

Hope was wearing thin. The classifieds, once a source of possibility, had become a ritual of futility. Each day felt like a race against time, my optimism dwindling with every unanswered ad. Then, out of nowhere, came a casual suggestion from Krishna, a friend of my cousin Vijay.

'You should check out AdventNet,' Krishna said. It was a simple nudge, offered in passing, but it planted a seed. Vijay forwarded my résumé and, soon, AdventNet called me for an interview.

Krishna didn't live to see the ripple effect of his words. A few years after I joined AdventNet, he tragically drowned while on a trip with friends. But his kindness opened a door that would change my life forever.

Chapter 9

THE interview was scheduled at Zoho's (known as AdventNet then) office on Velachery Main Road. Back then, Velachery wasn't the bustling tech hub it is today; it was a nondescript suburb, which felt remote. As my auto bumped along the narrow winding road, I wondered if I'd taken a wrong turn.

I had a second-hand Maruti Zen parked at home, but I chose an auto to avoid parking hassles. The journey seemed endless, every bump and turn amplifying my apprehension.

Finally, the auto pulled up in front of Kashyap Enclave, an ordinary apartment complex. There was no glitzy façade, no gleaming glass towers proclaiming corporate success. Instead, AdventNet's headquarters consisted of a handful of apartments reimagined as office spaces.

I stepped into the building, my curiosity mixing with uncertainty. The set-up was unlike anything I'd imagined. There were no polished receptions or carpeted floors, no carefully curated aesthetics. Instead, I found converted living rooms filled with workstations, black rolling chairs, and coffee-stained whiteboards brimming with flowcharts and ideas. Engineers sat in what had once been bedrooms, their heads bent in quiet concentration, the soft hum of computers filling the air.

It was unpolished and raw, and I loved it! Every corner spoke of ingenuity and effort. Nothing was wasted on appearances. This was a place where people rolled up their sleeves and *built* things. It wasn't about how things looked; it was about what they could become.

As I took it all in, I felt a faint thrill. This was different. This was real. It wasn't flashy or predictable, but it was alive with purpose.

The first two interviews began without fanfare: No small talk, no icebreakers. Sridhar Iyengar and Mathivanan jumped straight into the deep end—programming challenges and networking fundamentals. The questions were challenging and I drew on every scrap of my experience at HCL-Cisco to piece together answers. When I didn't know the answer, I improvised. I wasn't trying to impress them—I was just trying to survive.

Unknown to me, they already had a role in mind: TL1 protocol lead. TL1, or Transaction Language 1, was a telecom protocol I'd barely heard of, let alone studied. But they didn't seem concerned about my gaps in knowledge. They were testing something else: Adaptability, problem-solving and how I approached the unknown.

The third interview was supposed to be just a formality with HR, but Vardarajulu, the HR manager, had other ideas. He shifted the tone from technical to personal with a single question: 'Where do you see yourself in five years?'

Without hesitation, I replied, 'I'll be an entrepreneur again in five years.'

The words surprised even me. They weren't rehearsed or calculated. My recent attempt at entrepreneurship had ended in failure, but the fire hadn't been extinguished. If my answer came across as audacious, so be it—I wasn't going to fake my way through this.

Then came the salary question. I threw out a number: Five lakhs a year, roughly over ₹40,000 per month. It seemed fair for my experience, though it felt almost absurd as I glanced around. The HR manager's desk was crammed beneath a staircase, files stacked precariously around him, as though space itself had been an afterthought. This wasn't a gleaming corporate tower or a Silicon Valley campus—it was as bare-bones as it got.

But somehow, that didn't matter. As I sat there, a strange clarity washed over me. I didn't need sleek offices or inflated paycheques. I needed purpose—a chance to build something meaningful. AdventNet, stripped down to its essentials, offered that chance. Here, it wasn't about appearances. It was about potential.

At that moment, I was all in.

The next day, I got the call: Another interview, this time at a new address. 'It's our new office,' they said, the words carrying a sense of promise. This time, I was meeting Shailesh Kumar, AdventNet's VP of engineering.

Walking into the new office was like stepping into another world. Gone were the makeshift cubicles and workstations haphazardly crammed into living rooms and bedrooms. Instead, I found rows of neatly arranged desks, glass-walled conference rooms glowing under fluorescent lights and a receptionist's desk anchoring the entrance. It wasn't extravagant but radiated purpose—an environment where ambition had room to grow.

Shailesh was lean, short and bespectacled—the very picture of an IIT graduate. He didn't project authority in the traditional sense, but the respect he commanded was palpable. When I stepped into his spacious office, it was clear: This was a moment that could define the next chapter of my career.

He wasted no time. Shailesh laid out his vision for a new strategic projects group with sharp energy and deliberate words.

What he said struck a chord. This wasn't about routine coding or technical maintenance; it was about stepping into the client's world, understanding their challenges and crafting tailored solutions. It demanded domain knowledge, craftsmanship and fast execution.

Shailesh had a knack for steering the conversation, delving into areas where I felt confident and gracefully pausing when we touched on topics I hadn't mastered. The interview wasn't an interrogation; it felt like an exploration. He wasn't looking to expose gaps but to understand the depth of my strengths.

As he spoke, I realized this was more than just a job. It was a role that played to my strengths in ways I hadn't fully recognized. I'd never seen myself as a standout programmer, but this wasn't about sitting behind a desk writing code. It was about connection, about translating customer needs into solutions that felt uniquely theirs.

It hit me like a bolt of clarity. This was the intersection of creativity and technology, the blend of people and problem-solving that I hadn't known I was looking for.

I left the interview energized. I didn't know it yet, but this was the beginning of a transformation—not just in my career, but in how I approached every challenge that came after.

I didn't realize then that my journey to joining AdventNet was anything but typical. After my initial interviews, the team had decided they wanted me. But there was a catch—my salary expectations were higher than their usual range. That was enough to escalate my résumé up to Kumar Vembu, the founder himself.

Kumar didn't sift through résumés out of the need to micromanage. He did it because he believed in spotting something others might miss—a spark, a raw edge, potential that didn't scream from bullet points on a CV. When my profile landed on his desk, something stood out.

It wasn't my technical experience, though that's what I was being considered for. Kumar saw something else entirely. There were threads in my résumé—the way I had presented myself—that hinted at something different.

'If you hire him as a technical lead,' Kumar reportedly told the recruiters, 'he'll be bored in three months and leave.'

Kumar wasn't looking for someone to fill a position; he was looking for someone who could evolve, someone whose skills could the bridge gaps no one else was filling. Where others saw a tech hire, Kumar saw a marketer, someone who could connect the dots between product and customer.

That single insight—an instinct honed over years of reading people—changed everything. Kumar was crafting a role where I could thrive.

Kumar Vembu was unlike any leader I'd ever met. He didn't just manage people; he invested in them. He didn't focus on where you were; he focused on where you could go.

At AdventNet, stories about Kumar circulated like folklore. 'I owe my career to him,' people would say, not in whispers but with a heartfelt gratitude that came from being genuinely understood and empowered.

Kumar had a knack for spotting potential in places others might overlook. He called them 'corporate resources', the people he believed could become the backbone of the company. Once he identified them, he didn't hover or micromanage. Instead, he handed them the reins, gave them the freedom to lead and trusted them to succeed.

His approach was as unorthodox as it was transformative. The most critical projects and boldest initiatives always went to members of his corporate resources group—a select cadre that made up less than 10 per cent of the company. These weren't just employees; they were the architects of AdventNet's future.

Kumar had a distinct way of marking you as one of these pivotal players: The MVP tag in performance appraisals. Earning it wasn't easy. It came only after a meticulous review of accomplishments—a signal that you weren't just doing your job, you were shaping the company's trajectory. To be tagged as an MVP was a declaration that you mattered.

Under Kumar's leadership, the MVP tag was a ticket to opportunity, a sign that you were entrusted with the company's future. It wasn't about titles or hierarchy; it was about belief. And in that belief, Kumar built a culture where people didn't just work—they thrived.

Chapter 10

WALKING into AdventNet in 2001 felt like stepping into another world. It wasn't like HCL-Cisco, with its layers of hierarchy and polished corporate veneer. AdventNet was raw, unpretentious and alive with energy.

It reminded me of college—casual, chaotic and brimming with ideas. Nobody cared about titles. What mattered was getting things done, how deeply you cared and what you could do. Ownership wasn't assigned here—it was claimed.

Processes? There weren't many. Decisions weren't buried in approval chains; they were made in real-time. Problems were solved on whiteboards, sketched out in hurried conversations huddled around desks. Meetings were rare. When we brought in Marty Cagan, a prominent voice in product management, to train our team, he pointed out something that stuck with me.

'All your meeting rooms are empty,' he said. 'That means a lot of work gets done here.'

He was right. Work didn't wait for formality; it happened in the flow, in the act of creation.

That culture was the engine that powered AdventNet. Everyone, from junior engineers to senior managers, owned a piece of the puzzle. And with ownership came pride—a deep responsibility that drove us to push harder, think smarter and care deeply.

I was part of a culture that refused to settle. We weren't perfect, but we were relentless. It was a place where failure wasn't feared, where ideas weren't stifled and where ambition didn't need permission to grow.

Looking back, that was the foundation that kept AdventNet alive and thriving. It was more than a workplace—it was a proving ground, a space where you could test yourself, grow and build something meaningful.

Kumar had created a gritty, unpolished, but deeply purposeful culture where people could own their work and their futures. That simple truth made all the difference.

—

Shailesh, my first boss at AdventNet, wasn't one for handholding. His onboarding philosophy was simple: Throw new hires into the fire and see who comes out stronger. On my first day, he handed me my marching orders with no preamble.

'Start by answering customer support questions. That's the fastest way to learn the product,' he said matter-of-factly.

No introductions, no HR welcome packets, no glossy training manuals. Just a direct shove into the deep end. Sink or swim.

At first, it sounded simple enough. Answering emails? How hard could it be? But I quickly discovered these weren't your average support tickets. Each email was a labyrinth of technical questions about WebNMS—modules I hadn't even heard of, features I couldn't locate and edge cases that felt like they belonged to another universe.

These weren't frustrated users asking why their software wasn't working. They were developers dissecting the product, probing its innermost capabilities with surgical precision. Every email felt like a puzzle with a dozen missing pieces, and I didn't even know what the final picture was supposed to look like.

The first few days was pure chaos. I'd sit at my desk, staring at the screen as the cursor blinked back at me, mocking my confusion. Every answer I attempted seemed to spawn ten new questions I couldn't answer. It felt like being thrown into a raging sea with no lifeboat in sight.

Desperate for clarity, I began marching over to the engineers managing the modules. Some barely glanced up from their screens, rattling off jargon like a foreign language. Others paused to explain, their enthusiasm for their work shining through as they sketched diagrams on whiteboards or pointed me to hidden documentation. I scribbled down whatever I could, piecing together their insights like fragments of a treasure map.

It was overwhelming and exhausting, and, more than once, I wondered if I was in over my head. But there was an unexpected camaraderie in the chaos. Formalities didn't exist. If I needed answers, I could call ahead or just show up at someone's desk. Engineers would stop what they were doing, dive into my questions and send me back armed with enough understanding to tackle the next ticket.

Every email I answered was not only for the customer—it was for me. Each reply was a tiny victory, a marker in my uphill battle to understand the product.

Slowly, patterns began to emerge. A feature here, a bug there—the pieces started to fit together. With every email I sent, I was reconstructing WebNMS in my mind. It stopped being a chaotic collection of modules and started becoming a cohesive whole.

I was not only learning how to use WebNMS; I was learning how to think like the people who built it. Each query sharpened my instincts, teaching me not just what the product did but why it was built that way.

—

Looking back, Shailesh's method was unconventional, but it was genius. He didn't believe in spoon-feeding knowledge or wrapping new hires in a protective bubble. Instead, he trusted the product itself to be the teacher. By throwing me into the mess, he forced me to engage with the product at a level no formal training programme could have matched.

More than anything, Shailesh wanted me to take ownership. He wasn't just asking me to understand WebNMS; he was challenging me to own it.

By the end of those gruelling weeks, I didn't just know the product—I lived it. The chaos that had once overwhelmed me became the foundation of my confidence. Shailesh hadn't just taught me a job; he'd shown me how to approach challenges head-on, to let discomfort sharpen me and to thrive in the fire.

—

When I joined AdventNet in 2001 as a pre-sales engineer, one thing struck me immediately: Our demos were lifeless. They were functional, yes—efficient walkthroughs of features presented with polished templates—but they lacked soul. The screens could have been for anyone, offering a generic script that failed to connect with the client's story. It felt mechanical, impersonal and uninspired.

Then came my first demo for Riverbed Networks. As I prepared, the AdventNet WebNMS splash screen stared back at me for a full thirty seconds—our name, bold and unmissable. It was a proud statement of identity, but something about it felt off.

Why should the prospect see this? I thought. Why not start with their name, their story?

That thought sparked an idea. I called our designer and requested a quick change: A new splash banner featuring Riverbed Networks' logo and the title 'Element Management System' in bold letters. It was a small tweak, just a custom graphic with the same dimensions, but it planted a seed.

From there, we went deeper. We reworked the entire demo, tailoring it to what we knew about Riverbed's business. Every feature we showcased, every workflow we highlighted, was chosen with them in mind.

The next day, the screen lit up with Riverbed Networks' name and the room shifted almost instantly. Eyes that had been half-closed with disinterest opened wide. Shoulders straightened. People who had been passive listeners leaned forward, suddenly engaged.

For the first time, the product didn't feel like ours—it felt like theirs.

The energy in the room was palpable. The questions came quickly, each one sharper and more specific than the last. The demo transformed into a dialogue. The product's features weren't abstract—they were solutions to their challenges, tools for their success.

That single tweak—a splash screen—had transformed the demo from a dry presentation into a shared experience. It wasn't about dazzling them with our technical brilliance; it was about showing them that we understood their world.

That moment was a revelation. Customization was the key to building trust. It showed clients that they weren't just another calendar entry. It said: We see you. We hear you. We're invested in your success.

From that day forward, personalization became my guiding principle. Every demo became an opportunity to connect, to craft an experience that spoke directly to what mattered most to each client.

Looking back, that tweak was far more than a splash screen change. It taught me a fundamental truth: Even the smallest adjustments, when rooted in genuine empathy and understanding, can create the biggest impact.

The success of the Riverbed demo illuminated a stark truth: While we could impress clients with a great presentation, we left them to fend for themselves afterwards. Our demos sold the product, but onboarding often left them adrift. Clients needed more than features—they needed direction, tools and a clear path to solving their unique challenges.

That realization lit a fire in me. AdventNet didn't just need to sell solutions; we needed to teach clients how to build them. And that meant creating a training programme from scratch.

—

The foundation of the programme became a hands-on training workshop, centred on a fictional company I created called Skylark Networks. Each module simulated real-world challenges, guiding clients through step-by-step customizations of WebNMS to meet their needs. This wasn't a passive, dry manual—it was an interactive experience that turned users into creators.

By the end of each workshop, clients didn't just understand the product; they owned it. They left with the confidence to apply what they had learned, empowered to design solutions tailored to their businesses.

But a vision, no matter how clear, needs the right people to bring it to life. My first hire was Navaneetha Krishnan J., a sharp thinker whose knack for problem-solving would later lead him to co-found Voonik. Next came Neelam Chand, a natural go-getter who would go on to build Hippo Video. Together, we formed a nimble, driven team united by one goal: Revolutionizing how AdventNet connected with its customers.

We took a bold step—offshoring demo customizations to Chennai. By shifting the fine-tuning and personalization work locally, we freed the US sales engineers to focus on what mattered most: High-impact client interactions. Every detail crafted in Chennai was intentional, ensuring each demo felt tailor-made for the customer.

The shift wasn't without its challenges. Late nights and countless iterations became the norm as we worked to perfect every demo. But the effort paid off. Clients no longer saw just software—they saw solutions. Solutions designed for them, with their unique needs at the centre.

This wasn't about selling a product; it was about building partnerships. Every interaction deepened trust, showing clients we understood their challenges and cared about their success. With each demo, we were saying: We're here for you.

—

Looking back, those long hours, the training manual and the team weren't just tasks; they were the seeds of a cultural shift that would define everything that followed. The ethos was simple but powerful: Always design with the customer in mind. It became a guiding principle that shaped not only AdventNet but also the DNA of what would later grow into Zoho and Freshworks.

The lesson was clear: The smallest, most deliberate actions can drive the biggest transformations. Write the manual. Build the team. Solve for the customer first. Always.

Just three months into my tenure at AdventNet, I was handed an opportunity that was as exhilarating as it was intimidating: Training WebNMS resellers across Europe. The assignment felt monumental; and while a part of me was excited, another part whispered, 'Are you ready for this?'

Ready or not, there was no time for hesitation.

The training was to take place in Nice, France, a city as picturesque as its name. As the plane descended, the serene coastline stretched below like a postcard. But inside me, it was anything but serene—a mix of nerves and disbelief. Only months earlier, I'd been scanning job classifieds, uncertain about the next step in my career. And now, here I was, about to lead a room full of seasoned professionals.

The training room was packed. Rows of sharp, discerning eyes followed my every move. I'd spent days crafting a comprehensive manual, poring over every detail. But as I stepped to the front, a wave of doubt hit me. Could someone with just three months' experience possibly command the attention and respect of this audience?

Taking a deep breath, I started. Slowly, the tension began to dissolve. Questions flowed and, with each response, I felt the room warming to me. The nods of approval grew and a rhythm emerged—a dynamic back-and-forth that built trust. By the time I finished, I knew that the session was a hit with our resellers. In that moment, I learned a powerful truth: Authority isn't just about experience; it's about preparation and rising to the moment.

Just as I hit my stride, a curveball came from Germany. A last-minute addition to my schedule landed me in Hanover for a high-stakes meeting tied to a $500,000 deal. The client had specifically requested a WebNMS architect. But with no one else available, Shailesh, my manager, decided, 'Send Girish.'

At first, I thought it was another training session. But as I walked into the room, the atmosphere was unmistakably different—charged and expectant. This was a very sophisticated audience. These were engineers who had spent months customizing our framework. Their questions were razor-sharp, their tone relentless.

'Why this architecture?'

'Why JTables in Java?'

'Have you done performance benchmarks on loading times for JTable?'

I wasn't an architect—I was barely a pre-sales engineer. But there was no space for panic. I stayed calm, meticulously noted their concerns and admitted when I didn't have the answers. Instead of pretending, I assured them I'd follow up with the relevant people. It wasn't a flawless performance, but it was authentic.

By the end of that meeting, I walked away with a lesson that would shape my approach to every tough customer conversation thereafter: Not having all the answers isn't a failure—it's an opportunity. What matters is how you handle it. Being honest, capturing feedback and showing a commitment to follow through can transform scepticism into trust.

Looking back, those two moments in Nice and Hanover didn't just test me—they transformed me. They taught me that readiness isn't about time; it's about showing up, facing challenges head-on and learning as you go.

After the whirlwind of work and back-to-back challenges, I craved a break—a solo vacation to reset and recharge. My destination? Paris, the city of light and dreams. But as I arrived at Hanover airport, my plans unravelled. My flight had been booked for the previous day. To make matters worse, an air traffic control strike had grounded all flights to Paris.

For a moment, frustration bubbled up. This was supposed to be my escape! But I wasn't about to let circumstances dictate my story. A quick search revealed a last-minute flight to Rome. Without hesitation, I booked it, secured a modest hotel and decided to let fate chart my course.

Rome welcomed me like an old friend—warm, vibrant and timeless. The city pulsed with history, its cobblestone streets whispering stories of resilience and grandeur. I wandered through the ruins of the Roman Forum, felt the weight of time at the Pantheon and stood in awe before the Colosseum. Its towering arches loomed like a silent mentor, a testament to enduring strength. Beneath its shadow, I found a moment of clarity—an unspoken reminder that resilience is not bound by time; it's a timeless human trait.

Eventually, I reached Paris, where the Louvre became the highlight. Standing before the Mona Lisa, I marvelled at its brilliance, trading stories with a fellow traveller and rediscovering the joy of connection.

What began as a disrupted plan turned into a transformative journey of self-discovery. Navigating setbacks, embracing spontaneity and finding joy in the unexpected taught me something profound: Life isn't a straight road. It's a mosaic of detours, each filled with its own lessons and surprises.

When I returned to Chennai, I wasn't the same person who had left. Europe had tested me, shaped me and, most importantly, transformed me. The detours—the ones I hadn't planned—had been the most enriching parts of all. I came back sharper, more resilient and ready to face whatever came next with open arms.

In Chennai, the office buzzed with triumph. WebNMS 2.3 was live and the team celebrated as though they'd crossed the finish line of a gruelling race. But for me, Hanover's lessons still echoed and, amidst the cheers, I felt anything but victorious.

While the others revelled in accomplishment, I went straightaway to Kumar's office, unable to ignore the clarity that Europe had given me. I didn't mince words. 'Our customers don't care how many features we add,' I said bluntly, locking eyes with him. 'They need something reliable—a robust framework. Without that, all these features are just noise.'

Kumar listened intently, his expression steady. I could see he was weighing every word. The next day, he addressed the entire team at an all-hands meeting. 'Girish has given us a reality check,' he began, his tone serious. His words cut through the celebratory mood like a lightning bolt. 'We need to focus on strengthening the core before adding anything else.'

The celebration dimmed, replaced by reflection. It wasn't easy to hear, but the truth rarely is. That moment reframed my understanding of progress. Inside the company, moving the needle from 40 per cent to 70 per cent completeness felt like a win—a tangible leap forward. But to the customer, 70 per cent wasn't success. It was still failure.

It was a humbling realization. We saw our uphill climb—the hours, the effort, the incremental improvements. But customers didn't see the grind. They only saw the gaps. To them, our journey wasn't worth celebrating; they were waiting for results.

It felt like running a marathon, pausing at mile 20 to celebrate, only to hear the crowd shout: 'You're not done yet!' Effort didn't matter—only outcomes did.

This revelation left a lasting mark. Start-ups often fall in love with their own momentum, celebrating every feature release or milestone. But none of that matters if the customer's problem remains unsolved.

From that day forward, my perspective shifted. The foundation had to come first. The shine and polish could wait. What mattered was building something solid—something customers could trust without hesitation.

This lesson became a guiding principle—not just for how I built products but for how I led teams and companies. From that moment on, I carried this truth with me: progress isn't about internal milestones; it's about solving real problems for customers, meeting them exactly where they need us to be.

—

In 1999, I was running a modest Java training institute in Shenoy Nagar, juggling classes and dreams of building something meaningful. One of the students in that class was an engineering student from Coimbatore, D. She had come to Chennai for her holidays and had been referred to the course by her brother, one of my close friends from engineering. At the time, D was just a name on the attendance sheet, a quiet presence who blended into the crowd of eager learners. I taught the sessions, graded assignments and moved on, barely noticing her in the sea of faces.

Two years later, in 2001, life brought us together again—this time, under very different circumstances. I had returned from the US, navigating the challenges of building MindSphere, and often visited my friend's home. That's where I saw D again. Gone was the shy student from my Java class; in her place was a poised, confident young woman. She carried herself with an effortless charm that made her stand out in the lively atmosphere of her home, where dinners and conversations often stretched late into the night. I vaguely remembered her as my student, but now, she was more than that—a presence I couldn't ignore.

It's hard to forget my first meeting with D in her home. She had an air about her that immediately drew people in, cheerful, animated and effortlessly charming. Her smile seemed to belong to another world, one untouched by the weight of everyday worries. It wasn't just her cheerfulness that stood out, it was her presence. She had a way of making every conversation feel like it mattered.

Over time, the conversations extended beyond those dinners. During discussions, she'd lean forward, her hands punctuating her arguments, her eyes sparkling with conviction. Her voice carried a warmth that made even disagreements feel constructive, as though she could disagree without being disagreeable. It wasn't just what she said—it was how she said it, with an authenticity that made you listen.

Emails and phone calls turned into a connection that neither of us saw coming. What started as polite exchanges about work grew into deeper discussions about dreams, life and everything in between.

She was the youngest of three siblings, and you could tell. She had the light-hearted confidence of someone who'd grown up adored. She once told me, with a mischievous grin, 'My brothers never let me lift a finger at home.' Her stories from her childhood—of charming her way out of trouble or being indulged by her parents—always had us laughing.

The day MindSphere opened its office in Adyar was a moment of validation for me. The space was modest but filled with promise: Bare walls adorned with motivational posters, neatly arranged desks and the hum of computers that had just been set up. I had invited my family and a few close friends to mark the occasion, eager to share this achievement with the people who mattered most.

My father arrived early, his pride evident in the way he lingered over the details—examining the office layout, nodding approvingly at the set-up. My aunts came next, bustling in with their usual energy, followed by my cousins, who seemed more interested in teasing me than in admiring my entrepreneurial venture.

Then came D, accompanied by her parents and brother. She stepped into the room with her usual ease, her smile lighting up the otherwise subdued space. I introduced her family to mine and, for a moment, the room felt smaller, the chatter of introductions filling every corner. When I introduced D as my friend, my cousins exchanged knowing glances, their teasing smirks impossible to miss.

'So, who's this?' one of them asked, their tone dripping with mischief.

'She's just a friend,' I replied, brushing it off with a laugh.

But their teasing didn't stop. Throughout the evening, sly remarks and whispered jokes followed us wherever we went. 'Sure, just a friend,' one cousin muttered, loud enough for me to hear, as they winked in D's direction.

I laughed along with them, insisting there was nothing more to the story. And, at least at that moment, I believed it. But as the evening wore on and I caught glimpses of her chatting easily with my family, I couldn't shake the feeling that there might be something more—something I hadn't fully acknowledged yet.

When D left with her family, I found myself lingering at the door, watching as they disappeared into the night. The office still buzzed with life, but my thoughts were elsewhere, tangled in possibilities I wasn't ready to explore.

D joined AdventNet shortly after I did and we quickly became close. The long hours at work turned into shared coffee breaks, impromptu brainstorming sessions and conversations that stretched into the evenings. She had a knack for making the mundane feel special. Whether it was a simple cup of tea or a stroll to grab lunch, time spent with her felt lighter, easier—like the world had paused for a moment to breathe.

Amid the intensity of deadlines at AdventNet, her messages were my anchor. They reminded me of a world beyond metrics and milestones—a world of conversations that mattered.

The quiet hum of the evening filled the air as we strolled down a dimly lit road in Adyar. The rhythmic sound of her bicycle wheels seemed to echo my racing thoughts. The words tumbled out before I could stop them: 'I actually like you. I'd love to marry you.'

She froze, her expression shifting as my words sank in. For a moment, the silence between us felt heavier than anything she could say. 'I hadn't thought of it that way,' she murmured, her voice barely above a whisper. There was no edge to her tone, no immediate rejection—just hesitation.

It wasn't the answer I had hoped for, but it wasn't a definitive no either. The ambiguity of it hung in the air, pulling me into a place I didn't want to linger. Taking a deep breath, I met her gaze.

'I can't go back to being just friends,' I said, my voice firmer than I expected. 'It has to be all or nothing.'

Her eyes searched mine and, for a brief moment, I thought she might say something—offer clarity, closure ... Anything. But the silence lingered, speaking louder than words ever could.

That night, doubt wrapped itself around me like a cold fog. Had I misread her completely? Had I risked our friendship for something she didn't feel the same way about? The questions gnawed at me, keeping sleep at bay.

The next morning, I was startled by a knock at the door. When I opened it, there she was, standing on the threshold. Her usual confidence was replaced by something quieter, more vulnerable.

'Why did you say that?' she asked, her voice hesitant yet resolute.

I hesitated, unsure how to answer. But then she continued, her words tumbling out in a rush, as though she'd carried them all night. 'I can't stop thinking about you.'

For a moment, the world stilled. The doubt that had weighed so heavily the night before melted away, replaced by a warmth I hadn't dared to hope for. The uncertainty was gone and in its place was something undeniable—a connection we could no longer ignore.

—

In the early days, our relationship unfolded with an unspoken simplicity. Coffee breaks turned into long drives, and evenings stretched into hours of conversation on the sands of Besant Nagar Beach. There was a quiet magic in the way we existed together, untouched by time or obligation.

But life, as it often does, had other plans. A business trip took me to Europe and, when I returned, the air between us felt different. The warmth we had shared seemed overshadowed by something heavier.

Her family had intervened. Her brother—my friend—disapproved, his objections casting a shadow over what we had built. The disapproval didn't just strain our bond, it shook her confidence in us. I could see it in her eyes, the way her resolve wavered as she grappled with their expectations. What once felt certain now seemed fragile, slipping through our fingers no matter how tightly we tried to hold on.

Our final conversation unfolded in the AdventNet parking lot. 'If you stand with me, I'll fight for us till the end,' I said. 'But if you're unsure, I can't fight alone.' As I stood in the parking lot, her silence felt heavier than any words could. The hum of nearby conversations faded, leaving just the quiet ache of knowing that this was the end. Finally, she said, 'I'm not sure.'

The world didn't shatter; it simply dimmed.

We ended it on Valentine's Day—a cruel irony for something that had begun with so much promise. There was no anger, no blame, just the realization that sometimes, love isn't enough.

—

Life moved forward, as it always does. On 31 October 2002, we both married different people. It wasn't planned; it was life's peculiar way of weaving closure into the story.

D's chapter in my life was brief yet profound—a story of connection, hope and the bittersweet reality that not every love finds its forever.

—

Pre-sales had become a grind. Demo after demo, I was stuck in an endless loop, answering the same questions, running the same scripts. It felt like being on a treadmill—always moving but never getting anywhere. I craved something new, something that would reignite the spark. So, instead of waiting for an opportunity for change to present itself, I created one.

Over the following few weeks, I immersed myself in a new project: Building a library of forty 'canned demos', each tailored to specific industries—storage, Ethernet, optical fibre. Plug-and-play efficiency replaced repetitive customization. Time freed up. The grind eased. But for me, this achievement was bittersweet. It was satisfying, but it also cemented a realization: I was ready to move on.

Once the demo kits were live, I went straight to Kumar: 'I need something new,' I told him. Without hesitation, he offered me an opening in marketing—a role that promised uncharted territory. I didn't think twice before accepting it.

Marketing was a completely new challenge for me. Leading a small, scrappy team from Chennai, we tackled tasks that would free up a lot of time for our US folks—web design, trade show materials, polished brochures. It was fast-paced and impactful, everything I'd hoped for. At first.

Reality, however, had other plans. Each time we submitted work to the US team, it came back dripping with red ink. Feedback loops turned into frustrating cycles of perfection undone and my team felt like we were spinning our wheels. It was just tiring and demoralizing. Two masters, different visions and zero alignment.

I'd had enough. One day, I marched into Kumar's office and pitched a solution. 'Why don't I handle marketing for the rest of the world?' I suggested. 'Let the US team focus on their own.' It seemed like the perfect fix, but Kumar had other ideas.

Instead of discussing solutions, Kumar invited me to the roadside tea shop for tea. Over steaming cups of chai, he said something that stopped me in my tracks.

'Girish,' he began, 'do you know what the problem is? You're an authoritative person. Marketing is a consultative role. That's why you're frustrated. You're trying to make decisions that aren't yours to make.'

It stung, but I couldn't deny it. My natural instinct was to take charge, to lead. Marketing, though, demanded persuasion, patience and collaboration. I was in the wrong role for my strengths and Kumar wasn't afraid to tell me so.

Then, he flipped the script. 'Why don't you become a product manager instead?' he asked, as casually as suggesting lunch.

I was blindsided. Product management? The concept was barely on my radar. But Kumar saw something I hadn't. He reminded me of a conversation I'd had months earlier in Seoul. While training Telement Corporation, a Korean reseller, they'd questioned why we weren't building tools for businesses—affordable, user-friendly solutions for small and medium enterprises.

'Why don't you build that product?' Kumar proposed 'A network-management tool for IT departments.'

His challenge was simple but seismic. Clarity hit me like lightning. 'Yes,' I replied without hesitation. I had no idea what being a product manager entailed, but the idea of building something new, something transformative, was irresistible.

Back at my desk, I opened my browser and typed, 'Product Manager Roles and Responsibilities'. The adventure had begun.

The more I researched, the clearer it became: A product manager was a microcosm of leadership. You weren't confined to one department or function. You owned everything—sales, support, development and the delicate art of bringing them all together. It was like being the CEO of a single product.

The idea hooked me instantly. Every word I read pulled me in deeper, painting a picture of a role that demanded vision, grit and the ability to juggle chaos with clarity. By the end of the day, I didn't just understand the role, I wanted it.

I met Kumar soon after that, fuelled by the excitement of discovery. 'I'm in,' I said, the words spilling out with certainty.

'Okay, come back and present your strategy when you are ready,' Kumar replied.

Over chai and that brief conversation, my path shifted in a way I couldn't yet grasp. I didn't know it then, but I was stepping into the role that would define my career—one decision that would transform not just how I worked but how I thought, led and grew.

Weeks of research had consumed me—Gartner reports, customer feedback and competitor analysis. I pieced together every scrap of data into a detailed presentation, eager to impress Kumar with my strategy presentation. As I launched into my exhaustive rundown, he stopped me midway.

'Girish,' he said, leaning back in his chair. 'Don't just show me your homework. Tell me your insights.'

His words hit hard. I realized I was drowning him in data instead of delivering the story it told. I went back, stripped away the noise and focused on the essence: The *what* and the *why*.

When I returned, I pitched a vision: ManageEngine—a unified platform to simplify IT operations and services, making enterprise-level IT accessible to small and medium businesses (SMBs) and mid-market businesses. Initially, I'd called it *Em**power, short for enterprise-management power, but a quick search revealed the name was already taken by a waste-management company. ManageEngine felt sharper, capturing the heart of our mission: Managing the IT lifecycle for companies without enterprise budgets.

Kumar leaned back, nodding in acknowledgment. 'You are going to present this to the management team next week,' he said. I knew we'd hit on something real.

—

The insight came from dissecting the big players—BMC, HP and the rest.

They weren't just selling tools, they were offering integrated IT solutions: IT operations for managing infrastructure like servers and data centres; IT services for managing employee needs like helpdesk support and desktop management.

But these solutions were bloated, complex and priced out of reach for SMBs and most mid-market companies. A glaring gap sat untouched and it ignited something in me.

'We need to bridge that gap,' I proposed. 'An affordable, complete IT solution for SMBs and the mid-market.'

This was the core of the ManageEngine strategy and it was a game-changer. We weren't building another tool; we were levelling the playing field—delivering IT power to businesses the giants ignored. ManageEngine became more than software, it became a statement about democratizing network-management software.

ManageEngine was the start of a journey that would redefine how I thought, worked and led. That decision, born over a cup of chai, set the stage for everything that came next.

In May 2002, I travelled to Trichy to attend Pattai's wedding, a colourful affair brimming with music, laughter and the scent of flowers wafting through the air. The next evening, I visited my cousin Uma and her husband Shanky—my go-to person for work and business conversations—for a relaxed dinner. Over drinks, we swapped ideas and anecdotes late into the night and, at their insistence, I stayed over.

The next morning began with the comfort of filter coffee and a quiet newspaper session with Shanky. But an unexpected call from my father broke the stillness. 'There's someone who wants to meet you,' he said, urgency threading his voice. Intrigued, I borrowed Uma's Zen and drove over.

At the doorstep, I was greeted by a tall, lanky man in his fifties, glasses perched on his nose, and an air of dignity. 'He's here seeking an alliance for his daughter, Shoba,' my dad explained. After a polite exchange of pleasantries, it was agreed that later in the day, we'd visit his home to meet the family—and the daughter. This was the arranged marriage equivalent of a first date, with the added spectacle of both families in tow.

Before leaving, I offered him a ride home. He reluctantly agreed, but as we neared his neighbourhood, he gestured for me to stop on the main road. 'I'll walk from here,' he said, his voice casual, but I could tell he didn't want me knowing his exact address just yet. As he disappeared into the bustle of the street, I chuckled to myself, amused by the subtle theatrics.

The clock ticked to 3 p.m., the designated hour. In line with tradition, my entourage—Uma, Shanky and my parents—piled into the car, armed with good-natured chatter. When we arrived, their home was alive with activity. Shoba's younger sisters, Ramya and Meena, bustled around the room, arranging plates of snacks. The smell of freshly fried bajjis and filter coffee filled the air.

Then she entered—dusky, lean and striking, her sharp features radiating a quiet confidence. Her calm demeanour balanced the energy of the room, and I knew I had to know more about her. Polite introductions were made and I seized the opportunity to request a private conversation. We were ushered into a cozy side room, its walls adorned with family photographs and shelves lined with books.

What was meant to be a brief chat turned into an hour that felt suspended in time. We spoke about our quirks and dreams, but it was the effortless connection that struck me. Her quick wit, her curious questions and the way she listened—attentive, yet unpretentious—left me disarmed. When I asked her about her dream car, she mentioned a Mercedes E-Class. I grinned and told her about my 'Dream Book', promising to add a picture of the car to it. Later, she'd tell me that this simple gesture—folding her dream into my own—was the moment she knew I was the one.

By 15 May, we were engaged. Over the next five months, our daily phone calls became a lifeline, weaving a thread of intimacy. Shoba's detailed updates about her day amused me so much that I coined a term for it:

'phonecasting'. Her laughter became my favourite sound, her joys and worries my own.

On 31 October, surrounded by family and friends, Shoba became my wife. She stepped into my world with grace, embracing not just me but the chaos of relentless work hours and my quirks. Yet, she did so with a quiet strength that left me in awe.

And so began our story—one woven with shared dreams, late-night conversations and the understanding that love, in its truest form, is about finding joy in the everyday moments that make up a life together.

—

Tucked away in a corner of our Chennai office, six dreamers dared to reimagine how businesses monitored their networks—our ambition far outweighing our resources. Our mission: Transform AdventNet's developer-centric tool into a sleek, simple, user-friendly network-monitoring software. We brainstormed endlessly until 'OpManager'—short for Operations Manager—emerged, a name that encapsulated simplicity and functionality.

Our workspace became a battleground of caffeine, adrenaline and belief. Amid the haze of coffee and the relentless click of keyboards, our little corner buzzed with the sounds of possibility and exhaustion.

It wasn't about reinventing the wheel—it was about refining it. We polished the UI, highlighted key features and crafted a product that business users could embrace without technical hurdles. By April, we had an alpha version.

OpManager was proof of what we could build when we focused on what truly mattered: Delivering solutions that empowered customers. And it all started with a shift in mindset—from sharing homework to delivering insights.

—

April 2003: We took OpManager to the Interop Conference in Las Vegas, standing among industry giants like HP and BMC. As we stood in our modest booth, dwarfed by industry giants, our excitement mingled with a sense of vulnerability. This was our David versus Goliath moment. We had a bold promise: Unlimited device monitoring for just $795.

As I demoed the product, scepticism hung in the air. Veterans strolled by, their glances flickering between curiosity and dismissal. Then, a man from American Express stopped, his eyes scanning the screen.

'This can't be real,' he said, his voice tinged with disbelief. 'What's the catch?' His scepticism was a harsh reminder of how audacious pricing can breed doubt.

His words might have stung, but they exposed a harsh truth: The market equated quality with cost, and our audacious pricing seemed suspicious. I offered him a free trial, hoping the product would prove itself. He walked away unconvinced.

Back in Chennai, we dissected the Vegas feedback with growing clarity. One-size-fits-all wasn't a strategy—it was a limitation. We reimagined our pricing, striking a delicate balance between accessibility and credibility.

Vegas didn't just challenge us—it defined us. With every tweak and test, OpManager grew stronger, not just as a product but as a testament to what determination can achieve.

The months leading up to the launch blurred into a haze of sleepless nights and relentless bug fixes. Each step forward unearthed a new setback, tethering us to a cycle of triumph and exasperation. The date 31 October 2003 is etched into my memory for two profound milestones: My first wedding anniversary and the launch of OpManager. We were running on fumes, but the finish line was in sight.

That final night, the office was a hive of unspoken intensity. Hunched over our desks, my team and I ran test after test, each loop draining what little energy we had left. By 5.30 a.m., bleary-eyed but triumphant, we pushed the product live. A brief window of reprieve followed, just enough time to mark my anniversary with a few stolen hours. By 9.30 a.m., I was back at my desk, refreshing the screen obsessively, awaiting the flood of emails and sales.

Instead, silence.

Our screens stared back at us blankly, the reality sinking in: Launching wasn't the same as arriving. The product wasn't truly out there yet. And so, the wait for customers began.

The first two months trickled in with a modest $2,000 in revenue—barely a murmur by most standards. But for me, it was a start. I believed deeply in what we'd built—an intuitive, beautifully designed product that solved real customer problems at a fraction of the cost. I knew the market existed. We simply had to reach it.

That launch was more than OpManager's debut—it was my initiation into the world of product management, albeit 'accidental'. It came with sleepless nights and punishing lessons, but also the indelible reward of true ownership: Seeing a product through from concept to impact.

OpManager was proof of what passion and perseverance could achieve. That belief, tested and strengthened, became the fuel to carry us forward.

Chapter 11

IN 2002, AdventNet followed the traditional US corporate model: product management, marketing and sales were firmly entrenched in America, while India functioned as the engineering hub. But with OpManager, we rewrote the playbook.

For the first time, Chennai became the heart of innovation. Product management, marketing and engineering worked together under one roof. No longer a back office, Chennai became the nerve centre. The challenge, however, was formidable: Sustaining a global sales operation for a product priced at just $795.

In the US, enterprise sales reps, accustomed to six-figure deals, couldn't justify selling something under $1,000. We needed an entirely new approach. Demand generation, marketing and even sales had to shift entirely to Chennai.

It began with WebNMS. We had heavily invested in leased lines and phone infrastructure to set up a customer-service centre in Chennai. However, the centre never quite took off as intended, leaving Chennai's state-of-the-art infrastructure—Nortel leased lines, IPLCs and night-shift teams—underutilized.

What started as a pragmatic move to maximize resources quickly evolved into something much larger. Chennai began to shed its identity as a back office merely handling support calls and emerged as a hub of innovation.

Leveraging the infrastructure initially built for WebNMS, we expanded operations to include demand generation and deal closures for OpManager. Unknowingly, we were creating the foundation for an inbound sales engine—one that thrived on efficiency and focus, not expensive field reps.

Our strategy was deceptively simple: Keep prices low, quality high and let the product speak for itself. While competitors charged upwards of $50,000, we priced OpManager at $795. Yet, we didn't compromise on design, reliability or ease of use—qualities unheard of at our price point.

The turning point came in 2003 when I stumbled across a forgotten Google AdWords account with a $50 credit. Intrigued, we experimented, learning the basics of ad copy, campaigns and keywords. That curiosity quickly became a focused effort to drive traffic to our website—and it worked.

Instead of gruelling sales calls, we embraced what I called 'velocity sales'. Customers found us through Google, visited our website, downloaded the product and experienced its sleek UI. When they saw the price, it was irresistible.

There were no hard pitches or drawn-out demos. Prospects tried the product themselves, saw its value and bought it. Leads poured in—small businesses, teams within enterprises, grassroots buyers solving real problems. They discovered us, explored our product and, if it fit their needs, converted. This was product-led growth before the term even existed.

By 2004, our scrappy experiment had matured into a global operation. Chennai wasn't a limitation; it was the engine of a revolution. We proved that high-quality global solutions could not only be built in India but sold from India as well.

This pivot was more than a go-to market strategy change; it was a reinvention. The foundation of the company had transformed, setting the stage for a new era of innovation and growth.

Sridhar Vembu wasn't your typical CEO. He didn't sit behind a desk, buried in reports. Instead, he walked the floors—observing, listening and, most importantly, sensing. He had an uncanny ability to gauge the company's pulse, not through spreadsheets but through people.

One day, that intuition led him to the WebNMS 4 team. When he stepped into their corner, the air felt heavy with stagnation. Progress had slowed, the spark had faded and bureaucracy had dulled the edges of what was once a dynamic group. Sridhar later explained his observation succinctly: 'You can feel it—the energy. It's missing.'

Just a few steps away, the contrast was stark. A small team working on an experimental project buzzed with life. Whiteboards filled with scribbles, bursts of laughter and animated brainstorming sessions painted a picture of creativity in motion. Sridhar noticed the difference immediately.

The dot-com bust had devastated the market for WebNMS, AdventNet's flagship product. For most leaders, the grim numbers and dwindling momentum would have been paralysing. But Sridhar saw an opportunity. He made the call to shut down WebNMS 5 and splinter the team into smaller, more agile units tasked with pursuing new ideas.

The results were transformative. From these skunkworks, innovations emerged that would shape the company's future: WiFi Manager, Desktop Central and Event Log Analyzer. These weren't just products; they were bold experiments born from a culture of reinvention that Sridhar fostered.

This was Sridhar Vembu at his core—a quiet force of nature. Unorthodox and profoundly impactful, his decisions were sharp, his methods unconventional. He redefined how we approached problems, prioritized agility over structure and embraced chaos as fertile ground for growth.

Sridhar defied every stereotype. No corner office. No tailored suits. No corporate polish. He was the guy in a plain T-shirt and shorts, navigating Chennai traffic in a modest Toyota Innova. On trips, he avoided luxury—flying economy and staying in no-name motels. During one visit to Las Vegas, his hotel was so far away from the Strip that it barely qualified as part of the city. Frugality was a way of life, woven into the DNA of AdventNet.

Beneath his unassuming exterior lay a razor-sharp mind. Sridhar approached the world like a systems thinker. To him, economics, history and culture weren't abstract—they were blueprints for building resilience. He spoke of the self-reliance of Swiss cantons, the precision of German manufacturing and the discipline of Japanese work ethics, weaving these lessons into daily conversations.

'Companies are ecosystems,' he would say. 'They need to weather storms, not just chase sunny days.'

This clarity shaped AdventNet's evolution. When the company's backbone began to falter, most leaders would have clung to it, hoping for a turnaround. Not Sridhar. He redirected AdventNet's brightest minds to ManageEngine—a fledgling idea yet to prove itself. It was a bet on the future, and it paid off.

Sridhar's real magic wasn't control—it was empowerment. His philosophy was simple: 'People over process.' He let teams own their work, move fast and fail forward. Meetings were rare and documentation was nearly non-existent. It was a culture of trust and autonomy.

More than his decisions, it was this culture that defined Sridhar's legacy. He redefined what we believed was possible, showing us that leadership wasn't about micromanaging outcomes—it was about unlocking potential.

—

One day, Kumar sent me to Nungambakkam for an OpManager demo with Fullerton KCP, a cement manufacturer. The IT manager greeted me with polite indifference and the room seemed weighed down by apathy.

Halfway through my presentation, he casually opened another tool—TrackIT, an IT ServiceDesk product. The shift in his demeanour was instant. His voice filled with passion as he demonstrated its features, enthusiastically pointing out how it streamlined his workflows. It was a solution he loved, a tool that turned him into its advocate.

As I watched him practically sell me on TrackIT, a surge of clarity hit me. This was the kind of product I wanted to build—something that didn't just meet customer needs but inspired loyalty and excitement. The idea of an IT ServiceDesk was already part of my vision for ManageEngine, but, in that moment, it became personal. I didn't just want to compete with TrackIT. I wanted to beat it.

Back at the office, I interrupted Sridhar and his younger brother, Mani, mid-discussion, words tumbling out before I could stop them: 'I want to build an IT ServiceDesk and kill TrackIT.'

Sridhar didn't miss a beat. He turned to Mani and said, 'Girish is passionate about it. Let him build the product.'

I was ecstatic—until I told Kumar. His response was blunt: 'Why start a new product when your first one hasn't even hit $1 million? There are hundreds of helpdesks out there. How will you compete?'

It stung. Kumar was my mentor—someone I deeply admired and trusted. That night, I sought advice from Shoba, hoping for encouragement. Instead, she sided with Kumar: 'Do what your mentor says. Focus on one thing.'

But the idea wouldn't let go. Growth wasn't about staying in the comfort zone. Growth was chasing the challenges that scared you.

The next day, I went to Sridhar, torn between my doubts and my drive. His response was sharp and resolute: 'You asked for this. If you don't want it, Mani will do it.'

That hit me hard. This was not about the product—it was about the kind of leader I wanted to be. Would I step back or take the leap?

I made my decision. I told Kumar resolutely, 'I'm going to do it.'

That moment of tension gave birth to ServiceDesk Plus, a product that would go on to become one of our biggest successes.

We started small—a scrappy team determined to build something transformative from the ground up. Our first bold experiment? Introducing annual subscription pricing. It wasn't SaaS, but for an on-premise product, it was groundbreaking. The shift offered customers predictability in their budgets and gave us a steady, reliable stream of revenue. The response was electric and renewals quickly became the cornerstone of our growth strategy.

ServiceDesk Plus took off, rapidly outpacing OpManager to become one of our fastest-growing products. The surge in momentum reshaped my days into a whirlwind of activity, as I juggled two high-growth products. The relentless rhythm of building, launching and iterating didn't wear me down—it energized me. I thrived on the challenge, finding purpose in the sheer momentum of it all.

—

Building ServiceDesk Plus was consuming, but Kumar's knack for orchestrating customer engagements brought a new spark to my journey. One of these engagements—an OpManager demo with Wipro Technologies—turned out to be more than just another meeting.

As we delved into Wipro's requirements, a critical gap in OpManager became glaringly obvious: It lacked the ability to monitor and analyse WAN bandwidth traffic. Instead of dismissing this as a dealbreaker, Wipro posed a question that changed everything: 'Can you build this for us?' They even offered to collaborate on defining customer requirements.

That meeting didn't end with a polite handshake—it ignited a vision. Wipro's challenge highlighted a pressing need shared by countless IT teams, sparking the idea for a new product: NetFlow Analyzer, a tool designed to monitor and analyse network traffic.

The IT management space was fiercely competitive, but it offered endless possibilities for those ready to innovate. I returned to Chennai with a clear vision and a renewed sense of purpose.

However, turning this idea into reality was no small feat. We needed someone with a deep understanding of Cisco's internet operating system (IOS)—a person who could not only navigate the technical complexities but also drive the project at lightning speed. NetFlow Analyzer was going to be a bold step forward and it required a team ready to meet the challenge head-on.

That's when Shailesh stepped in and reassigned Shan Krishnasamy to my team.

Shan wasn't someone who announced his presence or drew attention to himself. In fact, you might not even notice him in a crowded room—at first. But once you did, you'd realize he was extraordinary. Shailesh's decision to move Shan wasn't random. Shan had already established a reputation for his deep expertise in Cisco-related projects. Now, he was tasked with leading the charge on NetFlow Analyzer.

Shan's journey was anything but conventional. When he joined AdventNet, he was fresh out of college, hailing from a rural village. He didn't fit the corporate mould—he spoke with a noticeable stammer and had zero programming experience. Yet, what Shan lacked in polish, he more than made up for with sheer grit and a relentless refusal to settle for mediocrity.

Incredibly, Shan taught himself programming after joining the company. He attacked his limitations with unyielding determination—polishing his English, mastering complex technologies and embracing every challenge thrown his way. While others sought recognition, Shan focused solely on delivering results.

Even during performance appraisals, his reserved demeanour stood out. I recall being puzzled by his silence, even when he received the highest raises on the team. At first, I wondered if he was dissatisfied. Over time, I came to understand that his silence wasn't discontent—it was quiet ambition. Shan didn't measure success by what he had accomplished; he measured it by what he could still achieve.

Shan turned every challenge into an opportunity, redefining brilliance. He never sought the spotlight—instead, he became the light, inspiring those around him to aim higher. NetFlow Analyzer stands as a testament to Shan's unspoken yet unstoppable drive.

Chapter 12

BY the end of 2006, a baffling restlessness had taken root in my life—a persistent hum I couldn't ignore. ManageEngine was scaling beautifully and, on the surface, everything seemed perfect. Yet, a question gnawed at me: What's next?

It was a strange, pivotal time—a mid-career itch that arrived uninvited. I had spent five transformative years at AdventNet, filled with growth, challenges and opportunities most jobs couldn't offer. Yet, a shadow lingered: My father's silent disappointment.

To my father, success wasn't about personal growth or passion—it was about tangible milestones. He measured life against the gold standard set by my engineering friends in the US. They were the golden children: Employed at prestigious tech companies, sending dollars home, buying houses in Trichy and flaunting shiny cars in American driveways. In contrast, I was the outlier—the one who walked away from the so-called American Dream to earn a modest salary in Chennai. To him, my story didn't add up.

One conversation etched itself into my memory. His disappointment was unmistakable as he asked, 'Why would you throw away the stability and success of the US for this?' His words replayed in my mind long after, leaving me wrestling with deeper questions: What does success really mean? Does my father think I'm a failure?

On the surface, my US-based friends seemed to have it all—shorter work hours, larger paycheques and the comfort of dollar salaries. Yet, every time I visited the US for work, I saw another side. Many of them were stuck in repetitive roles, financially secure but stagnating in personal and professional growth. They were earning more but doing less.

Back in Chennai, my life was the opposite of stagnant. I was constantly learning, building products, solving complex problems and expanding my horizons. The work was tough but exhilarating. It didn't come with societal validation or luxury cars, but it came with a deep sense of purpose. Yet, the questions persisted: Was I chasing the right kind of success? Was personal growth enough, or was I fooling myself into settling?

The internal conflict grew. Doubt crept in. Maybe I was wrong. Maybe I was missing out on something bigger.

It wasn't just my father's words or comparisons to my peers—it was the pull of a different life. Money was tight and the idea of combining the learning I loved with the financial security I craved began to take hold.

I started imagining life in the US again, this time with an H-1B visa. The thought didn't stem from dissatisfaction—it stemmed from restlessness; a whisper that asked: What if you could have both?

The decision wasn't easy. I loved what I was doing, but the questions loomed larger than ever: Could I be more? Could I do more? My father's doubts, the allure of the US and my own ambition converged into a single point of tension.

So, I decided to act. I applied for an H-1B visa, envisioning a fresh start. But fate intervened—the quota filled up before my application could even be filed.

At the time, it felt like a missed opportunity. But, in hindsight, it was a blessing in disguise. Leaving AdventNet for the uncertainty of a consulting role in the US would have been a mistake. Instead, life nudged me in an unexpected direction.

In 2007, during a business trip to the US, I visited Austin, where AdventNet was scouting for a new office location. By December, that idea had materialized. I was promoted to vice president of product management and marketing, tasked with heading ManageEngine's US operations.

The restlessness that had consumed me wasn't a sign of failure—it was a catalyst for growth. As I stepped into this new chapter, I realized something profound: Success isn't about choosing between two versions of it. It's about building a life where growth, purpose and fulfilment coexist—even if it doesn't come with shiny cars in American driveways.

—

For Shoba, leaving Chennai marked a heartbreak. I still remember the tearful look in her eyes as we packed up our life for a new chapter in Austin. For me, it was a calculated career decision—a step forward. For her, it felt like tearing away from the life she cherished: Family, friendships and the comforting rhythms of home. Starting over in a strange city didn't spark excitement; it brought a profound sense of loss.

Austin greeted us with its warmth and charm, but homesickness shadowed our early days, especially for Shoba. It wasn't just the big things she missed; it was the little comforts. The perfect coffee powder, the unmistakable taste of Aavin butter—these small pieces of Chennai seemed irreplaceable. Whenever friends visited from home, Shoba's first question was always the same: 'Can you bring some along?'

One day, as she unpacked yet another treasured item from Chennai, I couldn't help but tease her. 'Shoba, I'm pretty sure America has better butter than Chennai! But if you keep looking for Chennai in Austin, you'll never find happiness here.'

It was a realization. Moving wasn't about replacing what we had left behind; it was about discovering the new and letting it shape us in unexpected ways. I told her gently, 'If you keep holding on to what's gone, you might miss the beauty of what's right in front of you.'

That moment was about embracing change, letting go of the familiar and opening ourselves to new possibilities.

Despite the initial struggles, Austin slowly began to reveal its charm. For Shoba, it became a place of profound transformation. Back in Chennai, societal expectations often felt stifling, shaping decisions and curbing independence. But here, she discovered a new kind of freedom.

She began driving around the city—something she'd never fully embraced back home. She shopped on her own terms, free from the weight of judgement. These small but meaningful acts of independence weren't just adjustments—they were revelations, proof that she was thriving in ways neither of us had anticipated.

Austin itself buzzed with a unique energy. It felt like Silicon Valley's scrappy, younger sibling—dynamic, ambitious, but far more approachable. The tech scene was vibrant and conversations about ideas seemed to spark everywhere: in parks, coffee shops and even bookstores. Unlike the Bay Area, Austin offered a sense of balance. Here, owning a home didn't feel like an impossible dream, but an achievable goal within reach.

Life began to settle into its own rhythm. My elder son, Charan, had just started first grade and quickly found his footing, making friends with an ease that brought warmth to our days. Shoba, too, discovered her circle of moms, and weekends became a cherished ritual. Families gathered, children played with unrestrained joy and parents bonded over shared stories of adjustment, belonging and the quirks of life in Austin.

The sense of community deepened when we planned a move to a new apartment complex where some of Charan's friends lived. Shoba loved the idea and Charan was thrilled. For the first time, I began to feel that this life wasn't just a temporary stop—it was something we could build on.

Austin was no longer just a city; it was becoming home. Shoba's heartbreak had begun to soften into discovery, blossoming into a new-found independence. Stability, once elusive, now felt within reach. This was more than a change of address—it was a new chapter, reshaping us in ways we hadn't anticipated but so deeply needed.

—

As the business grew, we found ourselves stepping into an arena dominated by giants. IBM, CA, HP and BMC—the Big 4 of IT management—towered over the industry. Their reputations were so formidable, it often felt like they filled the room before we even walked in.

ManageEngine had the features to compete, but feature parity wasn't enough. We needed something bold—something that would make people stop and reconsider everything they thought they knew about enterprise IT software. That's when we landed on a daring, audacious tagline:

> The New 90-10 Rule of Enterprise IT Management: '90% of the features of the Big 4 at 10% of the price.'

It wasn't just a marketing slogan—it was a declaration of war. A line in the sand. It challenged the status quo and dared customers to rethink their loyalties. And it worked.

People leaned in, intrigued. The underdog story resonated and, for the first time, the industry's gatekeepers—the analysts—began to take notice. We weren't just competing; we were rewriting the rules of the game.

The shift became undeniable during a virtual call. A Forrester analyst introduced himself with a grin and said, 'Hey, Girish, I'm Peter from Forrester. We do 90 per cent of what Gartner does at 10 per cent of the cost.'

I couldn't help but laugh. Our tagline had become more than just words—it had entered the industry's lexicon. It was validation. Not just of the product, but of the strategy. Of the boldness. Of the belief that we could stand toe-to-toe with the titans and carve out our space.

It began as an ordinary conversation with Sridhar Vembu—updates, plans, the usual rhythm of work. But mid-sentence, a realization struck me like a thunderclap: What am I doing here?

The Austin office had started with grand ambitions—a hub for ManageEngine's global expansion, brimming with marketing and outbound sales energy. But the 2008 financial crisis changed everything. The collapse of Lehman Brothers derailed our hiring plans, leaving the office eerily empty.

Rodrigo Vaca and I often sat amidst rows of unoccupied desks, staring at what could have been. While the business thrived, I didn't. Managing from afar felt hollow, like watching a game through a window I couldn't open.

Meanwhile, the pull of Chennai grew stronger. Thousands of miles away, I longed for the electric energy of the team—the problem-solving, the camaraderie and the chaos. By 2009, as AdventNet transitioned into Zoho, the answer became clear: I needed to go back.

'Sridhar,' I said during that call, 'I think I need to return to Chennai.'

His response was immediate: 'I agree. Let's plan it.'

When I told Shoba, it landed with the force of a storm.

'We're moving back to Chennai,' I said.

Her expression said it all—shock, disappointment and a flicker of anger. Just days earlier, we'd been finalizing plans to move into a new apartment, further settling into Austin's rhythm. Now, I was asking her to uproot everything once again. It felt unfair, and I knew it.

Austin had been bittersweet—a chapter filled with growth, challenges and lingering homesickness. We had built something here—it was fragile but it was ours—and now I was asking her to leave it all behind.

Yet, as the decision took shape, Shoba and I began to see it not as an ending, but a reset. Austin had given us connections and discoveries, but it had also amplified what we missed most. Returning to Chennai was about returning to the pulse of the action, to a place where I could truly feel alive again.

We realized Chennai wouldn't erase what we'd built in Austin; it would expand on it. This wasn't a step back—it was a chance to start anew, closer to the heart of everything that mattered.

—

The birth of a company rarely comes from a single lightning bolt of inspiration. It's more like a series of sparks, each adding fuel to a growing flame. But if my next start-up had a defining spark, it all began with a broken TV.

It was August 2009. I had just returned to Chennai from Austin and, after two long months, our household goods finally arrived. Among them was my prized 40-inch flat-screen TV—the one indulgence I had brought back from the US, a small symbol of the life we'd left behind. Eager to reclaim a sense of normalcy, I opened the box, only to find the LCD panel shattered beyond repair.

What followed was a gruelling descent into the abyss of customer service. Emails, phone calls and follow-ups disappeared into a void of indifference. The shipping company had insured the TV, but getting them to honour the claim was like chasing a mirage. Days turned into weeks, and weeks into months. My frustration boiled over into fury and exhaustion.

In desperation, I turned to R2I Club, a community forum for Indians returning home, where I had originally found the shipping company. By then, I wasn't looking for a solution—I simply needed to vent. I poured every ounce of my frustration into a post, recounting my five-month battle in painstaking detail, fuelled by anger and disbelief.

I didn't expect much to come of it. But then, something incredible happened. The post struck a chord. People began commenting, sharing advice and recounting their own stories of frustration. The outpouring of support was unexpected, but what happened next was even more surprising.

Shyam Kumar, the president of the shipping company, apologized publicly on the forum. By the next day, the $750 insurance payout I had been chasing for months was sitting in my account.

It wasn't the money that stuck with me—it was the *how*. A single post, shared in the right place, had accomplished what months of futile calls and emails couldn't. I realized something profound: I wasn't powerless—I'd just been using the wrong tools to be heard.

This was a systemic problem. Companies were drowning in customer calls and emails, struggling to manage the growing noise. They reacted only when the loudest voices demanded attention, but by then, the damage to their reputation was often irreparable.

The broken TV was more than a personal ordeal—it was a crack in the system, a glimpse into an untapped opportunity. The traditional customer service model couldn't keep pace with the modern customer, whose complaints, tweets and reviews had the power to go viral and force accountability.

I couldn't stop thinking about it. For years, I had built helpdesks and optimized customer support systems, but now I saw their limitations first-hand. The irony wasn't lost on me. The system I knew so well had failed me and the lesson was clear: Traditional tools couldn't solve modern customer problems.

This was 2010—before viral complaints made daily headlines. And yet, my single forum post had cut through months of red tape. It was a prototype for a new reality where customers wielded power amplified by online communities and transparency.

The idea began to take root. What if customer service evolved from reactive phone and email responses to proactive engagement with customers online? What if a helpdesk became more than a tool? What if it became a platform for companies to truly listen, where every interaction mattered and every customer shaped the brand?

It wasn't just about building a better helpdesk. It was about reimagining the entire relationship between businesses and their customers. The broken TV was the start of something much bigger.

—

Returning to Chennai, I found myself stepping into a changed landscape. The products I had once nurtured were thriving under new leadership, their roots deep and branches spreading wide. My role had shifted—I was no longer the builder. Instead, I had become a management leader, stepping in to resolve conflicts and untangle the growing chaos within the ManageEngine portfolio.

The MSP product suite had grown, but with growth came complexity. Customers were confused by overlapping features, and sales teams were pitching the wrong solutions. It wasn't glamorous work, but it was essential. My days were filled with mediating meetings, troubleshooting issues and restoring order to the portfolio.

In the middle of this chaos, something caught my attention: SaaS was quietly but steadily rewriting the rules of the game. As I mediated discussions and triaged problems, a persistent question began to echo in my mind: What's next?

One meeting in particular captured the confusion. Voices clashed, arguments swirled and frustration hung thick in the air. Trying to ease the tension, I quipped, 'We're ManageEngine—where products are born, not made.' It got a laugh, but the truth of it lingered. While the wave of SaaS was rising, we were still tangled in the complexities of on-premise solutions.

Timing is everything in business—spotting the wave before it crests and positioning yourself to ride it. And, at that moment, I couldn't shake the feeling: We were standing on the shore, watching the future roll in.

A memory from Brazil reinforced this realization. On a trip to meet a potential customer, I was greeted with a question that stung: 'Zo-who?' To them, we were an afterthought—a footnote in an industry dominated by bigger names. But I filed that moment away.

A few years later, the SaaS explosion changed everything. Suddenly, the media that had ignored us started talking about Zoho in the same breath as Microsoft, Google and Salesforce. The question wasn't 'Zo-who?' anymore; it was 'What's Zoho doing next?' Respect had grown and, with it, our place in the SaaS narrative.

That shift stirred something inside me. It reminded me of the promise I'd made to myself during my HR interview when I first joined Zoho (then AdventNet): 'In five years, I want to start something of my own.' Those five years had turned into nine. I had stayed, grown and learned.

Zoho was a crucible in which I discovered my potential. Launching and scaling multiple products taught me how to take an idea from conception to success. Every challenge I faced reinforced my confidence. Crafting and mastering an inbound go-to-market strategy showed me the power of thinking differently and adapting for a global audience—all from right here in India.

Zoho became the arena where I honed my craft, shaping my identity as a creator and a problem-solver. With each product we built and every market we entered, I felt the pieces of my entrepreneurial dream coming back together—stronger and sharper than ever.

By then, I knew that I was ready to leap again, to venture into the unknown armed with the lessons I had learned and the confidence I had gained. Zoho wasn't the conclusion of my journey; it was the launchpad for what came next.

At the same time, SaaS was revealing its potential to transform the start-up landscape. It levelled the playing field, giving entrepreneurs the tools to compete with the giants.

The parallels to my early career were striking. When I learned Java, I recognized its potential as a platform and jumped on that wave early. It shaped my trajectory. Now, as I looked at SaaS and the cloud, I saw another fundamental shift. The writing was on the wall—on-premise software was not the future. Its growth would slow, maybe even stagnate. The momentum was elsewhere.

And then, Wayne Gretzky's timeless advice echoed in my mind: 'Skate to where the puck is going to be.'

SaaS was an opportunity to ride another wave. The realization refused to let go, teasing the edges of my thoughts until it became impossible to ignore.

The question grew louder: Was there something bigger waiting to be built?

The answer, I knew, wasn't in fixing the past—it was in chasing the future.

—

It began on a lazy afternoon, the kind that drapes over you like a warm blanket after lunch. My desk at Zoho was its usual mess—scattered notes, half-formed ideas and the hum of a routine I knew too well. I wasn't planning to start a company that day—or any day, for that matter. But sometimes, the universe catches you off guard when you're ready, even if you don't know it yet.

I was scrolling through Hacker News, my trusted source for inspiration and distraction, when an article about Zendesk caught my eye. They had raised their prices by 300 per cent—not for new customers, but existing ones. It was a move so audacious it bordered on reckless.

The fallout was swift. Comments sections were ablaze, forums echoed with protests and Zendesk's own community was drowning in dissatisfaction. TechCrunch dissected the backlash, while frustrated customers vented everywhere they could. Amid the chaos, I saw something else: An opportunity.

One comment stood out like a flare in the dark. A stranger named Mark Ransom wrote: 'It just shows how someone could come up with the right product at the right price and take all of Zendesk's customers away.'

That line hit like a match to dry kindling. A customer service company with unhappy customers? The irony was glaring; the challenge irresistible. My mind ignited: What if I built something better? Smarter? Something fresh?

Some ideas simmer slowly, brewing in the background until they're ready. This wasn't one of those. This idea demanded action.

I walked over to Shan, my closest ally in tech and a friend I trusted implicitly.

'Shan,' I began, 'what if we built a customer service software company? I haven't figured out the details, but the idea came to me today. Would you join me?'

There was no hesitation. 'I'm game,' he said. Two words—and just like that, we were co-founders.

Shan was more than a colleague. He was family in the way only friends who share late-night drinks and family dinners can be. Earlier that year, we had even signed up for Rs 50 lakh home loans to buy apartments in the same complex. It was a bond built on trust, shared dreams and a mutual willingness to take risks.

Now, we were about to leap into the unknown together.

On paper, it was the worst time to start a company. I was thirty-six, with two kids, a stable job and a mortgage that felt like an anchor. But that spark from Hacker News wouldn't let me rest.

One morning, as Shoba stirred something in the kitchen, I decided to tell her. 'I'm thinking about starting a company.'

She froze mid-stir, her eyes searching mine. 'Why now? Everything is going so well. Why risk it?'

'I haven't finalized anything,' I said, softening the blow. But deep down, I already knew. The decision was made.

When I decided to start something of my own, I thought I could ease into it—build quietly on the side, get a few customers, generate some revenue and then resign once things felt stable. It seemed logical. Safe.

But that plan didn't last a week.

I'm not wired that way. I'm an all-in kind of person. Trying to juggle both was torture. My mind was already consumed by my new idea—yet, I was still showing up at Zoho, trying to give my best. It felt wrong. Zoho was a place I loved, a place I had poured my heart into. Half-measures weren't fair to the company or to me.

Zoho had given me everything: Opportunities, mentorship and a confidence in my abilities I hadn't known before. But no matter how much I owed to Zoho, the fire to build something of my own hadn't dimmed. Each day became a reminder of the dreams I'd put on hold. Walking away wouldn't be easy—it meant leaving behind what felt like a second family. But it also meant stepping towards a future that was entirely my own.

The breaking point came when a business trip to Canada was being planned. I couldn't shake the guilt. How could I board that flight, knowing I'd already decided to leave? It wasn't right.

That's when I made the call to Sridhar Vembu.

'I'm quitting,' I told him, 'to start my own company.'

Sridhar surprised me. 'My respect for you just went up,' he said. 'You're not leaving to join a competitor. You want to build something of your own.' His words meant more to me than I could express.

That evening, I came home early and said it outright: 'I've informed Sridhar. I'm quitting Zoho.'

Shoba was stunned. We had just taken on a massive mortgage. She wasn't working, and the stability she so cherished had just been ripped away. 'How will I explain this to people?' she asked, her voice filled with worry.

I met her eyes and said, 'If the start-up fails, I'll find another job. But I'm not starting a company to buy a BMW for myself. I'm starting because I want every employee to be able to buy a BMW. That's the dream.'

It wasn't the answer she expected, but it was the one that resonated. Slowly, she began to see the purpose behind the risk, the deeper meaning driving my decision.

Through it all, Shoba stood by me, even when the uncertainty felt overwhelming. In those moments, I realized something about

Girish at the AdventNet stall at Interop Las Vegas, April 2003

The cake says it all: Freshdesk reaches $50 million in annual recurring revenue (ARR)

Freshworks celebrated the $100-million ARR milestone with another cake—and a public announcement of its revenue for the first time

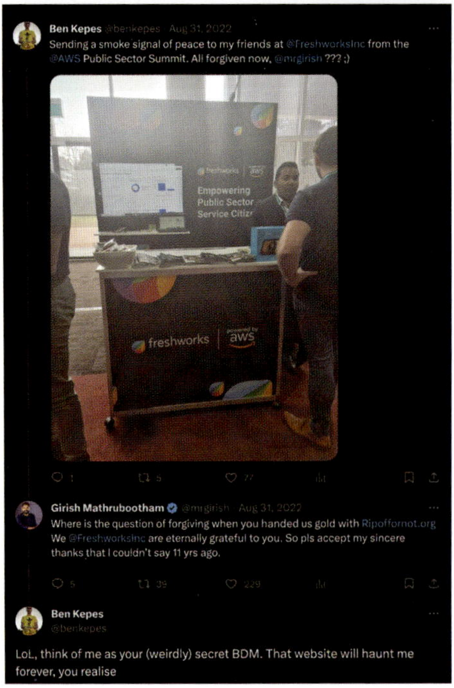

When cloud analyst Ben Kepes accused Freshdesk of unethical behaviour (because of Zendesk, which paid him as a blogger), Girish responded with a fitting reply—and a microsite, ripoffornot.org, which went viral

Screenshot of the microsite ripoffornot.org set up in response to Zendesk accusations

Freshdesk founding team after winning the Microsoft Bizspark competition: (Left to right) Parsuram Vijayasankar, Shan Krishnasamy, Girish Mathrubootham, Shihab Muhammed, Kiran Darisi and Vijay Shankar

The 40-inch flat-panel TV that arrived broken when Girish moved back from Austin to Chennai in 2009. The five-month ordeal of claiming its insurance made him realize that the traditional customer service was broken too.

Shan and Girish receiving the Economic Times' Startup Award in 2016 from Nitin Gadkari, Union Minister of Road Transport and Highways

The blimp that stole the show at Salesforce's flagship conference in San Francisco in 2018

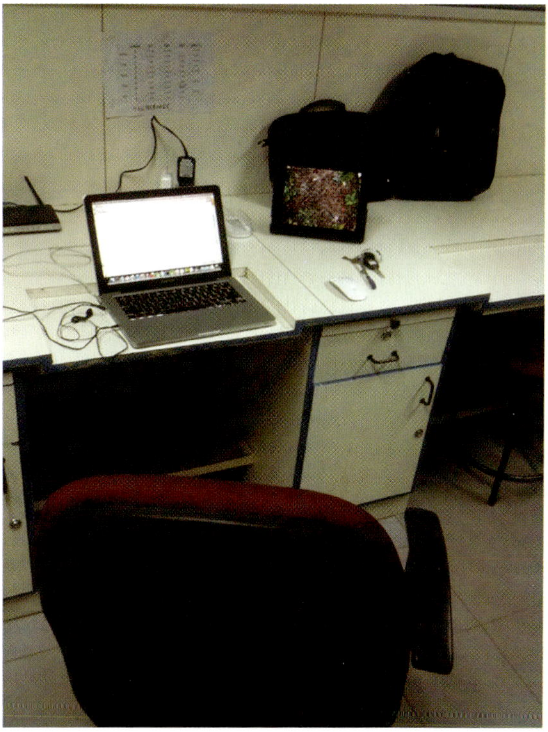

Girish's desk in the conference room of Sekar Vembu's office at Kashyap Enclave in Chennai's Velachery. This is where Freshdesk took its first breath.

Kumar Vembu, Girish's mentor in his Zoho days, cutting the ribbon for Freshdesk's first office

Shan and Girish at the latter's home in Chennai. The 2011 power crisis in the city forced the Freshdesk team to work from home when WFH wasn't trending.

Girish interacting at the SaaSx event in Chennai

Girish with wife, Shoba, and their sons, Charan and Sanjay

Girish with his maanaseega guru, Superstar Rajinikanth

Girish with a prop next to one of the beautifully decorated walls of Freshworks' SP Infocity office

entrepreneurship: It wasn't just my leap—it was hers too. And like always, she took the plunge with me.

—

My last day at Zoho felt surreal—like standing at the edge of a precipice, staring into the uncertain future of what lay ahead.

Just a week earlier, *Enthiran* had hit theatres and Rajinikanth, India's superstar, had delivered a cinematic spectacle. I watched it with Arvind Parthiban and friends, soaking in the energy of the crowd. Lunch that day was Thalappakatti biryani—comforting, familiar and delicious. But, by the afternoon, as I walked into Zoho's office, the weight of the moment had settled in.

The news of my departure had spread. Arvind, standing next to me, looked blindsided. We'd spent the morning together, but he hadn't known.

The day unravelled in vivid snapshots. I handed over the keys to my company-leased Honda Civic, each gesture underscoring the finality of my decision. At my desk, I packed years of memories into two bags, condensing a transformative decade into a few physical tokens.

Looking back, those years were an incredible training ground—a mix of failures and breakthroughs that shaped my identity. MindSphere taught me humility. The relentless job hunt honed my grit. And Zoho showed me the value of purpose over polish. Each step, no matter how uncertain, had brought me closer to the person I wanted to become. As I took my final steps away from Zoho, I knew I was ready to build again—this time armed with lessons only experience could teach.

I hugged colleagues who had become family, their words of encouragement a bittersweet reminder of everything we had built together.

'It's like Sachin Tendulkar walking back to the pavilion,' Sreelesh, a colleague, had said. The words lingered. I didn't feel like Tendulkar, but the sentiment resonated—a decade of work, friendships and growth distilled into one final moment.

As the day wound down, Gerald, our pre-sales manager, offered to take me home on his two-wheeler. I sat behind him, clutching my two bags awkwardly on either side as we navigated Chennai's traffic. The ride felt cinematic, like the interval scene of a Rajinikanth movie: The hero loses everything, heads into the unknown and readies himself for a second act.

When I reached home, reality hit hard. There was no title, no team, no plan. Life was a blank slate again, with only one burning question left to answer: What's next?

INTERSTITIAL 1

Kumar Vembu: Through the Eyes of a Mentor

by Pankaj Mishra

TO understand the leader and entrepreneur Girish Mathrubootham is today, it's helpful to look through the lens of someone who saw his potential early on—Kumar Vembu. I interviewed Kumar to trace Girish's journey and explore the (often unseen) layers of mentorship that shaped him during his years at Zoho and beyond. Kumar, himself a remarkable leader, offers a raw, unfiltered and insightful view of Girish. His role in Girish's evolution wasn't just about coaching—it was about recognizing traits and talents in Girish that others may have missed.

Kumar's reflections highlight the pivotal role Girish's time at Zoho played in his transformation from a bright and ambitious young lad into one of the most prominent voices in the SaaS world. Under Kumar's watchful guidance, Girish honed his ownership mindset, relentless curiosity and entrepreneurial spirit. Also, it was Kumar who saw in Girish the traits of a product visionary, a leader capable of wearing multiple hats and thriving in different roles.

What makes Kumar's insights even more noteworthy is the firm conviction with which he speaks about Girish's contribution to Zoho's success. The way he recounts Girish's tireless push for better UI, his knack for understanding customer needs and his fearlessness in questioning norms underscores Girish's significant, sometimes overlooked, role in shaping Zoho's trajectory.

Kumar's words do more than help us see how Girish grew as a leader. They allow us to peek into Kumar's own exceptional mentoring and leadership qualities—and how he practiced values such as empathy, responsibility and a keen sense of purpose. In the following pages, Kumar's perspective becomes key in understanding the making of Girish Mathrubootham—an entrepreneur who built successful companies and left a lasting impact on those he worked with.

—

It was the most compelling résumé I had ever seen. Every word seemed to say something about Girish—what he cared about, what drove him. It wasn't just a list of jobs or projects. It showed me his passion for teaching and his knack for communication. That one-page document told me more than any interview could.

He had already worked in India and the US for about four years. He had also run a training centre. So, I would say there was not one word that was boring about it: It was a very well-crafted résumé.

The résumé had personality. It said who he was! He listed his strengths, interests and goals, so they were all very clear.

Teaching is a lot about communication—about simplicity in communication. And I could see that simplicity, that passion, in the résumé.

It's not like somebody preaching something, claiming something and then not doing that—when he said this is what he loved, you could see that in the résumé!

We were looking for somebody in pre-sales who could actually demonstrate the product. In the résumé, he also talked about designing, and we could see how well the résumé was structured.

Every Saturday, without fail, I'd sit down and review the week's interview notes. I wasn't just looking for skills—I wanted to see who had the right mindset for what we were building. For me, that review was like a huddle, a chance to understand each candidate beyond their résumé and see if they'd fit into the culture we were nurturing.

This approach wasn't common, but it reflected how I liked mentoring. It was about being hands-on and understanding each person as a potential team member, not just another hire. It's a practice that I think kept us rooted in our purpose.

—

When Girish asked me how I decided to proceed to make him an offer without meeting him, I told him that all the interviewers' comments—we used to have three rounds of interviews and an HR interview—were in favour of hiring him.

So, there was no reservations about hiring him. In all the roles we had assessed him for, there was no doubt about his calibre—in terms of competence, skill and other things.

The only decision to be made was whether we should go ahead with the salary Girish was asking for or not. We had not seen anybody clear all the parameters so well in the many interviews we had done. And here was a candidate who had cleared everything—and so low-balling him did not seem right.

—

He questioned everything: Why do we hire only freshers? Why is our office *here*? Why don't we pay more? But Girish's questions were never just complaints. He genuinely wanted to understand and make things better.

I liked people who questioned everything. I don't think there is anything that I do or I do not do that Girish hasn't questioned me about [laughs].

But that is very refreshing. He would question you, but when you explained [it to him], he would stop. At least I assumed that he was convinced [laughs].

See, he is full of positive energy, and he questions things to understand and improve. If somebody wanted to cause trouble, they would gossip and create nuisance, right? With Girish, it was always direct, always one-on-one. The intention was to improve, contribute more and help the company grow faster.

So basically, Girish's intent was always to help us progress together, to help us do things better and do bigger things faster. Even if he was critical of some things or didn't understand or agree with something, I don't think you can ever doubt his intention.

—

Most of us lose that spark of curiosity as we grow older. Not Girish. Even when the stakes get higher, he keeps that childlike enthusiasm [alive]. It's something I've always admired about him.

It's not like all my conversations with Girish were pleasant; sometimes, I probably exerted authority. I might not have had the maturity of age, but he is like a child to me. A lot of times, when I meet Girish, the enthusiasm and playfulness of a child shine through.

He always speaks his mind and speaks from the heart—whether he is happy or unhappy or irritated, or wants to question or appreciate something ... Whatever it is, he doesn't hold back.

I have many inhibitions about discovering the child in me, maybe because of my social upbringing or the way I was taught. But Girish has kept that child in him alive.

Our meetings at Mama's Mess were our ritual. I'd sit back and listen to whatever Girish wanted to share, but I never felt the need to interfere. It wasn't my place to give advice unless he asked for it. For me, being a mentor meant respecting his independence and giving him the space to make his own decisions.

—

We always encouraged an ownership mentality and Girish embodied that from day one. He didn't just do his job; he approached everything as if the company was his. That kind of mindset is rare, and it's why he stood out.

Most of those who worked with me were around my age, and I had very little experience at the time. My exposure was limited to some companies in India and a year in the US, so it was not like I had managed teams and built companies. But we always encouraged people to take ownership, to do the work like it was their own company.

From the very beginning, the people who were respected were the ones who responded well when given responsibility; people who were promoted demonstrated an ownership mindset and commitment—which Girish definitely had in abundance.

—

Girish would say, 'This product isn't good enough. We need to fix the UI.' Or, 'We're not hiring the right people.' And you know what? He was right. He pushed us to improve things, making a huge difference in how the product was received.

We had our own resource limitations and our own image when recruiting people from the market. It was not like highly talented people wanted to come and work in a product company in India in 2001 or 2002. Nor could we promise them US trips or foreign assignments.

But Girish would honestly share his opinions, suggestions and feedback in a very positive way. To some of his suggestions, I would tell him my inability; to others, I would tell him why he should work with what we had. For example, we did not go for lateral hires or pay people much higher [salaries] because we didn't have the confidence of future revenues to make such decisions.

We were all engineers. My primary experience is in back-end software. I can say I've never used a graphical user interface until I started a company, and even when we were building the company, we had never done anything with the GUI. Girish was the first guy with some aesthetic sense, and a talent and appetite for UI, UX and things like that.

In fact, he was initially on the pre-sales team and would constantly complain about or criticize our UI. Given our constraints on hiring, I often told him that beggars can't be choosers, but that didn't keep him from redefining the way we did things.

In pre-sales, when we had to demo a product to a customer, Girish would go to their website, get their logo and find out their product profile. He would then simulate that, and he and his team would work on it for a couple of days. When the customer was shown the demo, they would feel like they were seeing *their* network management system, not *our* product. It definitely increased our customer win rate.

So Girish quickly gave the product the right facade in pre-sales to make sure we started winning more customers. That was refreshingly new and had a positive impact on business.

—

Girish insisted on quality in user experience, no matter the limitations. He had a knack for working within limits, but wouldn't settle. The user sees the product first before they get to anything else, so it has to shine.

For most of us who focused on back-end engineering, Girish's approach to UX was refreshing, if sometimes a bit relentless. We were all engineers; honestly, GUI wasn't our strong point. But Girish was different. He had this sense of how things should look and feel. He'd question, critique and come up with improvements. He'd find ways to make the product stand out visually even if resources were thin.

Girish's persistence wasn't just about aesthetics but the overall user journey. He'd say things like, 'If this isn't up to the mark, what impression are we making?' That drive to get it right and make the product memorable is something I respect deeply.

—

We used to have our annual employee event for some entertainment. Since I was busy with other things, I remember giving Girish the free hand to organize it. And he organized it very well, branding the event as Amistad with a theme of three Ps—Passion, Pride, and Progress! That was a very apt caption.

Usually, when an engineer organizes such an event, people's expectation or involvement is not always great. But Girish ensured that employees bought into the idea, created skits, stories and music medleys all aligned to the theme of Passion, Pride and Progress.

The event was very well-marketed, and it totally energized the team. Although such things were outside his role, he definitely made a positive contribution.

We used to have an internal event in the evening for some entertainment. Since I was busy with other things, I remember giving Girish a free hand in terms of decorating the office and organizing it with logistical support from the admin [team]. And he organized it very well, branding the event as 3Ps—Passion, Pride and Progress! That was a very apt caption.

Normally, when an engineer organizes such an event, the people's involvement is not as great as it should be. So Girish ensured that some employees formed music troops and arranged for some other performances for the evening.

The event was very well-marketed and it totally energized the team. Although such things were outside his role, he definitely made a positive contribution.

I used to tell him, 'You could do my job better than I do.' And it was true. He thought of the big picture, had empathy for users, and possessed the ability to make fast and smart decisions. The only thing he lacked at first was patience with people.

When the telecom market was in trouble, we wanted to use our developer expertise in network management to build an end-user product that IT teams in organizations could use. That is how ManageEngine was born.

So when the question came about as to who would create the product, I really wanted Girish to steer it.

I remember that he used to tell me we were driven too much by back-end engineering and did not focus much on design, UI/UX and marketing—and I would say he was more competent to do my job than me! He just needed to work a bit on how to carry people along.

Sometimes, it is difficult to manage high-energy people, right? Maybe if I challenged him all the time, it would not have worked. Sometimes, surrendering is a better way to make someone work.

So, my strong recommendation was to have him build the product independently, where he had the authority to hire the people, build the team and give enough importance to design.

And you know what? The product was released in ten months flat—which is fast even by today's standards, especially because it addressed a complex problem.

We had the development platform on top of which it was built. Girish's key strengths are his comprehension skills, ability to get a good view of the market and ability to build a good user interface. He scanned the competitive landscape, sized up the competition, and—knowing that 20 per cent of product features can give you a foot in the door in that market—got the product out in ten months. Over time, we kept building on it.

Girish was responsible for ManageEngine as a product manager end to end—from market research to minimum viable product to its launch and go-to-market motion.

—

When Girish told me he wanted to start his own company, I asked him, 'Why take the stress? You're already a diabetic.' He just smiled and said, 'We're all going to die someday. Let me die doing what I love.'

I remember thinking he was jumping without a parachute. I've always leaned towards safety—making sure there's a fallback plan. But Girish? He was all in, full throttle. For him, it was about doing what he loved, even if it meant taking a risk that, to me, seemed almost irrational. Over time, watching him taught me something: You can be deeply committed and still be at peace with having just a one-year runway.

With the passion with which he works, Girish likes to pursue the best talent, paying the price. Whatever he told me I should have done earlier at AdventNet, he made sure he had the resources to do that when he started his own company.

In terms of the quality of the work environment, he always invested early. He made sure he could afford it: Whatever we put as an outcome, he would put in as an ingredient to create success. So he sort of lived true to his words and wisdom—and he had the tolerance to put up with [the fact that] his ideas have not been listened to for so long.

And he remains the same, going by how he invested in the football club, the way he invests in start-ups, the way he relates to people and how his network is ... I didn't change him much [laughs].

As a person, Girish retained his spirit of optimism. For example, if I had started with the resources he had, would I have spent like he had and looked for capital? No. That means, even when he knew he had a one-year or eighteen-month runway, he was going full speed, carrying on with hope. It's like he jumped without a parachute.

Imagine the stress when you have only a runway of a few months and you have discussions [lined up] with investors!

For someone like me, who always prioritized safety, I would have considered it irrational or irresponsible fifteen or twenty years ago. But working with and knowing Girish helped me change my stance: I can now understand that you can be very sincere, committed and careful, and [still] be comfortable doing something with a one-year runway. You can be at peace and focus on solving the problem at hand.

Girish's biggest risk was starting Freshworks. After that, he took incremental risks, and with each risk, he emerged stronger and richer.

—

Girish has tremendous empathy. He doesn't use his background to inflict suffering on others—he is [in fact] opposed to it. Because of his background, he does not want another person to suffer emotionally. I have seen this many times. When he had a rough experience with people, sometimes I saw him in tears—the sort of tears that say that is not who he really is.

I cannot tell [you] what he goes through personally, but in terms of his attitude in relationships or [his] behaviour with people, because of his suffering, he goes the extra mile to better relate with others.

It is natural to talk to him because whether you agree or disagree with him, whether you do or do not do what he wants you to do, it doesn't change your relationship with him.

—

Girish wasn't just an engineer. He could market, design and manage, and he could tell stories. Most people need a team to do all that, but Girish could do it all himself.

Many other ex-employees from Zoho founded a company as a team of two, three or four people. But Girish was [the whole] combo—good at marketing, messaging, storytelling, product management, design and people management. Of all the people I worked with in Zoho until 2004, Girish was among the best. It is very hard for somebody to be a package like that.

Girish was more than a go-getter; he could think beyond engineering because he had actually engineered the product and trained people in writing the code. He had an overall perspective in terms of doing the marketing—product marketing or digital marketing—positioning the brand, looking after the user experience and managing channel sales.

You can call him a full-stack or a full life-cycle entrepreneur.

—

Freshworks is a playbook [in itself], one that is easier for today's entrepreneurs to follow than Zoho's model. Girish showed others that it's possible to start and scale a SaaS business—and that's no small thing.

There is an intersection of the Zoho playbook and the Freshworks playbook, wherein you learn how to build the product and how to have a go-to market motion predominantly out of India. It's like SaaS from India for the developed world. Another way to build a SaaS business is to do it as a lifestyle business. Yet another way is to bootstrap it and scale it without external capital.

Many successful businesses have followed the intersection, plus the Freshworks playbook.

While Zoho has a playbook, replicating it in today's context is very different. In Zoho's case, there was another revenue stream—through

ManageEngine—which was not SaaS. All said and done, SaaS is a capital-intensive business, and most companies take anywhere from six to ten years to become cash-flow positive.

With the Freshworks playbook, replication is easier by an order of magnitude, as are the chances of success, and what the founding team and management must do.

That ease of replication is what has made Girish a role model for so many entrepreneurs and made them follow the path that Freshworks has traversed.

It took so many Olympics before Jim Hines broke the ten-second barrier in the 100 metre sprint. But after that, at least one guy was breaking it in every subsequent Olympics. Then, all the top three were breaking it. Now, probably everybody is breaking it. Similarly, how long did it take for somebody to climb Mount Everest? Now, people are doing it multiple times because of their faith and belief, and they know how to get there. Somebody is there to tell you.

So now, there is a playbook—from a start-up to listing on the Nasdaq. People have the belief. Before Girish, people would say, 'Not possible.' Or, 'Is it possible?' The doubt was there.

See, I put effort into it when I know it's possible, right?

It is always the first-timer who has to overcome the doubts, uncertainty and fear—and the moment they do it, it makes it 50 per cent easier for the second guy, who is not chasing an improbable or uncertain goal. He knows it's possible. It's only how and when.

—

It's not about who wins. It's about building something bigger than ourselves. Zoho and Freshworks are both creating thousands of jobs. The world has enough space for both.

I used to tell people in Zoho frequently that our work has to be purposeful, and you have to always put the purpose first.

So you compromise your ego, or you give in, because the purpose is larger than the individual, right? And now, see the impact of having two successful companies from Chennai instead of one! Today, Freshworks may probably be half of Zoho. Let's say Freshworks didn't exist—would there be any guarantee that Zoho would have done 50 per cent more? Highly improbable. Freshworks has created another 5,000 jobs in Chennai, which is a big bonus for the ecosystem.

—

Girish brought skills and leadership to Zoho that didn't exist before. Whether Zoho accelerated or delayed what he did next, the seed was already there inside him.

Girish was already a start-up founder before he joined Zoho. That urge to do something on his own—the aspiration, the ambition—was already inside him.

It is also a question of what perspective you look at your alma mater.

For example, I studied at AC College of Engineering, Karaikudi. My college played a defining role in shaping who I am. I walked in as a directionless, raw boy and left with values that have guided me ever since. That's why I've stayed closely involved with my alumni association, giving back in any way I can.

When it comes to Zoho without Girish, I would definitely say he brought in competencies and skills that did not exist in the company at that time. Now, whether the company would have figured out all those how many years later—and what opportunity cost it would have had—is something we cannot predict.

So definitely, he was there at the right time with the right kind of competencies.

INTERSTITIAL 2

Shoba: The Heart behind the Dream

PEOPLE often dismiss arranged marriages as old-fashioned, maybe even unromantic. To me, they're a leap of faith—a moment when you trust something bigger than yourself to make one of life's biggest decisions. Shoba is proof that, sometimes, fate knows you better than you know yourself.

I met Shoba in 2002 when love was the last thing on my mind. After a heartbreak, I had poured myself into work, letting my family take charge of finding a match. What I didn't expect was that Shoba would become the axis around which my life would spin—a partner whose quiet strength and boundless resilience would hold everything together when I needed it most.

From the moment we met, Shoba's calm confidence stood out. During our first conversation, she casually mentioned her love for Benz cars. Without hesitating, I said, 'Give me a picture of your favourite model. I'll add it to my dream book.'

That dream book was my private map of aspirations—cars, homes, single malts, even a yacht. Shoba's eyes lit up at the mention of it. Later, she told me that moment sealed it for her. It wasn't about the car but the way I shared her dreams as if they could become ours.

I lost that dream book years ago but never lost the dreams. Together, Shoba and I have built a life that far exceeds anything I ever imagined.

Shoba likes to joke that I'm Shrek. 'If you're Prince Charming, everyone likes you at first glance,' she says. 'But Shrek—an ordinary guy—nobody notices. People need time to see how amazing you are.'

It's a funny comparison, but it's also true. Shoba has always seen beyond the surface and understood the person behind the roles. She's my anchor because she sees me—not just the entrepreneur or the leader but the flawed, dreaming, determined man beneath it all.

I often call Shoba a 'shopping tsunami'. It's a joke, but it holds the truth. She doesn't just shop for herself—she shops for everyone. When Andrew, a Zoho colleague from India, visited, Shoba casually asked about his family. By the time he left, his suitcases were bursting with gifts for parents, siblings, nieces and nephews. He hadn't planned any of it, but Shoba's gentle nudges made it happen. That's her magic—she influences people effortlessly in ways they don't even realize.

Since we got married, I've moved her across cities and continents at least a dozen times. Each time, she left behind familiar comforts but carried friendships and relationships with her, building new ones wherever we landed. Whether in Chennai or Seattle, Shoba creates a sense of home for us and everyone around her. She could walk into a room full of strangers and leave with their life stories.

But Shoba is more than a steady presence; she's the bambaram in my life. She moves through the chaos like a spinning top, keeping everything in motion. Her days start before the rest of us are awake. She's in the kitchen, planning the day, preparing lunch and juggling a hundred tasks while making it look effortless.

She's also my mirror. Whether I'm speaking at a public event or in meetings, Shoba watches closely. Later, she offers candid feedback—everything from softening my tone to improving how I explain a point. Her observations are sharp but always delivered with care. She's helped me refine my words and how I show up for others.

She's a Montessori teacher who gives her students the same attention and care she gives our family. Between workouts, hosting friends and keeping everything running, I've often asked myself: How does she do it?

But that's just Shoba—her energy endless, her strength unshakable, her ability to turn chaos into calm unmatched.

One of her greatest acts of resilience came when I told her I wanted to quit Zoho to start Freshdesk. She was shocked. 'Why leave a stable job?' she asked. 'You've built something incredible; and we have everything we need.' Her fears were valid. Walking away from stability to chase a dream was a massive risk. But, despite her reservations, Shoba trusted me. She stood by me, even when it scared her because that's who she is.

That trust carried us through another leap in 2019 when we moved to the US to prepare for Freshworks' IPO. Leaving Chennai meant stepping away from a life of comfort—a rented bungalow, household help and a tight-knit community. Suddenly, in the US, every task, no matter how small, was ours to handle.

I told her, 'This isn't about us anymore. It's about the thousands of employees who depend on Freshworks. If we get this right, we can change lives.'

Her response was immediate: 'If it's for their dreams, we'll move.'

That's Shoba. She sees the bigger picture, even at a personal cost. Her strength, adaptability and unwavering support keep our family—and me—grounded.

Entrepreneurs are often celebrated for their grit and determination, but the truth is, we're only as strong as the people who stand beside us. I've been incredibly fortunate to have Shoba. She's the quiet force behind every decision, sacrificing her comfort without hesitation for our collective dreams.

The story of Freshworks wouldn't exist without Shoba. But more than that, the story of my life wouldn't exist without her. She's my bambaram, my anchor and the heart behind every dream.

SECTION 4

KUDUMBA

Making It All Count

Chapter 13

THE morning sunlight slipped through the blinds, soft but insistent, like it had a mission. Half-awake, I hovered in that hazy space between dreams and reality. The day ahead loomed heavy with the expectations I'd placed on myself. The hunt for an office—it was the cornerstone of a vision that refused to fade; yet, it felt too big. Too much. Too impossible.

And then, the opening notes came.

Rajinikanth's '*Vetri kodi kattu*' burst through my headphones, shattering the silence with electric percussion. The rhythm pulsed with life, the words pierced through my doubts like a beam of light through thick fog. I'd heard it a thousand times, but this time, it wasn't background noise. This time, it was a command.

'Vaazhkaiyil aayiram thadaikkallappa,
thadaikkalum unakkoru padikallappa'
(Life has a thousand hurdles, but each one is a stepping stone)

The words struck a chord deeper than ever. My heart synced with the beat, each lyric reinforcing the resolve I didn't know I had. Rajinikanth's stride filled my mind—bold, unrelenting, unstoppable. His eyes burned with purpose, daring me to match his fire.

By the time the chorus thundered, I was sitting upright. Clarity cut through the fog in my head.

'Vetri kodi kattu, malaigalai muttum varai muttu, lathchiyam ettum varai ettu'
(Fly your flag of victory, break through mountains, reach for your dreams)

I swung my legs off the bed, my feet touching the cool floor. The doubts that had gripped me moments before now seemed laughable. The hunt for an office wasn't a burden anymore—it was the first step in claiming my dream.

'Vettukkili alla, nee oru vettum puli endru'
(You're not a grasshopper; you're a roaring tiger)

That line hit like a surge of electricity—a raw reminder of my strength and purpose. It wasn't the time to hesitate. It was the time to roar.

By the end of the day, the office hunt hadn't turned up much. Yet, strangely, it didn't matter. I had the song, the fire, the promise. Exhausted but undeterred, I went to bed with my headphones still within reach, ready to hit play again the next morning.

And I did. Every morning after. '*Vetri kodi kattu*' became my anthem, my rallying cry. With every note, every lyric, I felt it: The tiger within me, ready to charge, ready to win.

—

The weeks that followed were a blur of decisions—brainstorming frameworks, business structures and names. ActiveDesk? SugarDesk? TrueDesk? Each one felt off, lacking the energy and clarity I was searching for.

Then, like a nudge from the universe, I stumbled upon 'Freshdesk'. The name stood out—simple, direct, alive with possibilities. The domain had been dormant for years, practically forgotten. It was listed for $11—a bargain that seemed too good to be true. I placed a bid, bracing for disappointment. But days passed and no one else claimed it. Freshdesk was ours.

When I told Shoba, she laughed. 'Freshdesk? Sounds like a vegetable shop,' she teased me. But to me, it was perfect—fresh ideas, a fresh start and a fresh take on what customer service could be.

A fresh start, not only for our future customers but for us too. With an $11 domain, a borrowed desk and a spark that refused to fade, Shan and I set out to build something that would eventually become Freshworks.

We didn't have much, but we had enough—a dream, a name and the will to see it through.

The spark had found its flame.

—

The morning after I walked out of Zoho for the last time, I woke up to a new kind of silence—no emails pinging, no calls to make, no meetings to prepare for. But this wasn't the unsettling void people warn you about when leaving a steady job. This silence felt alive. The day stretched out before me like a blank canvas, daring me to fill it.

I reminded myself: I wasn't starting from scratch. I was starting from possibility.

First on the list? Find a space where Freshdesk could take its first breath.

My search began at Kashyap Enclave, a place tangled with personal history. Years ago, I was interviewed for Zoho in this very building. It looked exactly as I remembered—a cluster of residential apartments clumsily rebranded as offices. Inside, the air carried the unmistakable scent of bureaucracy: Stale coffee, aging paper and the faint whiff of too many ambitions cramped into too little a space.

Sekar Vembu, an old acquaintance and fellow entrepreneur, welcomed me warmly. 'You can use our conference room,' he offered, gesturing to a modest set-up: A table, a few chairs, reliable Wi-Fi, and an endless supply of coffee and tea. 'Stay as long as you need.'

It was generous, and I was grateful. But as I looked around, something didn't sit right. The space didn't match the vision I had in my head. Freshdesk wasn't just a name or an idea—it was a leap into the future. And if we were going to leap, we needed to land somewhere aspirational.

That weekend was a whirlwind of leads and disappointments.

My first stop was Velachery, where my tennis buddy Murali had just opened a bright, modern office for his training company. From the outside, it radiated the energy of a place where great things happen. But as I stepped closer, reality hit: The ground floor housed a bustling chicken shop, its red-and-yellow sign proclaiming 'Sadiq Proteins'. Clucking hens and clanging knives created a cacophony that even the pristine office upstairs couldn't escape.

Murali listened patiently as I outlined my plans, then shook his head. 'Sorry, Girish,' he said, genuinely apologetic. 'I'll need the space soon.'

Strike one.

Next, I visited Vignesh, a former Zoho colleague, who had converted a residential apartment into an office for his automotive blog, *Vicky.in*. The setup was functional but cramped—PCs cluttered the living room and a bedroom had been hastily repurposed as a meeting room. He offered me a spare room, but as I stood there, imagining Freshdesk's future, all I could see were obstacles. Limited parking. No sense of permanence. It felt more like a bachelor pad than the headquarters of a company with global ambitions.

This wasn't it.

By Sunday night, I was exhausted. The limitations of Chennai's office market were glaring. Co-working spaces like WeWork hadn't arrived yet and serviced offices like Regus were out of reach—both financially and geographically.

I needed something closer to home, within 10 kilometres in South Chennai.

That night, as I lay awake, Sekar Vembu's offer came back to me. Maybe the conference room wasn't perfect, but it was a start. Monday morning, I walked back to Kashyap Enclave, right next door to my apartment.

'We'll take it,' I said.

The space wasn't much—a simple conference room in an unassuming building. But as I stepped inside, something stirred. The air buzzed with a quiet hum of potential, the kind that quickens your heartbeat and whispers, 'This is where it begins.'

This was where Freshdesk would start.

The journey had officially begun.

---

13 October 2010: This was it—the day Freshdesk officially began. Our 'office' was a borrowed conference room with a desk, an iPad and the faint hum of air conditioning. It wasn't much, but it was enough.

With Shan still serving out his notice period at Zoho, I was alone that day. The room was eerily quiet—no team, no buzz of activity. Just me, an idea and the faint smell of instant coffee lingering in the air. My iPad, propped up like the centrepiece of some grand workstation, felt almost comical. But it didn't matter. This was a start.

I couldn't let the day pass unmarked. Freshdesk deserved its first stamp on the world, however small. I opened a blank page and began to type, the words coming naturally: 'Freshdesk is Born'.

The post wasn't long. Just a few paragraphs, accompanied by a simple image of a chick hatching from an egg—a visual that felt both symbolic and deeply personal. This wasn't about crafting the perfect message. It was about planting a flag, however small. It was about saying, 'We're here.'

I leaned back after hitting publish, letting the weight of the moment sink in. The spark, ignited in a moment of frustration over Zendesk, was now tangible.

That first day wasn't glamorous. There were no press releases, no champagne toasts, no high-fives in the hallway. Just the stout determination of beginnings. As I stared at the iPad, I didn't know then what Freshdesk would become. But I knew one thing: This was real.

And so, we began—with borrowed space, borrowed time and a vision that demanded to be realized.

Every company has a first team—the group of people who take the leap when there's nothing but an idea and a dream. For Freshdesk, that team started with Shihab Muhammed.

Shihab was the first to reach out. A developer at Zoho turned start-up explorer, he showed up unannounced one day, curiosity written all over his face.

'You're starting a company?' he asked, a glimmer of excitement in his voice. But there was a catch that made me smile.

'I'll work weekends and evenings,' he offered casually. 'Just give me a laptop, and I'll help however I can.' He had assumed we couldn't afford a salary.

Part-time help wasn't what we needed, though. Shan and I both knew Shihab—his sharp thinking, his dedication, his ability to get things done. Why settle for weekends? 'If you're this interested,' I said, 'why not join full-time?'

Shihab hesitated. It wasn't an easy decision. After long conversations and a lot of back and forth, he said yes. He came on board as employee number three, bringing with him a fire that matched ours. Six years later, he walked away with a well-earned single-digit equity stake, proof that we were building something significant.

Next came Parsuram Vijayasankar—'Parsu' to everyone. A talented front-end developer and passionate gamer, Parsu was sharp, creative and ready for a challenge. He didn't need much convincing. With him on board, Freshdesk was no longer just an idea; it was game on.

Then came Kiran Darisi.

Kiran and I had worked together at Zoho before he moved to Accenture in Bangalore, chasing the typical IT dream of going abroad. But the world of IT services didn't match his energy. One day, he messaged me on Facebook: 'Keep a seat for me. Someday, I'll join you.'

I didn't let it sit as a casual remark. 'Why not now?' I typed back.

Kiran hesitated. 'What's your tech stack?' he asked cautiously.

'Ruby on Rails,' I replied.

He frowned. 'I've never worked with Ruby.'

'Neither have we,' I said. 'But you're a great programmer. The question isn't whether you know Ruby. It's whether you believe you can learn.'

That wasn't the only hurdle. Moving back to Chennai—leaving his close-knit Telugu-speaking circle—was another. But the pull of building something meaningful won out. Kiran packed his bags and joined the team.

Finally, there was Vijay Shankar, a customer support professional I'd worked with during our OpManager days. Vijay had started his own business in Trichy, but it wasn't taking off. Newly married, he was splitting his time between Trichy and Chennai, a routine that was wearing him down.

When I heard he was looking for a change, I reached out. Freshdesk didn't have customers yet, let alone the need for a customer-support hire. But I knew Vijay was a rock star. 'Let's bring him in,' I told Shan. 'He can help with QA for now and, when we're ready, he'll lead support and pre-sales.'

The timing was perfect. Vijay said yes and the Freshdesk team grew to six—each person bringing in their expertise, stories and faith in what we were building.

With Shihab and Parsu, the four of us had managed in the cramped conference room. But now, with Kiran and Vijay joining, we were out of space. It was time to find a place we could call our own.

The hunt for Freshdesk's first real office was about to begin.

Finding an office wasn't just about space—it was about laying down roots for Freshdesk. The shiny tech parks, with their glass façades and manicured lawns, weren't just out of budget, they felt out of sync with the scrappy dream we were building. Instead, our search began the old-school way: Scouring property listings in the Saturday edition of *The Hindu*, red pen in hand like treasure hunters marking a map.

One morning, Shihab, my trusted partner in this adventure, waved a freshly clipped ad in front of me. 'Seven hundred square feet in Keelkattalai,' he said, his voice tinged with cautious excitement. 'It's not fancy, but it might work.'

That was all the push we needed.

The drive to Keelkattalai was unexpectedly smooth, thanks to the newly constructed Pallavaram–Thoraipakkam road. As we approached, the city's chaos gave way to a quieter, humbler vibe.

The building, tucked in front of a small church, was unassuming—its plain exterior a stark contrast to the ambitious ideas in our minds. The ground floor housed a bustling automobile workshop, where grease-smudged mechanics worked under creaky ceiling fans. The air was thick with the tang of oil and metal, the clanking of tools providing a gritty soundtrack to our visit.

We climbed a narrow staircase, Shihab leading the way. The first floor had three small offices, each with its quirks.

The first was a chaotic storage room for air-conditioning ducts, a tangle of pipes and insulation. The second belonged to an interior designer, though the uninspired walls and mismatched furniture told a different story.

And then, we found it: The third space.

A room—just 700 square feet, with a single attached toilet and stark white walls. It wasn't much, but it was enough. Standing there, I could feel the possibilities waiting to be unlocked. Freshdesk's first home wouldn't come gift-wrapped; it was up to us to shape it into something remarkable.

The space wore its past like a faded scar. A failed business had left behind mismatched furniture: Worn-out desks, creaky chairs and odd knick-knacks. We scooped it up for a bargain, grateful for the savings even as we saw how much work lay ahead.

The walls, dull and lifeless, seemed to bear witness to countless abandoned dreams. That wasn't going to be our story. If this space was to house Freshdesk, it needed to embody who we were: Bold, optimistic and fresh!

So, we got to work. Bright greens and yellows replaced the dreary white, breathing life into the walls. The vibrant hues were a promise, a declaration that something extraordinary was about to begin here.

We divided the space into three sections. The front became a modest reception area with a sofa borrowed from my home, offering a warm welcome. The centre was the heart of the office, where eight desks sat shoulder-to-shoulder, close enough for ideas to bounce off the freshly painted walls. The back corner became our multipurpose area: A dining table and chairs that served as a cafeteria by lunchtime and extra desk space when work spilled over.

The quirks of the location became part of its charm. The clanging tools from the workshop below, the hymns drifting over from the church behind and the scent of chai from a nearby tea shop aptly called 'Dreams', blended into our daily rhythm.

In that humble 700 square foot space, with second-hand furniture and freshly painted walls, we found a home for Freshdesk—and the beginning of a journey that had only just begun.

The early days of Freshdesk were a chaotic blend of creativity, camaraderie and challenges. In that tiny, overworked office, we were building a story, one chapter at a time. It was relentless and messy, but it was also oddly beautiful.

Kiran was the first to surprise us. His initial hesitation about moving to Chennai melted away faster than we expected and, before long, he became the heartbeat of the team. His Andhra-style pappu became a lunchtime tradition. On certain afternoons, the scent of home-cooked comfort filled the office, grounding us in food and connection.

Dinner was Kiran's time to unwind. Sitting with his plate, he'd light up the screen with video calls to friends in Telugu, his laughter ringing through the walls, bridging the miles with ease.

Then there was Vijay, the dynamo. Picture someone scanning Twitter with laser focus, hunting for unhappy Zendesk customers—that was Vijay. Quick to swoop in with a bold pitch for Freshdesk, he turned complaints into opportunities. His energy was infectious, sparking the team to chase the next big win.

Days blurred into nights as we wrestled with code, designs and strategy. The green and yellow walls, painted in an outburst of optimism, seemed to absorb our energy and reflect it back. Lunches were communal—a mix of banter, ideas and Kiran's aromatic pappu. Weekends, however, were sacred—non-negotiable time for family. We had learned that avoiding burnout wasn't just practical; it strengthened us as a team.

But start-up life has a way of throwing curveballs, and ours came with quirks that could make anyone laugh—or cry.

One morning, the motor that pumped water to the building broke down. No water meant no restrooms—a humbling challenge for a global start-up in the making. Enter Shihab, our unsung hero. His apartment next door became our emergency pit stop. Awkward at first, it quickly turned into another shared joke. On tougher days, Domino's Pizza merged lunch and restroom breaks into one bizarrely efficient solution.

Parking was its own daily adventure. Leaving cars on the street was a gamble and deflated tires became a recurring theme when the cops showed up. Thankfully, the mechanics downstairs patched us up with knowing smirks.

Then came Chennai's 2011 power crisis. Two–three-hour long outages turned our office into an oven. When the air conditioning stopped, we huddled in the reception, sweating and chatting until the lights returned. A petrol generator—our first 'luxury' purchase—became our lifeline. Every few days, someone hauled a red can to the petrol station to refill it, keeping our dream alive.

When outages stretched too long, we moved operations to my apartment. The fans kept us going, even if the ACs couldn't. Shoba adapted her days around our chaos, as we turned the dining table into a communal desk and the living room into a brainstorming hub. Far from ideal, but it worked.

Looking back, it's almost comical. We were coding the future in a space held together by petrol generators, borrowed bathrooms and makeshift workstations. Parking tickets and power cuts were as much a part of our start-up story as our first lines of code.

But, in all the chaos, there was camaraderie. We were like a family, finding joy in absurd moments and strength in small victories.

Those early days weren't perfect, but they forged the foundation for everything Freshdesk would become.

—

Amid the grind, a glimmer of hope emerged—the Microsoft BizSpark Start-up Challenge, a competition with an attractive cash prize of $40,000. It wasn't the money that made us hungry to win. It was a stage to prove that Freshdesk mattered, that we weren't just another start-up but a serious contender.

With 438 start-ups in the running, making it to the final fifteen was a moment of pride. But the real challenge loomed ahead: Presenting in front of 450 people—venture capitalists, industry veterans and seasoned entrepreneurs who had seen it all. The stakes were nerve-wracking.

The day of the finals arrived, buzzing with ambition and tension. Founder after founder took the stage, weaving technical brilliance into their pitches. But the audience? They were blank, disconnected, lost in a fog of dense jargon and over-polished slides.

Watching them, my years at Zoho clicked into place. Speaking wasn't about dazzling people with features; it was about making them care. Our moment wouldn't come from specs or slides—it would come from connection.

When my turn came, I tossed aside the script. I stepped onto the stage, not as a polished founder, but as a storyteller.

'I'm thirty-six years old,' I began, letting the silence settle. 'I have two kids and just one wife.'

Laughter rippled through the room, breaking the tension.

I continued, drawing them into my world. 'In my previous job, I drove a Honda Civic. Life was comfortable, predictable. Then I launched a start-up. Now, I drive a Ford Figo hatchback.'

The chuckles grew louder. I paused, then delivered the punch.

'My kids ... They used to fall asleep in the back seat of my Honda. Now, in the Figo, there's no space for them to lie down. And I can't explain to them why life has changed. As a father, that's tough.'

The room fell silent—the kind of silence that means people are listening, not to the pitch, but to the person. From there, I pivoted to Freshdesk, showing a brief demo of our product.

When I finished, the applause was electric.

And then, we won.

Winning wasn't just a trophy or a cheque—it was proof. Proof that the sacrifices, sleepless nights and relentless belief were worth it. It was a turning point for Freshdesk, and for me. We had shown the world—and ourselves—that we belonged on that stage.

Chapter 14

THE $40,000 prize was more than money—it was momentum. It validated our idea, gave us breathing room and allowed us to think bigger. Bootstrapping had taught us to stretch every rupee, but this windfall felt like permission to take calculated risks.

Over the next two months, we poured the funds into marketing experiments—Google Ads, Facebook campaigns, content marketing. Every dollar spent was a gamble, every campaign a lesson. Some flopped spectacularly; others hinted at scalable growth.

By the time the money ran out, we weren't just a fledgling team with a product—we were a company with a plan. The Microsoft BizSpark win had ignited something bigger than we'd imagined.

The buzz hadn't even settled when the first calls from venture capitalists came. Among the jury that day was Anand Daniel from Accel Partners. After the event, he introduced me to Shekhar Kirani, a connection that would change everything.

Three offers stood out.

The first came from an agritech fund. The partner was supportive and personable, offering $500,000 for a 15 per cent stake. But as much as we appreciated his enthusiasm, the fit felt off. We weren't building tractors; we were building global tech.

The second offer came from Fidelity Ventures. The numbers were tempting, enough to smoothen our growing pains. But the price? A staggering 40 per cent of the company.

Then there was Shekhar Kirani from Accel. Shekhar didn't rush. He listened, probed and connected with our vision. His offer wasn't just about money; it was about alignment.

At the time, I didn't grasp the full weight of Accel's brand or their history with start-ups like Flipkart and Facebook. What I did know was that their approach felt right—not just financially, but strategically.

Choosing Accel marked a turning point. The first offer from the agritech fund was less dilutive and the second one offered more money, but Shekhar brought something deeper to the table: Belief. Accel's network, credibility and experience gave us a pathway to take Freshdesk from a small Chennai start-up to a global player.

The Microsoft BizSpark win had been transformative, but the real shift came with Accel's investment. It signalled that Freshdesk wasn't just a dream cobbled together in a sweaty office over chai breaks—it was a real business with global ambitions.

We now had validation, funds and the backing to dream bigger.

—

Our office in Keelkattalai was noisy and cramped—a hive of energy where every conversation became a team discussion. Privacy was a luxury no one gave much thought to. But that closeness became our strength. Every voice was heard and every decision felt like a collective effort to shape Freshdesk.

When Shekhar Kirani arrived to meet us, I knew this wasn't just another investor pitch. This was a chance to prove that Freshdesk was scalable. I picked him up from his hotel, recounting Freshdesk's lean beginnings during the drive—the trickle of beta signups, the big ambitions we nurtured in our tiny, bustling office. By the time we reached the building, his curiosity had sharpened into something more deliberate.

Shekhar climbed the stairs, taking in the sights and sounds of our 700-square-foot set-up. He paused at the door, surveying the space. Later, he would laugh about it: 'The first thing that struck me was the furniture. It was so ... barebones. The chairs didn't match the tables and the colours were all over the place. It looked like you'd salvaged whatever you could find.'

He wasn't wrong. Our furniture was a mismatched collection of second-hand desks and chairs left behind by the previous tenant. It screamed scrappy, not sophisticated.

But then something else caught his eye. 'You all had MacBook Pros,' he said later, chuckling. The sleek Apple laptops stood out like beacons amidst the clutter. 'That told me everything I needed to know about your priorities. You didn't care about appearances; you cared about getting the work done.'

Hearing that from Shekhar was an affirmation of the choices we'd made. We weren't here to look the part; we were here to build something that mattered.

Inside, I introduced Shekhar to the team, who were trying their best to appear busy while clearly hanging on to every word exchanged. After a brief demo of Freshdesk, Shekhar wasted no time. His questions came fast, precise and relentless.

'How big is this market?'

'Who is your customer?'

'Why will they buy your product?'

'What problems are you solving for them?'

He cut through the fluff, drilling straight to the heart of our strategy. I scrambled to answer with the clarity he demanded.

'Who is your customer?' he asked again.

I replied, 'Any small business.'

He raised an eyebrow. 'So, can the hotel guy next door be your customer?'

The simplicity of the question threw me. For a moment, I paused, then recalibrated. 'Our ideal customer,' I said carefully, 'is someone managing a customer service team of two to ten people, who is actively searching for a helpdesk solution online because they've outgrown email and are ready to make a purchase.'

Shekhar nodded, but his expression told me the work wasn't done.

After Shekhar left, I gathered the team for a debrief. This wasn't just my decision—it had to be ours. I wanted their raw, unfiltered take.

Shihab didn't mince words. 'Girish,' he began, 'with the other investors, you were in control. They agreed with everything you said. But Shekhar? He challenged you. He asked the tough questions. Maybe that's what we need—someone who won't just agree with us but will push us to be better.'

He was right. Shekhar's questions weren't just hard; they were necessary. They forced me to think deeper about our assumptions and strategies. That kind of partnership felt invaluable.

Beyond the practicality, there was also the optics. I imagined the headline: 'Freshdesk Raises $1 Million from Accel Partners'. It wasn't just about funding—it was a stamp of legitimacy; the kind of story that could help us attract talent, customers and attention.

The team's clarity and Shekhar's relentless curiosity made the choice obvious. I called Shekhar and told him we were going with Accel. This was about partnering with someone who believed in us and wasn't afraid to challenge us to reach our potential.

With Accel's funding and the validation from Microsoft BizSpark, Freshdesk was no longer just an underdog. For the first time, it felt like we were stepping out of the shadows and into the spotlight.

Those early decisions—choosing Shekhar as a partner, stretching the $40,000 prize into bold experiments and listening to the instincts of a young team—laid the foundation for everything that followed.

The flame had begun to burn brighter and, now, for the first time, it felt like we had the wind in our sails. Freshdesk was set to embark on its journey.

—

When Freshdesk was just an idea—fragile yet buzzing with possibility—I knew I couldn't do it alone. Building something this ambitious needed more than talent or effort; it needed belief. And two names immediately came to mind: Rajesh Rajasekar and Ravi Raman, my closest friends from college.

They had stood by me before. Back in 2001, when I started the training business, they invested in me. That venture barely got off the ground, but their support had stayed with me—not as a debt of money, but as a debt of trust. This time, I wanted them to be part of the journey, not just to raise funds but to finally give them a return on the faith they had placed in me years ago.

Rajesh wasn't in an easy place to invest. Just a month earlier, he had lost his father, leaving him with heavy hospital bills and a weight of grief. On top of that, he was juggling an executive MBA at Georgia State University, managing personal loss with academic rigor.

Yet somehow, he made it work.

'I pulled money from my 401K,' he told me later, almost casually. 'I don't know anyone who's done that—taking money out of retirement savings to invest in a start-up. But I believed in you, Girish, and I'm so glad I took that risk.'

Even now, I get goosebumps thinking about it. That was an act of faith, far beyond the dollars it represented.

Ravi Raman, my other college anchor, came on board without hesitation. Ravi had always been a steady presence—the kind of friend who doesn't need to say much to make you feel secure. Knowing that both Rajesh and Ravi were with me gave me something money couldn't buy: An emotional ballast.

Looking back, I realize how much I wanted them both to invest. Yes, the money was crucial but, more than that, I wanted to repay their belief in me—a belief that had stayed unwavering, even after my earlier failure.

They believed in me. And that belief became the foundation on which Freshdesk began to rise.

—

Some days are unforgettable, like 7 June 2011, when we officially launched Freshdesk. But 10 June was something else entirely—the day we got our first paying customer.

In the days after our launch, we checked the dashboard obsessively, watching trial signups trickle in. Each one felt like a small victory, but the silence on payments was deafening. We told ourselves it would take time, that customers needed to explore the product. Still, the wait tested our patience.

Then, on a quiet afternoon, the email came in. It was from Atwell College in Perth, Australia. Someone had stumbled upon Freshdesk through Google, signed up for a trial, and spent two-and-a-half hours exploring the product. Without a single call or email, they entered their credit card details and paid $38 for two agents.

For a moment, we just stared at the dashboard in disbelief. A complete stranger halfway across the world had trusted us enough to pay for our product. No pitches, no demos—just our software quietly doing its job.

The room erupted. It wasn't about the $38; it was about validation. Someone we'd never met had seen value in what we'd built and chosen us over every other option. It was a wow moment that electrified the entire team.

We were officially in business.

With $40,000 from the Microsoft BizSpark Challenge, we had some breathing room—but not much. Every rupee had to count and every experiment carried the weight of our hopes for Freshdesk's future.

Our first attempt was Google AdWords, but it proved too expensive for our lean budget. So we pivoted. That's when I discovered BuySellAds, a network of blogs offering tiny, stamp-sized ad spaces. Individually, no single blog drove significant traffic, but collectively, they became a lead-generation machine. For as little as 50 cents to $1 per lead, we found quality customers.

We also listed Freshdesk on the Google Apps marketplace, which brought in additional exposure. Other experiments, like LinkedIn ads and Facebook campaigns, didn't perform as well. LinkedIn was too pricey and Facebook didn't resonate with our target audience.

By August, our scrappiness was paying off. We had seventy paying customers contributing an average of $30 each, giving us a monthly recurring revenue (MRR) of $2,100. For a start-up less than three months old, it felt like momentum.

But momentum wasn't enough—we needed stability.

Accel hadn't yet come back to us and our runway was shrinking fast. I called Shekhar Kirani with a direct message: 'If you're ready, let's finalize the deal and take us off the market.'

Accel's initial offer was $1.5 million for 26 per cent of the company. While exciting, I wasn't comfortable with that level of dilution. After back and forth negotiations, we settled on $1 million for 22 per cent. It was a compromise I could live with.

On 28 August 2011, we signed the term sheet. Relief mixed with nervous energy. But one phrase echoed in my mind: 'The term sheet is not a legally binding document.'

The next two months tested me like nothing else. Our marketing experiments had burned through the $40,000 prize and we were running on fumes. Confident the funds were coming, I had already paid an advance for a new office and started hiring.

By October, the coffers were dry. On 1 November, I wouldn't have enough to run payroll.

I called Shekhar constantly, voicing my worries. His response never wavered: 'Don't worry. We've never walked out of a term sheet. The money will come. It's just a process.'

Finally, on 28 October—Diwali day—the funds hit our account. Relief washed over me, profound and bright, like a burst of light cutting through the darkness.

On 1 December 2011, we announced the funding with the headline: 'Freshdesk Raises $1 Million from Accel Partners'.

Between June and December, we went from bootstrapping in a cramped office to securing funding from one of the most recognized VC firms in the world. Along the way, we learned to adapt, experiment and trust the people around us.

Freshdesk was now a thriving start-up poised to become something bigger. We closed 100 customers in 100 days, then 200 in 200 days. For the first time, I could see it—the outlines of something global, significant and, most importantly, fresh.

—

By August 2011, Freshdesk was hitting its stride. We had launched our first product, secured a $1 million term sheet with Accel and felt the buzz of momentum. That's when Shekhar Kirani, our lead investor, began pressing me to move the company to Bangalore.

On paper, it was hard to argue with him. Bangalore was the undisputed epicentre of India's start-up ecosystem. A magnet for ambition, companies like Flipkart, Myntra and Cleartrip thrived in the city. Deals were made over coffee, partnerships formed in buzzing coworking spaces and networks grew like wildfire.

Chennai, by comparison, felt comfortable but isolated. I joked about it at a start-up pitch event, opening my talk with: 'I'm from Freshdesk, based in Chennai. Chennai has a beach, which Bangalore can never have. Our traffic is better. And the sambar isn't sweet.'

The crowd laughed, but beneath the humour, I felt the pull of Shekhar's advice. Not only did Bangalore seem a better location, it also felt like a bigger stage. On a visit to the city, I noticed how effortlessly founders and investors mingled. 'There's the Cleartrip founder,' someone whispered. 'That's the Flipkart team.' It struck me that in Chennai, I only knew logos. In Bangalore, they knew faces.

Back home, I laid it out for Shan, my co-founder. 'If we stay here, we'll always be Freshdesk, the Chennai start-up. But if we move to Bangalore, we'll meet the people driving the ecosystem. Let's go.'

Shan wasn't as sold on the idea. His family wasn't thrilled about the thought of moving either. To ease the decision, I suggested, 'Let's visit first. See the companies, explore some homes, meet the people, feel the energy. Then decide.'

We made it a family trip, bringing our wives and kids to explore the city, while Shan and I explored its start-up scene.

Our first stop was Koramangala, the heart of Bangalore's start-up culture. There, we met Pallav Nadhani, the young CEO of FusionCharts, who had built his company at just seventeen and was now pulling in nearly $5 million a year. As he drove us around in his sleek BMW, I couldn't help but feel inspired—and slightly envious.

The city buzzed with ambition. Cafes were filled with founders sketching out plans and pubs hummed with start-up chatter. Bangalore was more than just a city; it was a mindset. I was ready to move.

Back in Chennai, the team's reactions were mixed. Parsu, our free-spirited designer, embraced the idea—it meant new adventures and independence. Vijay, on the other hand, was torn even though he was personally excited. His wife's family lived in Bangalore, but his parents were in Chennai. The move wasn't easy for him.

Others, like Shihab and Kiran, weighed personal and professional factors. Meanwhile, I began planning for new hires in Bangalore. Two candidates, Bharath from Yahoo and Navaneetha from Aryaka, were already excited to join us once we made the move.

But not all hurdles were professional.

Parsu's enthusiasm masked one significant obstacle: His mother.

At twenty-six, Parsu still lived with his parents, and his mother was deeply concerned about him moving to Bangalore. She was not willing to let it happen without trying to intervene. One day, I got a call from her.

She didn't hold back. 'He left a job that paid ₹10 lakh a year to join your company for ₹25,000 a month. Is this a good idea?' she asked bluntly.

Her words hit hard. I respected her perspective—it came from a place of love. But I also knew this was a pivotal moment not just for Parsu but for Freshdesk.

'Madam,' I said, choosing my words carefully, 'I was the same manager at Zoho who gave him the ₹10 lakh salary. At Freshdesk, we offered him ₹45,000, but Parsu chose to take ₹25,000 to show his commitment. In return, we doubled his stock options from 2.5 per cent to 5 per cent.'

Her voice softened slightly and she didn't know how to respond, but I could tell she wasn't convinced. So I took a different tack.

'Madam,' I said, my tone firm but respectful, 'should I discuss Parsu's compensation with him or with you?'

That question landed. After a pause, she assented, letting the decision rest with him.

With that, I thought, our plan to move to Bangalore was on. But that conversation reminded me that start-ups weren't just about rational logic or business decisions; they were about people and their families, and their collective belief in building something bigger than themselves.

And then, everything seemed to fall apart.

The first hiccup came when my younger son, Sanjay, was rejected from Head Start Montessori in Bangalore. Their strict policy wouldn't allow him to enrol in first grade because he missed the cut-off by a few months.

Next, I found what seemed like the perfect office in Oxford Towers, near Old Airport Road. But just before signing the lease, the landlady suggested waiting a week. It felt off, like a bad omen.

Later that day, with hours to kill before our flight back to Chennai, Shoba, the kids and I strolled through Forum Mall. The buzz of the arcade, the aroma of coffee and the clatter of trays all blurred into background noise. I felt guilty. Why was I wandering aimlessly here when I should be building Freshdesk? Every step felt like a waste, each passing second an accusation.

Leaning against the railing, watching the crowd below, I made a promise to myself. This waiting, this stalling—it ended here. We'd find our space. We'd build Freshdesk. No more distractions.

The final blow came from Bharath, one of the candidates excited to join us. He called to say he'd accepted another offer—one with better pay and a US trip.

As I sat on the return flight to Chennai, I couldn't shake the feeling that these weren't coincidences. They were signs.

When I landed in Chennai, I met Shan. 'Why are we forcing this move?' I asked. 'Look at everything that's happened. Parsu's mom wasn't happy. Vijay's family isn't thrilled. Bharath has backed out. Why don't we build Freshdesk right here, in Chennai?'

It wasn't superstition. Chennai was our home, a place that had shaped us, supported us and grounded us.

So we stayed.

Looking back, staying in Chennai was one of the best decisions we ever made. Freshdesk didn't need Bangalore's buzz to grow into Freshworks. What we needed was belief—in ourselves, in our team and in what we were building.

In the end, the beaches, better traffic and sambar that wasn't sweet weren't just jokes. They were part of who we were. Staying home not only kept us grounded, it also gave us the freedom to dream bigger.

And from that foundation, we built something global, impactful and unmistakably fresh.

—

The days leading up to our move to SP Infocity were filled with a sense of urgency and determination. Freshdesk was taking root, and with the Accel term sheet in hand, it was time to find a home worthy of our ambitions.

We had outgrown our modest set-up. The constraints of space and infrastructure were beginning to stifle our aspirations. Finding a new office, however, was easier said than done. Chennai, with all its bustling promise, offered little in the way of suitable, affordable office spaces. Most commercial buildings required massive leases far beyond what our young start-up could justify.

After countless dead ends, our search brought us to SP Infocity—a gleaming IT park that seemed to encapsulate everything we were dreaming of. From the moment we stepped in, the place felt alive with potential. It had ample parking, reliable power backups and a polished modernity that resonated with our vision. But reality came crashing down soon after. The smallest space available was 3,000 square feet, and the costs for fit-outs and the hefty ten-month security deposit were simply beyond our reach.

For a while, it felt like yet another missed opportunity. But this time, I couldn't let it go. On a sleepless night, I decided to write to the marketing head, Jair D'Souza, explaining our position. I told him about Freshdesk, our constraints and our relentless belief in what we were building. His response came the next morning—a short but encouraging note asking me to meet him later that day.

Sitting across from Jair, I saw a professional who genuinely listened. He didn't brush us aside with policies or impersonal guidelines. Instead, he worked to understand our situation and began piecing together a solution. That's when he proposed an alternative—a compact 1,150 square feet in the middle of what used to be a dining hall for Amazon. It wasn't just the space—he also highlighted how this arrangement would save us on fit-out costs. The flooring and ceiling were already done, and the AC ducts were in place; he even reduced the security deposit to six months, throwing in two months rent-free during the fit-out period.

It was more than what we could have asked for. By the end of that meeting, we had signed the lease and our journey at SP Infocity began. The move marked a turning point. It wasn't about relocating as much as it was a leap of faith into a future we were eager to create. The office became more than just walls and desks; it was a symbol of possibility, a place where our ideas could breathe and grow.

Looking back, I realize Jair's approach embodied the essence of great customer service—understanding a problem deeply and working earnestly to solve it. His willingness to make exceptions, to see the human behind the client, taught us a lesson we would carry forward in our journey of building a customer service company.

Freshworks would go on to become an anchor company and take more than 250,000 square feet of office space in SP Infocity. We are still there, fourteen years and counting.

—

In 2011, the customer service market was fiercely competitive, with over 600 helpdesk providers battling for attention. Zendesk, the Danish frontrunner, was racing ahead, winning clients like Adobe and Sony Music. Salesforce, the industry giant, had over 100,000 customers and the distinction of being Forbes' 'most innovative company'.

This was the arena Freshdesk entered—an underdog staring down giants. Our competitors had years of experience, deep pockets and market dominance. But if I've learned one thing, it's this: You don't wait for an invitation to the table. Sometimes, you crash the party.

That's exactly what happened on a chilly December day in 2011—on Twitter, no less.

It started with a seemingly offhand tweet from tech blogger Ben Kepes: 'Seems to me that #Freshdesk is an unethical troll trying to cash in on #Zendesk's good name. But that could just be me ...'

To most, it might have seemed minor, but I knew better. Kepes was a respected cloud analyst; his words carried weight. This wasn't a casual remark—it was a calculated jab.

I decided to respond.

'A pretty harsh comment from someone we respect and follow at CloudAve,' I tweeted. 'Have you tried Freshdesk? An objective review will help all.'

Before Kepes could reply, another user chimed in: '@benkepes Bunch of Indian cowboys #Freshdesk.'

The room fell silent. The comment wasn't just an insult; it was a thinly veiled, racist dig.

I steadied my hands and replied: 'Making an unsolicited attack on our nationality reflects badly on you, not us. We're Indian, and we're proud of that.'

Short. Clear. Defiant. Then I added one more line: 'Freshdesk is six months old. I am sure both of us will be around to see how this plays out.'

What followed was unexpected. Kepes escalated the exchange, tagging Zendesk CEO Mikkel Svane. Mikkel's response lit the fuse: 'You know what they say? Imitation is the sincerest form of WAIT-WHAT-A-FREAKING-RIPOFF! ;-)'

The tweet went viral. Suddenly, Freshdesk—a fledgling start-up from Chennai—was in a public spat with the industry leader.

Vijay was fuming with anger and wanted to respond to the tweet.

But I saw the moment for what it was: An opportunity. If Zendesk felt threatened enough to punch down at us, it meant we were on their radar.

I called an all-hands meeting. 'This isn't a problem,' I said. 'This is a stage. And we're going to own the narrative.'

Within hours, we launched ripoffornot.org, a microsite detailing the entire Twitter exchange. In a blog post, I addressed Kepes' accusations head-on: 'So, according to Ben Kepes, we're unethical trolls because our name includes "desk". Does Zendesk own the word "desk"? What about companies like eStreamDesk, ReadyDesk and WonderDesk—are they ripoffs too? By that logic, maybe Zendesk is the ripoff.'

Then came the kicker: Kepes was a paid Zendesk blogger, a fact missing from his critique.

We added a call-to-action at the bottom of the page: 'Sign up for a free Freshdesk demo.'

And we signed off with the famous quote:

> First they ignore you, then they ridicule you, then they fight you, then you win.

The fallout was immediate. The microsite and blog post went viral, drawing attention from start-ups, media outlets and even Zendesk customers. Many sided with us, praising our transparency and boldness.

That week, our website traffic surged, signups spiked and we gained more attention than we could have ever bought.

Gawker Media captured it perfectly: 'Freshdesk brings gun to a knife fight,' they wrote, ending with, 'Freshdesk 1 - Zendesk 0.'

For all their bravado, Zendesk handed us the ultimate gift: An audience. More than that, the episode gave Freshdesk a personality—defiant and unafraid to stand up to Goliaths.

The Twitter spat became our unofficial coming-out party. Freshdesk was no longer just another CRM start-up; we were the underdog with a voice, ready to take on the giants. We didn't just crash the party. We left with the spotlight trained firmly on us.

—

By late 2011, Freshdesk's momentum was undeniable. The Microsoft BizSpark win and Accel's investment had drawn attention, our viral Twitter spat had put us on the map and paying customers were signing up faster than ever. More investors were starting to notice us.

One day, a prominent VC from Mumbai reached out. 'We'd love to meet,' they said. 'We know you've just closed a round with Accel, but we're really interested.'

I politely declined. 'We're not raising money right now,' I told them.

But they didn't give up. Their persistence was flattering. They even offered to fly me to Mumbai, but I declined that offer after consulting Shekhar. 'Go meet them,' he advised, 'but pay for your own flight. That sets the tone.'

When I arrived at their office, I was ushered into a room filled with their entire partnership team. By then, Freshdesk had crossed 200 paying customers—nearly double what we had just months earlier. I walked them through our story, our traction and the growing buzz around the product.

One of their US partners leaned in, his eyes sparkling with excitement. 'Girish,' he said, 'we know you'll hit 2,000 customers soon. Just name the valuation you want and we'll make it happen.'

It was flattering, but the India partner's comment on my way out stopped me cold.

'Girish, you just closed your round in October. We can offer a 30 per cent markup on your last valuation,' he said casually, as though it were a foregone conclusion.

I turned to face him, standing in their reception area. 'Look,' I said, my tone firm but calm, 'I'm not here to raise money. But if we do, it won't be for a 30 per cent markup.'

I paused, letting the silence hang.

'Treat us like a Silicon Valley start-up. In the Valley, companies raise their next round at least three times their last valuation. That's the benchmark. If you're serious, and can match that, then let's talk.'

And with that, I walked out.

I wasn't being arrogant. I was setting the tone.

We were building something global—something with the potential to make a wide impact. We deserved to be valued for what we were becoming, not just where we had started.

This moment wasn't just about negotiating with investors. It reflected everything we stood for: Belief in the product, belief in the team and belief in the journey we were on.

Our global strategy, bold campaigns and how we handled investors boiled down to one thing: Confidence. We weren't just taking the stage. We were proving we belonged there for good.

Chapter 15

BY January 2012, Freshdesk's momentum was undeniable. We'd attracted customers, secured funding and generated buzz. But the next step was critical: Finding the right investors to scale our vision.

One day, a Mumbai-based VC firm offered $2 million on a post-money valuation of $8 million. For an early-stage start-up, it was a solid number. But something didn't sit right.

I remembered advice from *Venture Hacks*: If you want to discover the true valuation of your start-up, you need to clear the market. That meant engaging multiple investors simultaneously—not settling for the first offer.

I called Shekhar Kirani, our partner at Accel. 'We've got an offer,' I said, 'but I want to test the waters. Can you connect me with a few other investors?'

Shekhar didn't hesitate. Among his introductions was Lee Fixel of Tiger Global—a name I knew but whose weight I didn't fully grasp at first. Tiger Global was fast becoming a force in the start-up world, known for its speed and decisiveness.

Lee was in Chennai for another investment (which, I later learned, was CaratLane). He had agreed to visit our modest office in SP Infocity, but plans changed. The day before the meeting, he emailed: Back-to-back meetings meant we'd need to meet at the Crowne Plaza hotel instead.

The next day, I stood in the sleek lobby, iPad in hand, ready to pitch.

—

Lee was already there, wrapping up another meeting. He was lean and sharp, with thin rimless glasses and an understated intensity. He didn't fit the typical image of a high-powered investor—young, calm and commanding without trying.

I dove straight into my pitch: My journey from Zoho to Freshdesk, our traction, the hurdles we'd faced and the vision driving us forward. Lee listened intently, asking precise, pointed questions. Unlike others, he wasn't there to impress or overwhelm. He wanted to understand.

When the meeting ended, I had no idea where I stood. There were no promises, no hints. As I walked out of the hotel, I chalked it up as just another pitch.

The next day, I was in Bangalore, waiting for a flight at the airport, when my phone buzzed. It was Lee.

'Girish, the numbers don't make sense,' he said, straight to the point.

My heart sank. With just $10,000 in monthly recurring revenue, I knew Freshdesk's metrics weren't dazzling. I braced myself for the rejection that seemed inevitable.

But then, he said something I'll never forget.

'I'm taking a bet on you. If you agree, we'll offer $5 million on a $12.5 million pre-money valuation. Let's skip the term sheet and go straight to due diligence.'

I was stunned.

VCs typically took weeks—or months—poring over financials and forecasts before making an offer. Lee cut through all that with a single phone call. He wasn't betting on numbers; he was betting on the team, the vision and what Freshdesk could become.

The deal was finalized the next day.

—

For Freshdesk, it was an unimaginable sum at that stage. For me, it was a lesson in trust and decisiveness.

Lee's style was unlike anything I'd experienced. Other firms sent teams of analysts to dissect every detail, trying to predict every scenario. Lee moved with instinct and speed. He trusted his gut—and he trusted me.

The news of Tiger's interest set off a chain reaction. VCs who had been hesitant now rushed to reach out. One even contacted my former boss, Kumar Vembu, hoping to sway me. Kumar's response was simple and supportive: 'Girish knows what he's doing. If you give him a good valuation, he'll consider it.'

But my mind was made up.

With Lee, there was no drawn-out dance, no second-guessing. A handshake carried the weight of a signed contract.

The partnership wasn't just about the money. It was about believing in Freshdesk's potential—not as a scrappy Chennai start-up, but as a global player with impact. Lee's trust didn't just validate our journey; it propelled us forward, proving that sometimes, bold bets and quick decisions are the keys to transformative growth.

—

The Tiger Global investment marked a seismic shift for Freshdesk. For the first time, money wasn't a constraint. The days of cramped offices and mismatched furniture were behind us. We upgraded to a 5,800 square foot space in SP Infocity—a professional set-up that reflected the company we were becoming.

Lee Fixel's advice was refreshingly straightforward: 'Keep hiring engineers with your eyes closed.' And we did.

We scaled aggressively, forming specialized teams to tackle critical components of the product: Core help desk, integrations, mobile, knowledge base and more. We even ventured into gamification—an innovative idea at the time that gave us an edge in the market.

Yet, amid this growth, one thing stayed the same: We didn't build a traditional sales team. Every customer came through the product's organic pull. No outbound calls. No aggressive pitches. Just the strength of what we had built.

By the end of 2012, Freshdesk was evolving. The company felt different—more ambitious, more united and more attuned to the global stage. As 2013 loomed, one thing was clear: Freshdesk wasn't just growing; it was transforming into something its competitors couldn't easily replicate—a team forged in the trenches and a product crafted by people who cared deeply.

When we hit 500 paying customers, every dollar of revenue came from inbound leads—people already curious about the product. Customers found us, explored the product and signed up—often without speaking to anyone. If someone wanted a demo, Vijay or I would jump on a call. It was organic, efficient and manageable ... Until it wasn't.

As leads poured in, it became clear we needed help. We needed someone to dive into the growing interest and convert curious people into paying customers.

In May 2012, we hired our first salesperson: Periyaswamy Palanikumar, or Peri.

Peri, a former colleague from Zoho, had moved into IT services but was eager to return to the product world. Bringing him on board was a no-brainer. His impact was immediate. In his first month, Peri sent daily email campaigns to trial users, followed up on responses, arranged demos and closed deals. By the end of that month, our revenue had doubled.

It felt like striking gold. The inbound leads we'd been nurturing for months weren't just interested—they were ready to buy. Peri showed us how to unlock that potential.

Encouraged by Peri's success, we expanded the sales team.

Next came Irshad, a cold-calling veteran whose grit and resilience were honed in IT services. At Freshdesk, he faced a different game: Handling inbound leads. Irshad mastered the product, engaged trial users and adapted his approach to their needs.

We divided territories: Peri focused on the US, while Irshad managed the rest of the world. Together, they handled over 3,000 leads a month. Each month, we raised their targets by 15–20 per cent—and each month, they hit them.

Then there was Abdur, whose background was as unconventional as it was impressive. Before Freshdesk, Abdur sold international SIM cards to travellers at airport security gates—a job that demanded instant rapport with strangers. At Freshdesk, that skill became a superpower, especially as we targeted global markets.

With Abdur on board, it felt like the sales team was complete. His knack for connecting with international customers added a new dimension to our process and, together, the team turned inbound leads into a revenue machine.

Peri, Irshad and Abdur weren't just a sales team—they were a force shaping the future of Freshdesk. Watching them work, I realized a critical truth: Great hiring isn't about filling roles; it's about finding people who amplify what you've built—people who make the company better in ways you never anticipated.

Month after month, our momentum grew, fuelled by a team that believed in the mission and a product that spoke for itself.

Freshdesk was charging full steam ahead.

By mid-2012, we set our sights on a milestone that felt audacious, yet tantalizingly achievable: $1 million in annual revenue. For Freshdesk, crossing that threshold would prove we weren't just a promising start-up—we were a viable, growing business.

I mapped it out in an Excel sheet, weaving together numbers, assumptions and targets. How many customers would we need if each spent an average of $30 a month? What traffic would the website require? How much marketing spend would it take? Every figure had a purpose, every calculation a direction. It was precise, logical and foolproof—or so I thought.

What I hadn't accounted for was the magic of expansion revenue.

At first, it crept in unnoticed—a 2 per cent monthly growth in customer spending. Some added users, others upgraded plans. Small increments compounded into something massive.

By the time we hit $1 million, expansion revenue wasn't just padding the numbers—it was rewriting our growth strategy.

This wasn't about chasing new leads endlessly. It was about growing with the customers we already had, nurturing relationships and scaling alongside them. That realization shifted everything.

By December, we were just shy of the $1 million mark. But in January 2013, the numbers tipped, and we crossed it—with far fewer customers than I'd planned for.

That $1 million wasn't just a financial milestone; it was proof that Freshdesk was a force to reckon with.

—

Ripoffornot.org had thrust Freshdesk into the global spotlight, but attention alone wouldn't sustain us. We needed something bolder—an audacious move to cement our place in the market.

It was November 2012 and the bustling NASSCOM Product Conclave in Bangalore buzzed with India's brightest tech minds. Amid that energy, I met Sameer Gandhi, the US-based Accel partner who had championed Freshdesk's investment.

Sameer was on the board of Dropbox and had witnessed firsthand how the freemium model could be the rocket fuel for growth. Dropbox had proven that giving something valuable away for free wasn't just generosity—it was strategy.

We sat down and I walked Sameer through Freshdesk's progress: Milestones hit, customers won and the buzz we had generated. He listened intently, nodding along. Then, in his quiet, deliberate way, he leaned forward and cut to the chase.

'I want to focus on one metric,' he said. 'The number of freemium customers. See what you can do to 10x that.'

His words lingered long after the conversation ended. The power of freemium wasn't new to me—we had already launched a free plan earlier that year, offering start-ups the first agent, free on all plans. The results were promising, but we'd treated it as an experiment.

Sameer's challenge made it clear: Freemium wasn't just a feature. It was *the* strategy.

If we could grow our base of free users, we wouldn't just expand our pipeline of potential paying customers. We'd create an army of brand ambassadors—users who would carry our name into every conversation, every recommendation and every corner of the market.

Back in Chennai, I gathered the team. 'We're doubling down on freemium,' I said. 'Sameer wants us to 10x our free customers and I think he's right. This is how we stand out.'

The question was: How?

We revamped our approach, introducing the 'Forever Free' plan, offering start-ups three agent licenses free for life. Marketing campaigns were reimagined, product messaging simplified and word-of-mouth marketing became a central focus. Every free plan came with a Freshdesk branded URL and email signature, turning every support ticket into an ad for us.

To ensure users experienced the product's full potential, we made onboarding frictionless—no calls or handholding required. We wanted the product to speak for itself.

The impact was immediate and electric. It had taken us twenty-one months to reach our first 5,000 customers. After doubling down on freemium, we added another 5,000 in just four months.

The freemium strategy changed how the market saw Freshdesk. From start-ups to mid-sized businesses, we became the go-to name for customer support. Every free account was a seed for the future—some grew into paying customers, while others spread the word, pulling new users into our orbit.

Sameer's challenge wasn't just about freemium. It was about thinking bigger, acting bolder and trusting the exponential power of a single good idea.

More than a mere feature, Freemium became our marketing engine. By betting big on it, we didn't just play to compete—we played to win.

—

Momentum is addictive. By the summer of 2012, we'd hit 100 customers in 100 days. By April 2013, the number had skyrocketed to 5,000 and, by August, it doubled to 10,000. Freshdesk had become the fastest-growing customer support software in the world, used in 180 countries.

Our secret? Listening.

We focused on small businesses—the ones giants like Zendesk overlooked—and delivered what they needed at prices they couldn't resist.

I borrowed a lesson from Saravana Stores—a Chennai icon known for selling quality goods at unbeatable prices. Their superpower was scale: Thriving on slim margins and high volumes. If they could bring affordability to families, why couldn't we do the same for small businesses?

So, we built Freshdesk to be accessible—a tool for the underdog. 'Start small, grow with us' became our mantra.

Chapter 16

BY mid-2012, Freshdesk was on a roll. Deals were closing, revenue was climbing and our reputation was growing. But my mind was restless, always searching for what would come next. I wanted Freshdesk to be more than just a single-product company—I envisioned a suite of solutions, each starting with the word 'Fresh'. In fact, I'd already bought forty domain names starting with 'Fresh'. To me, each one represented a market opportunity we could exploit successfully with our inbound customer–acquisition model.

One of those ideas was Freshmarketer, a marketing automation tool. The category was still in its infancy, with no clear SaaS leader. It felt like the perfect opportunity. I put together a small team and started prototyping the product.

I could see it clearly: Freshmarketer would complement Freshdesk, creating a seamless flow between customer service and marketing. The potential was enormous.

But that excitement didn't last long.

Around that time, Shekhar and I flew to Palo Alto to meet Andrew Braccia, a seasoned investor at Accel. I pitched Freshmarketer to him, walking him through the idea, the market opportunity and how it could fit into the Freshdesk ecosystem.

Andrew listened patiently, nodding occasionally. Then he leaned in and said something that stopped me cold: 'Girish, you haven't even hit $1 million in revenue with Freshdesk yet. It's too early to think about a second product. Focus on dominating customer service first. Otherwise, new investors might think you're pivoting because Freshdesk isn't working.'

His words stung. I believed in Freshmarketer. I *knew* it had potential. But Andrew's advice made sense.

As much as I wanted to pursue the vision of a multi-product company, the timing wasn't right. Freshdesk wasn't yet strong enough to support the weight of another product.

I flew back to Chennai with a heavy heart and called the team. Reluctantly, we shut down the Freshmarketer project.

It wasn't an easy decision. For months, I had envisioned Freshmarketer as the next step in Freshdesk's evolution. Letting go felt like a setback. But Andrew's advice was clear, and I trusted his experience.

This wasn't us abandoning the dream—it was us ensuring our foundation was unshakable first. It was a hard lesson, but an invaluable one: Timing matters as much as the idea itself. Sometimes, the most strategic move is holding back.

With renewed energy, we turned our focus back to Freshdesk. We pushed harder, refining the product and doubling down on customer service. By January 2013, when we crossed $1 million in annual revenue, it was clear we had made the right call. Investors were thrilled, the team was energized and the path ahead was clearer than ever.

The experience stayed with me. It wasn't just about timing or focus—it was about understanding that discipline is as important as ambition. Freshdesk's success proved that when you get the foundation right, the possibilities don't just wait—they grow stronger.

—

Managing people is hard. It often requires decisions rooted in belief rather than data. I've always seen myself as a coach, not just a manager—someone who uncovers talent and aligns it with the right opportunities. There are no bad employees, only untapped potential waiting to be unlocked.

One of the most striking examples of this came with Annapoorna Venkataraman—'Anna' to us—who joined Freshdesk in 2012. We hired her fresh out of college during an off-campus drive at SASTRA University. Bright, articulate and full of promise, she impressed us in her interview. I told her, 'We'll help you find what you're good at.'

We gave Anna a start in marketing, but things didn't click. Her content writing lacked impact and her shift to SEO writing was even more frustrating. Six months in, she was struggling and in tears, feeling like she was letting everyone down. But I reminded her of my promise and suggested something new: customer support.

Anna was hesitant, and so was our small, mostly male support team. But she embraced the role, taking on day-shift tickets for customers in India and Europe. The early days were tough—learning the product, managing demanding tickets and working without much support.

Then, her natural strengths began to shine. Anna's empathetic communication turned every customer interaction into a positive experience. She didn't just resolve issues—she owned them, ensuring customers felt heard and valued. Soon, they were asking for her by name, leaving glowing reviews and even tweeting about her.

By 2014, Anna had transformed into a standout performer. Her exceptional work earned her the Customer Success Hero Award at the CS Summit, a testament to how far she had come. From a lost fresher unsure of her path, Anna became a global symbol of excellence in customer success.

Her journey proves a simple truth: When you invest in people, believe in their potential and give them the right opportunities, they can achieve extraordinary things.

—

For years, inbound sales had been our lifeline at Freshdesk. Customers found us, signed up and our pipeline flowed. But as revenue climbed, one question gnawed at me: Could outbound work for us, too?

I didn't want Freshdesk to become a cold-calling machine. That wasn't who we were. If we were going to do outbound, it had to be thoughtful, personal and genuinely valuable—something that made prospects think: *That was different. That was worth my time.*

So we launched an experiment with Yashvanth Rajendran—one of our early sales stars. Instead of blasting generic pitches, we crafted highly personalized outreach emails, each focusing on a prospect's specific needs. 'Let them remember Freshdesk as the company that never wasted their time,' I told the team.

It worked. Prospects responded. Conversations started. This wasn't a volume game—it was about meaningful engagements with the right customers.

But I wanted more than an experiment. If outbound was to be a true growth engine, we needed a strategy. That's when I brought in Madhu Lakshmanan, a seasoned sales consultant from Bangalore.

In February 2013, after reviewing our numbers, Madhu made a bold prediction: 'You can hit $2.2 million in revenue by the end of the year.'

It was ambitious—more than double what we had achieved so far. But deep down, I wasn't satisfied. Why stop there?

Then, something unexpected happened.

In March 2013, Bessemer Venture Partners hosted a hackathon in Bangalore, inviting developers to build apps using APIs from their portfolio companies like Twilio and SendGrid. It was an exciting opportunity to flex our creative muscles. We quickly assembled a team, rented a van and set off for Bangalore.

The journey, however, was chaotic. Halfway through, near Kanchipuram, the van broke down. Exhausted but determined, we called home for help, summoned our cars, split into two groups and continued the journey by car. By the time we reached the hackathon, we were tired but inspired by the event's energy.

For over twenty-four caffeine-fuelled hours, we used Twilio's APIs to build a prototype for a cloud-based call centre solution: FreshCaller. Simple but functional, it caught everyone's attention.

By the end of the event, we'd won the first prize. The victory felt incredible—not just for the recognition but for what it represented: An idea with potential, a seed waiting to grow.

The hackathon sparked something even bigger. During conversations with their team, I got a glimpse into the revenue trajectories of their portfolio companies. One had scaled from $1 million to $5 million in a year; and another, from $1.5 million to $6 million. Hearing those numbers lit a fire in me.

Could Freshdesk do the same?

Crossing $1 million in January 2013 had felt monumental. But now, a new dream took shape: Hitting $5 million by December 2013. It wasn't just a revenue target; it was a statement.

I didn't share this dream immediately. For our developers, revenue was an abstraction—they focused on building great products. But the goal gnawed at me. Back in Chennai, I mapped out a plan. Customers were signing up, outbound leads were showing promise and the team was evolving. But $5 million wasn't going to happen with business as usual.

We needed to scale—fast. Marketing, sales and product development had to level up.

Early on, we set sales targets based on the number of seats sold, prioritizing customer relationships over upselling. But, by April 2013, it was clear we needed to pivot. Revenue-based targets aligned more directly with our growth goals, energizing the sales team and sharpening their focus.

By May, we set an audacious goal: $5 million in annual revenue by December. At the time, we were at $2.2 million. The gap felt insurmountable, but the team embraced the challenge.

December came, and we did it. Freshdesk crossed $5 million in revenue.

The celebration was electric—a mix of disbelief, pride and exhilaration. In just eleven months, we had quintupled our revenue, proving what once seemed impossible.

But more than the numbers, the journey had reshaped how we thought about growth.

Momentum. It was the only word to describe what we were experiencing in 2013. Each new million in revenue seemed to come faster than the last, like we were on a rocket ship gathering speed.

I started tracking how quickly we were hitting each milestone and the trend was undeniable: The first million had taken eighteen months after launching the product. The second came in just 4.5 months. The third arrived in three months. The fourth? In 2.5 months.

These shrinking milestones weren't just numbers—they were proof that Freshdesk was evolving into something far bigger than we had imagined. Each milestone reinforced our confidence and fuelled even bigger dreams.

The year 2013 wasn't just about growth. It was the year we realized we were building more than a product—or even a company. We were building a force that could truly go the distance. And, for the first time, it felt like the world was starting to notice.

Amidst this whirlwind of growth, an email landed in my inbox that shook everything up. A global company based in Europe had taken notice of us. They weren't just curious—they were serious.

Their offer? $80 million.

The breakdown: $50 million upfront and $30 million tied to revenue milestones. The proposal was very similar to what Salesforce had offered to acquire Assistly (Desk.com). But there was a catch: They were only interested in our ticketing solution.

I remember sitting with Shan, laying out the details. The numbers were staggering, especially for two guys who had started this journey just a few years ago. 'This will make you and me very rich,' I told him. 'But the team? They won't benefit nearly as much. And worse, we'd have to abandon everything else we dreamed of. Freshdesk wouldn't be Freshdesk anymore.'

Shan listened quietly, taking it all in. His response, as always, was calm. 'I'm fine with whatever you decide, Girish,' he said.

It wasn't his words that made the decision easy—it was the unspoken trust. Shan believed in the bigger picture as much as I did.

For us, it was never just about the money. We didn't set out to build ticketing software. Freshdesk was always about a broader vision: A suite of tools that could redefine the future of customer engagement.

So, we turned the offer down.

That decision wasn't just about rejecting $80 million. It was about choosing the future we wanted to create. In a world obsessed with exits, we chose to double down. We chose belief over a big payout.

Turning down the offer became a defining moment—not just for Freshdesk but for me, personally. It reaffirmed why we had started this journey in the first place and what we wanted to achieve.

As I walked out of that conversation with Shan, the path ahead felt clearer than ever. Freshdesk wasn't just growing—it was becoming unstoppable.

Chapter 17

WHEN we shut down Freshmarketer in 2012, it felt like closing a door on a dream. But even then, I knew it wasn't the end. The vision of Freshdesk as a multi-product company stayed with me, a quiet but persistent reminder of what we could achieve. In a few months, I pitched another idea to our board. This time, the pitch was clear and grounded in data.

'The story doesn't need to change,' I told the board. 'It's still a helpdesk, but for internal customers instead of external ones. Think about it—23 per cent of Freshdesk customers already use it for internal ticketing. I know this market inside out. ServiceNow dominates the enterprise space, but the mid-market is wide open.'

The response was immediate. Lee Fixel, always sharp and instinctive, nodded as I walked through the plan. With his support, we got the green light to move forward.

For the project's leader, the choice was obvious: Shihab Muhammed. Shihab understood IT helpdesks better than anyone on the team. Together, we crafted a product that would cater to the mid-market with the same care and innovation that had powered Freshdesk's success.

We named it Freshservice. And, in January 2014, it went live.

The launch wasn't flashy. There were no grand announcements or massive marketing campaigns. Instead, we focused on building a product that delivered value from day one.

The results spoke for themselves.

Within its first year, Freshservice generated $1.5 million in revenue. By the second year, that number had soared to $6.5 million. It was growth that could only be described as explosive.

Freshservice's success was more than just numbers—it was validation. It proved that our multi-product vision wasn't just possible; it was powerful. We could solve distinct problems for different audiences while staying true to our brand's essence.

More importantly, it cemented what Freshdesk—Freshworks, now—was becoming. We weren't just building tools; we were crafting purposeful solutions. Whether it was Freshdesk or Freshservice, every product shared a common thread: fresh, innovative ideas built for businesses ready to grow.

With Freshservice, we'd launched our second rocket and it was soaring higher than we ever expected. But as exciting as it was, I knew this was only the beginning.

The success of Freshservice reignited something I had felt back in 2012—a belief in the power of building not just one great product, but an ecosystem of tools designed to transform how businesses operate.

In October 2013, an email landed in my inbox that felt different. It was from Sherjan Husseini at Google Capital. They had been tracking companies on the Google Apps marketplace, and noticed one with glowing customer reviews and a steady rise in popularity: Freshdesk.

Sherjan wanted to meet. I wasn't actively fundraising, but this was Google. You don't say no to them.

The meeting with Gene Frantz, one of their partners, was scheduled at their office. What was supposed to be a forty-five-minute session stretched into two-and-a-half hours. Gene was polite but thorough, diving into our story, numbers and vision. It wasn't an interrogation—it was a genuine, thoughtful conversation.

By the end of it, Google Capital was ready to invest.

But I wasn't. We'd just closed an internal round with Accel and Tiger. I told Gene we'd reconnect for the next round, leaving the door open. At the time, it felt like just another productive meeting. I didn't realize it would become a turning point.

By mid-2014, Freshdesk was on fire. Revenue was climbing and it was time to raise another round of funding. Both Accel and Tiger, our existing investors, wanted to lead. Sameer Gandhi from Accel's US office was eager to double down and Lee Fixel from Tiger was equally enthusiastic.

But I believed that bringing in a new investor would add validation and credibility. Accel and Tiger had been incredible partners, but a fresh name on the cap table could signal to the market that Freshdesk was evolving into something much bigger.

Google Capital was still interested, offering a pre-money valuation of $100 million. But Lee wasn't one to back down. Tiger countered with $125 million and, in the end, we let them lead the round, with participation from both Accel and Google Capital.

The decision to bring Google Capital on board was strategic. Their name carried immense weight, especially in India.

One moment stuck with me. During campus placements at SASTRA, we'd made an offer to a brilliant engineer. She was thrilled to join us but later declined after speaking to her parents.

'Why join an unknown company?' they'd asked. They couldn't fathom why she'd choose Freshdesk over giants like TCS or Infosys.

That frustration stayed with me. I wanted Freshdesk to be a name that parents recognized and respected. With Google Capital on our side, I could confidently walk into the next campus placement with a slide that read: Freshdesk: A Google Company.

It wasn't just a logo on a deck—it was validation. If Google trusted us, so could everyone else.

By the end of 2014, the round was complete. Google Capital joined Tiger and Accel on our cap table, a trio of investors that gave us both the resources and credibility to scale further.

Their name opened doors we hadn't even knocked on, from attracting top talent to gaining credibility with enterprise customers. For me, it was deeply personal. Freshdesk was becoming a company people believed in—not just customers and investors, but sceptical parents too.

With Google Capital on board, we were ready to redefine what a global tech company from India could achieve.

—

There's a peculiar ritual to boarding an airplane, one I knew all too well from my years at Zoho. Every trip—whether to the sprawling cities of the US, the historic avenues of Europe or the vibrant markets of Asia—began with the same march. As an economy-class passenger, you walk through the hushed luxury of the business-class cabin. Plush seats that could cradle you in sleep, elegantly dressed passengers sipping champagne or reading—this was a tantalizing glimpse into a realm that seemed reserved for another kind of traveller. Each time, as I settled into my cramped seat at the back of the plane, I made myself a promise: Someday, I'll know what it feels like to sit there.

For years, that dream remained unfulfilled, tucked away like an unread book on a high shelf. Until October 2014. Tiger Global, our investor, invited me to speak at their internet conference in New York City. The email alone was enough to send a jolt of excitement through me. But what followed felt like stepping into a dream. They had invited my entire family to join me and they were covering all our expenses—flights, accommodation, everything.

The real surprise came when the itinerary arrived in my inbox. I clicked it open and there it was: Business class. Not just for me but for my family. I stared at the screen, my heart racing. This wasn't just a step up; it was a leap into a world I had only imagined.

When the day finally came, we boarded our Emirates flight from Dubai to New York. The anticipation was electric as we made our way down the jet bridge. But there was a twist I hadn't foreseen. We didn't enter the plane through the business class section. Instead, we were routed through first class.

First class! I couldn't help but gape at the private suites, the gold-trimmed details and the sheer opulence that bordered on absurdity. Passengers reclined in cocooned luxury, as if floating through the skies in a palace. The stewardesses moved gracefully, offering flutes of champagne as if it were the most natural thing in the world.

And then we reached our section—business class. The seats were everything I'd dreamed they would be, and more. Wide, reclining chairs with legroom that seemed almost wasteful, gourmet meals served on fine china and the kind of service that made you feel not just comfortable but cherished.

My children were excited as they explored the amenities, and my wife and I exchanged glances that spoke volumes: 'Can you believe this?' It was a moment of wonder, a taste of a life we had worked so hard for but never quite dared to expect.

The surprises didn't end there. Tiger Global had booked us rooms at Mandarin Oriental, a hotel that stood like a shimmering jewel overlooking Central Park. When I checked the room rates out of curiosity, I nearly fell off my chair. For someone used to a $100 per diem budget and sharing rooms, this was a dazzling, almost surreal experience of luxury.

As the plane took off and the lights of Dubai faded below, I looked around and savoured the moment. Here I was, living a dream I had chased for years. But as I leaned back, a glass of sparkling water in hand, the humour of it all hit me.

The way airlines route economy passengers through business or first class? That's no accident. It's a sales pitch, one I know all too well. Show me something I can't afford—a luxury, an unattainable treasure, even an overpriced Adidas sneaker—and it's only a matter of time before I find a way to get it.

So, as I passed through first class on my way to business class that day, one thought stayed with me: You may be out of reach now, but someday, I'll be back. This time, I'll be sitting right here.

—

By 2013, Freshdesk was punching far above its weight. From our modest office in Chennai, our inbound sales team was closing deals with global giants like Burger King, Schneider Electric, 3M and Pearson Education. It felt surreal to see entire divisions from these companies discover us online, sign up for trials and convert—often without a single face-to-face meeting.

But for every deal we won, another slipped through our fingers.

One conversation still stings. A UK prospect told me, 'Salesforce is coming on Monday, Zendesk on Wednesday. Can you come on Tuesday?'

I swallowed hard, forcing out an apology. 'Sorry, I can't. I don't have a visa, but I'll come as soon as I get one.'

The silence on the other end was deafening. They liked our product, but they couldn't shake off their hesitation. Without someone local they could see, trust and call on short notice, they couldn't justify the risk.

We weren't losing deals because our product wasn't good enough. We were losing them because we weren't physically there. That realization hit me hard. It wasn't just frustrating—it was unacceptable.

We needed boots on the ground in the US to build credibility and show the world that Freshdesk wasn't just an ambitious upstart from Chennai. It was time to plant a flag.

The search for our US presence took me to Dreamforce in late 2013. Salesforce's annual gala was more than a tech conference—it was a spectacle. For Freshdesk, it was our debut. We had a modest booth to showcase our Salesforce integration, but the real action unfolded on the sidelines.

Introductions from Accel and Tiger Global led me to meet several candidates, but one stood out: Dilawar Syed.

At the time, Dilawar was running a media-tech company operating between the US and Turkey. His experience scaling a global operation immediately resonated. But what truly struck me was his presence. He wasn't a flashy salesperson or a big-talking executive. He was a builder—a strategist who could see the big picture without losing sight of the details.

We scheduled an hour, but our conversation stretched to three. By the end of it, I knew I didn't want just a VP of sales. I wanted a leader who could help us build a complementary US operation without compromising our inbound-first DNA.

Hiring Dilawar was a turning point. Under his leadership, Freshdesk was no longer just a Chennai-based start-up selling globally; we were becoming a global company.

This decision set the stage for everything that came next: Bigger deals, deeper market penetration and the ability to stand shoulder to shoulder with SaaS giants. It was the bold step we needed to break through to the next level.

Dreamforce wasn't just about connections. It also offered a masterclass in showmanship, courtesy of Salesforce's larger-than-life CEO, Marc Benioff.

I vividly remember Marc's entrance: Sporting custom sneakers emblazoned with clouds, he exuded confidence as he commanded the room. His presence was magnetic, but his message was even more powerful: Salesforce owned the cloud.

Then came the demo.

Marc introduced Service Cloud's integration with Google Glass—a cutting-edge but impractical device at the time. On stage, a technician used the Glass to snap a photo of malfunctioning medical equipment, upload it to Service Cloud and resolve the issue in seconds.

The crowd erupted in applause. But here's the thing: Almost no one in the audience was using Google Glass. Marc knew that. The demo wasn't about immediate utility; it was about showcasing innovation. He wasn't selling what Salesforce could do today—he was projecting what it could lead tomorrow.

I can still hear his words: 'Trust us. We're ahead of the curve.'

That moment stayed with me. Start-ups, mine included, often focus on solving today's problems with precision. But Marc taught me the power of showcasing possibilities. It's not enough to sell a product—you have to sell confidence.

I left Dreamforce with a lesson to carry forward: A great company doesn't just solve problems—it inspires belief. Marc reminded me that trust is built not only on what you deliver today but on the confidence that you'll still be leading tomorrow.

This shaped how I approached Freshdesk—and later, Freshworks. It wasn't just about showing what we could do. It was about inspiring trust in what we'd become.

Chapter 18

BY 2015, Freshdesk stood at the edge of transformation and was evolving into a global company. North America led the charge as our largest market, with Europe following close behind. It was time to plant flags in key regions and establish a physical presence that matched our growing ambitions.

So, we took the leap.

We opened offices in North America and London simultaneously. Dilawar Syed, with his steady leadership, took the reins in the US, anchoring our presence there. In London, our first hire was Simon Johnson, an experienced sales leader with a deep understanding of the European market. Simon quickly got to work, laying the foundation for our operations across the region. But Europe needed more than a London foothold. To truly scale, we needed a leader with both vision and precision to orchestrate our growth across the continent.

That's when I met Arun Mani. It was a rainy day in Chennai and Arun arrived at my office looking nothing like the polished New York–based, ex-McKinsey consultant I'd expected. He wore shorts, flip-flops and a rain-soaked T-shirt. But appearances quickly faded into irrelevance the moment he opened his deck.

Arun had crafted a meticulous and bold plan to scale Freshdesk to $200 million. His analysis was thorough, his vision ambitious. I was impressed. 'Would you consider leading Europe?' I asked, sensing he was the right person for the job.

In true consultant fashion, Arun didn't jump at the offer. Instead, he took his time, analysing three potential cities for our European hub—Dublin, Amsterdam and Berlin. A week later, he returned to present his findings.

Before he even began, I smiled knowingly. 'I already know what you're going to say: Berlin.'

He laughed. 'Why do you think that?'

'Your wife is German,' I said with a grin. 'No matter what the data says, I know Berlin's your pick.'

Arun chuckled but walked me through his analysis anyway. By the end of his presentation, Berlin wasn't just a personal choice—it was the clear strategic winner. It had the right mix of talent, accessibility and potential to scale. And so, Berlin became our European hub, with Arun at the helm.

While we were expanding west, our inbound demand gen leader, Sreelesh, was looking east—for a challenge. One day, he approached me with an idea.

'Can I start our outbound operation in Australia?' he asked, his enthusiasm unmistakable.

I agreed, but with one caveat. 'Find your replacement first,' I said.

True to form, Sreelesh hired Ramesh Ravishankar from Google Malaysia to lead our inbound demand-gen operations in Chennai—a very capable successor and an excellent people manager—while he hit the ground running in Sydney. His energy and determination transformed Australia into a promising new frontier for Freshdesk.

By the end of 2015, Freshdesk had gone from a single product in Chennai to a global operation with offices in the US, London, Berlin and Sydney.

With that growth came an avalanche of fires—big and small—that demanded immediate attention. Escalations from customer support, sales discount requests, salary negotiations, offer letters—everything seemed to land on my desk. I had become the bottleneck, trying to make decisions across every function. It was draining and, deep down, I knew it wasn't sustainable.

Sensing my struggle, Subrata Mitra of Accel suggested I reach out to Sachin Bansal, Flipkart's co-founder. 'He's scaled before you,' Subrata said. I was eager for guidance and scheduled a conversation with Sachin. His advice was simple yet transformative.

'Do you have a leadership team?' he asked.

'No,' I admitted. 'I have managers overseeing functions, but I'm still making most of the decisions.'

'That's your problem,' he said. 'Without a layer of leadership, you can't scale. As a CEO, your job is to focus on the strategic items and keep yourself free to jump in to put out fires that show up in different parts of the organization. Let your leaders handle the day-to-day operational decisions.'

His words hit home. I realized that while I was trying to do everything, I was holding the company back.

Inspired by Sachin's advice, I started building a leadership team. I sought out people with impressive résumés, conducted extensive interviews and trusted that their prior experience would equip them to thrive. But it wasn't that straightforward. Some hires didn't fit; others struggled to adapt.

Experience, I learned, wasn't always transferable. A leader's past successes didn't guarantee success in a fast-growing start-up. It was a lesson I had to learn the hard way.

By 2017, after navigating these early missteps, I had a sharper understanding of what leadership meant in a chaotic, high-growth environment. At a SaaSBoomi session that year, I shared this hard-earned insight, which resonated deeply with other founders.

There's a well-known fable in Indian villages: When a cow falls into a ditch, there's a sequence to follow. First, lift the cow out of the ditch. Then, fill the ditch with sand. Only after that do you teach the villagers how to prevent cows from falling into ditches in the future. The order is critical.

This simple story became a metaphor for my leadership philosophy. In a fast-growing start-up, there are countless 'cows in ditches'. Everyone is already overwhelmed, trying to solve pressing problems. When a new leader arrives and starts lecturing on prevention—or worse, declares, 'Everything is broken'—they don't inspire the team; they alienate them. Leaders who rely entirely on past playbooks, attempting to apply them wholesale, often miss the mark.

The leaders who succeed are the ones who ask the critical question: Which cow, which ditch? They focus on identifying the most urgent problems—the 'cows' stuck in the deepest 'ditches'—and solve those first.

By addressing what matters most and demonstrating impact early, these leaders earn trust and respect. They prioritize, adapt and show the team they're there to help, not disrupt.

This experience reshaped my understanding of leadership.

Leadership, I realized, is about prioritizing what truly matters, rolling up your sleeves and leading from the front, and earning the trust of your team.

—

In Tamil Nadu, there's a legendary biryani chain called Dindigul Thalappakatti Biryani. What began as a humble shop in a tier-two city quickly grew into a destination for food lovers across the state. The reason? Consistency. Every plate of biryani carried the same rich flavour, the same perfect balance of spices and the same unforgettable taste. Word spread and, soon, travellers went out of their way—sometimes miles off course—just to savour this biryani.

Over time, the business grew. Today, the second generation of the family has taken it global, with outlets in major cities like New York, San Francisco and Dubai. Their focus has shifted, understandably, to metrics—single-store profitability, footfall and average spend per meal.

But here's the fundamental truth that drives their success: No matter how many outlets they open or how sophisticated their metrics become, the business will collapse if the biryani—the core product—isn't consistently exceptional. The secret of Thalappakatti Biryani isn't their ASP per meal or their footfall; it's the care, attention to detail and passion that go into every single plate they serve.

This lesson isn't limited to restaurants. In start-ups, especially VC-funded ones, it's easy for leaders to obsess over metrics: Revenue targets, conversions, MRR (Monthly Recurring Revenue). These numbers often become the guiding stars for decision-making.

But here's the danger: When these metrics are handed down to frontline teams without context or alignment, they risk becoming an endless treadmill—numbers to hit, devoid of meaning.

Imagine telling a salesperson to hit $2,500 in MRR this month, then $3,000 the next. Sure, it's a necessary goal, but to that salesperson, it can start to feel like a mechanical grind, stripping the joy from their work. Similarly, a pre-sales engineer who crafts an innovative pitch or a marketing team that produces brilliant ad copy shouldn't see their contributions reduced to a percentage point on a conversion chart.

Celebrating these creative, impactful contributions—the 'biryani' of the business—is what keeps teams motivated and inspired.

This is where middle managers play a crucial role. Their job isn't just to enforce numbers—it's to bridge the gap between high-level metrics and the meaningful activities that drive them. They're the ones who can turn a revenue target into a mission that inspires creativity and pride.

For example:

- A marketing team should be recognized for discovering innovative negative keywords or crafting ad copy that resonates deeply—not just for lowering CPC (Cost Per Click).
- A pre-sales engineer should be celebrated for designing a demo that leaves prospects in awe—not simply for nudging up the conversion rate.
- An engineer should feel proud of making the product faster or more secure—not just for meeting a sprint deadline.

When teams feel that their craft is valued, their work becomes meaningful. Metrics might guide leadership, but the energy—the spark—comes from celebrating the 'biryani'.

As founders and leaders, it's easy to get caught up in billion-dollar valuations and revenue milestones. But for a DevOps engineer, a pre-sales associate or a designer, those metrics often feel abstract, far removed from their day-to-day work. What they care about is what they're building every day—the biryani they're creating.

The secret to scaling successfully lies in this balance: Celebrating the craft while focusing on growth. Metrics are important, yes, but they're not the heart of a company. The heart is its people and the exceptional work they do.

So, as you scale your business, don't just count the numbers. Celebrate the process. Celebrate the craft. Celebrate the biryani.

—

The atmosphere in 2015 was tense. Freshdesk faced a challenge that wasn't about competition in the market—it was competition for our people. Start-ups like Housing.com were offering astronomical salary hikes, doubling or even tripling what our employees earned, to lure them away.

It wasn't just the loss of team members that kept me up at night; it was the doubt those offers planted in the minds of those who stayed. The narrative was shifting. Employees began to equate these 'jump offers' with their true market value, and I could see the ripple effect it had on morale. Questions like 'Am I being undervalued?' and 'Should I leave too?' hung in the air.

I knew we had to address this head-on—not with corporate platitudes, but with clarity and honesty.

At the next all-hands meeting, I stood in front of the team, determined to shift the conversation.

'Let's clarify this,' I began, my voice calm but firm. 'Jump value—that big salary hike you get when you switch jobs—is tempting. It's the premium companies pay to bring in someone with your skills and experience. But don't confuse that with your *real* market value or the long-term worth of your career.'

I could see their curiosity shift into focus.

'To explain, let me give you an example,' I continued. 'Say you're earning ₹10 lakh a year here at Freshdesk. A competitor might offer you ₹15 lakh to lure you away. That's your jump value *today*. But if you stay here, grow with the company and reach ₹50 lakh in a few years, your jump value could skyrocket to ₹80 lakh or more. That kind of leap doesn't come from chasing the next big paycheque. It comes from building real skills, creating impact and being recognized for your growth over time.'

To help the team see the bigger picture, I introduced what I called the 'Career Tripod'—a simple framework for building a balanced and sustainable career.

A strong career, I explained, rests on three legs:

1. Knowledge: The skills, expertise and the learning you gain on the job.
2. Challenges: The responsibilities and problems you tackle that push you to grow.
3. Compensation: The salary and benefits you earn.

'If only one leg grows—say, your salary—but the others stagnate,' I told the team, 'the tripod becomes unstable. Jumping for money alone might feel rewarding in the short term, but it can stunt your long-term growth.'

The room was quiet, the kind of silence where you know people are reflecting. I leaned in.

'Think of your career as an investment. Would you put your money into something that gives you 15–20 per cent steady annual returns? That's what a balanced career does. If you're learning, tackling meaningful challenges and seeing your salary grow steadily, you're already in a great place.'

To drive the message home, I shared my own story.

'When I worked at Zoho, I wasn't paid the highest salary,' I admitted, 'but the learning and exposure I gained were invaluable. Those experiences laid the foundation for everything I've built at Freshdesk.'

I paused, letting the thought settle. 'The skills and insights you're gaining here will become your strongest asset.'

I didn't shy away from acknowledging the other side of the coin. 'Sometimes, leaving *is* the right choice—if you feel undervalued, lack respect from your team or don't align with your manager. But if you're working with smart people, earning respect *and* making a real impact, the grass isn't necessarily greener elsewhere.'

I wanted them to see that Freshdesk was about more than just paycheques and promotions.

'We're building careers with purpose,' I said, 'where learning, respect and meaningful work matter just as much as compensation.'

I closed with a challenge: 'The real question you should ask yourself isn't about numbers. It's this: Are you learning? Are you respected? Are customers loving what you're building?

'If the answer is yes,' I said, meeting their eyes, 'then you're already in the right place.'

—

By 2015, Freshdesk was scaling rapidly, but our challenges were growing alongside our success. We weren't looking to acquisitions for revenue—our organic growth trajectory was strong. Instead, we saw acquisitions as a way to solve two pressing issues: Acquiring top-tier talent and accelerating our technology capabilities.

At the time, Freshdesk's valuation had risen to nearly half a billion dollars, giving us the currency to explore strategic acquisitions. We focused on start-ups with exceptional tech or talent, especially in areas where hiring alone couldn't keep up with our pace of growth. Many of these acquisitions brought founders into our fold, people who made a significant impact on Freshdesk with their ownership mindset.

One of our biggest challenges was hiring specialized talent, particularly in areas like mobile development. The best mobile developers gravitated towards consumer-focused companies like Swiggy and Ola, where the mobile was central to the product. For Freshdesk, mobile felt secondary to our core desktop-first approach, despite increasing customer demand.

This was where acquisitions became more than a strategy—they became a necessity. It wasn't about acquiring companies for market share or revenue; it was about bringing in people who could help us scale faster and smarter.

The turning point came with our first two acquisitions—1Click and Konotor.

I still remember meeting Srikrishnan, the founder of Konotor, which had built a voice and messaging SDK (software development kit). While the team and product were excellent, they were struggling to scale. Sri was weighing funding options or an acquisition. When I introduced him to Lee Fixel to explore funding, Lee's advice was eye-opening: 'Why fund them when you can acquire them? This is exactly the team you've been struggling to hire.'

Konotor became Freshchat, which scaled to $10 million annual recurring revenue (ARR) within two years. It wasn't just a product acquisition; it was a people acquisition and it changed the trajectory of our mobile strategy.

Around the same time, we acquired 1Click, a co-browsing solution for real-time troubleshooting. While the product itself wasn't revolutionary, it filled a tactical gap in customer support. These early acquisitions taught us that the real value lay not just in the product but in the people behind it.

The most transformative aspect of these acquisitions was the influx of founders into Freshdesk. Between 2015 and 2017, we brought in start-ups like Frilp, Chatimity, Airwoot, Framebench, Pipemonk, JoeHukum and Zarget. These weren't just acquisitions—they were cultural infusions.

The founders we brought in didn't think like employees. They operated with an owner's mindset, taking initiative, solving problems and driving change without waiting for instructions. They had skin in the game too—most of our acquisitions were structured with 80 per cent stock, ensuring a shared commitment to Freshdesk's—and later, Freshworks'—success.

This founder-driven culture elevated the calibre of our team. It introduced a dynamic where fresh perspectives met our existing DNA, creating a synergy that accelerated innovation and execution.

As Freshworks scaled, my days became a blur of back-to-back meetings, with a line of people often forming outside my office. They'd wait patiently—sometimes ten or fifteen minutes—before giving up and returning later. Watching them come and go, I couldn't help but feel a pang of guilt. Was I becoming the bottleneck?

It was clear I needed help. Managing my time, coordinating with visitors and ensuring no one's time was wasted required someone who could bring structure to the chaos. That's when I decided to hire an executive assistant.

Delane became my first EA, and her arrival was a game-changer. Suddenly, my meetings were streamlined, my schedule was manageable and Freshworks visitors were greeted with professionalism. It was transformative. But while Delane brought order to my calendar, something else was missing.

Around the same time, Satya Padmanabham entered the picture. Satya had come to Freshworks through the Pipemonk acquisition and joined as a business development leader in our Channel and Partnerships team. He was brilliant and had a knack for breaking down complex challenges. Watching him in action, I began to see an opportunity—what if Satya could be more than just a leader in his domain?

My days were an endless sprint from one meeting to the next. I'd walk into rooms with no time to prep, relying on the presentations in front of me to make decisions on the spot. I couldn't dive into ground-level research or truly understand the implications of key product, people or business decisions. What I needed was a thought partner—someone to help me think ahead, provide context before meetings and ensure follow-through on decisions.

That's when the idea of a chief of staff started to take shape. The challenge? I didn't know exactly what the role entailed, and neither did Satya.

Satya was intrigued but apprehensive when I first approached him about stepping into this undefined role. 'What does a chief of staff actually do?' he asked. I didn't have a clear answer. So, I gave him his first assignment: research the role.

Over the weekend, Satya dug into the responsibilities and expectations of a chief of staff, mapping out how the role could work at Freshworks. Once we both understood its potential, we agreed to give it a shot.

Over the next seven years, Satya became far more than just a chief of staff. He was my thought partner, my sounding board and the person who ensured our meetings weren't just efficient but effective.

Before every major decision—whether it was about people, products or business strategy—Satya did the groundwork. He provided the context I needed to make informed choices. Together, we prepped meticulously for board meetings, anticipating questions and crafting responses. His presence allowed me to focus on leading while he managed the details that could otherwise overwhelm.

What started as an undefined role grew into a critical function at Freshworks, one that I credit Satya with shaping entirely. His work was about ensuring we made better decisions as a company.

Looking back, Satya's journey was about creating a blueprint for a role that's now indispensable. Today, I can articulate the purpose and value of a chief of staff because of him.

Delane brought order to my calendar. Satya brought clarity to my decisions. Together, they helped me lead Freshworks with focus and intent, transforming what could have been bottlenecks into breakthroughs.

Looking back, acquisitions are always a gamble—not every one of them works out. But when they do, the impact can be transformative. For us, the right acquisitions weren't about short-term gains like market share or plugging product gaps. They were about long-term value: Accelerating our ability to scale, strengthening our culture and keeping our growth aligned with our vision.

The biggest lesson? Acquiring founders and their teams is more than just a strategic move—it's an investment in chemistry, culture and ownership. This approach didn't just add to Freshdesk's capabilities; it reshaped our trajectory, proving that the right people can move the needle in ways no metric or product ever could.

At Freshdesk, life wasn't just about building products or hitting milestones—it was also about finding pockets of joy amidst the chaos. The 'Married Bachelors Club', as I cheekily called it, became one of those rare oases of camaraderie during a particularly intense period of scaling the company.

It all started with the founders we acquired. Many of them had their families living in different cities. For instance, the JoeHukum founders' families were in Delhi, but they set up a rented beachside villa in Chennai, commuting to work daily from there. Sameer Goel, a product leader, and Ravi, co-founder of Pipemonk, commuted back to Bangalore every weekend. The thread connecting this group was that they were all living away from their families.

In Chennai, they formed their own little fraternity—a group bound by shared circumstances and the strange freedom of being 'married bachelors'. Weekdays became a blur of work, but evenings were reserved for their escapades. Tuesday movie nights. Wednesday beach outings. Midweek dinners that stretched late into the night. Sometimes, they'd throw a party at the beach villa, where the ocean breeze carried their laughter into the night.

I wasn't part of their escapades—I was too busy juggling the relentless demands of scaling Freshdesk and the duties of family life. My day always ended with me heading back home to my wife and kids. But I couldn't resist poking fun at them. 'So, the *married bachelors* are out again, huh?' I'd tease. They'd laugh and play along, wearing the title with pride.

Their adventures weren't just about having fun; they were about creating a sanctuary in the middle of an exhausting grind. These were founders and leaders who were pouring everything they had into Freshdesk. Away from their families, juggling the weight of their roles, they found solace and energy in each other's company.

By Friday, the villa would empty out as they boarded flights back to their families. But from Monday to Thursday, Chennai became their playground, offering a slice of freedom and a break from the responsibilities waiting back home.

The Married Bachelors Club wasn't just a quirky nickname; it was a testament to how people adapt, bond and find joy even in demanding circumstances.

—

The Economic Times' Start-up Award in 2016 was a surreal milestone. Winning Start-up of the Year was a validation for both the performance and the promise that Freshdesk demonstrated. Held at the majestic Leela Palace in Bangalore, the event was buzzing with luminaries from India's entrepreneurial ecosystem. My wife, Shoba, had joined me, and the pride we felt that evening was unforgettable.

When the emcee asked me about my dream, I didn't hesitate. 'I'd love to meet Rajinikanth,' I said. It wasn't just an offhand remark; it was a connection to my roots and a tribute to the cultural icon who has inspired millions—including me.

But as memorable as the awards night was, the real magic happened afterwards.

Back in my hotel room, I was ready to call it a night, but my friends had other ideas. Calls poured in, insisting we celebrate properly. With Shoba's blessing, I headed to Pallav's home, where he and his wife, Puja, were hosting an impromptu gathering.

That night, amidst laughter, spirited conversation and flowing drinks, was easily one of the most memorable parties of the Daaru Pe Charcha (DPC) group. DPC was started earlier that year as a casual WhatsApp group and it quickly evolved into something much more: A vibrant, tight-knit community of founders sharing unfiltered insights, banter and hard-earned lessons.

DPC wasn't about formal networking; it was about trust and vulnerability. Whether in Delhi, the Bay Area or Chennai, members would organize smaller gatherings—'mini DPCs'—to keep the spirit alive. The focus wasn't just on celebrating wins but on dissecting failures, exchanging strategies and offering advice on everything from venture capital negotiations to product pivots.

That night at Pallav's, the conversation flowed as freely as the drinks. I vividly recall meeting Sachin Bhatia, who was then building InsideSalesBox. Freshsales, our sales CRM, was still in development, and I playfully teased him, 'We're going to kill you,' while showing off a demo. It wasn't a threat—it was the kind of friendly rivalry that sharpens ideas and sparks innovation.

Sachin wasn't discouraged. He asked question after question, eager to learn, and that exchange epitomized the magic of DPC. It wasn't just a social gathering; it was a crucible where founders refined their ideas, challenged one another and grew together.

DPC quickly became an underground nerve centre for India's start-up ecosystem. It wasn't unusual for stories of unfair venture capital practices or product challenges to spread through the group, followed by practical solutions or shared warnings. The speed and depth of insight shared within DPC were unmatched.

What set DPC apart was its celebration of vulnerability. Founders didn't need to pretend they had all the answers. Instead, they could openly share their struggles, knowing they were surrounded by peers who had faced—or were facing—the same challenges.

That night at Pallav's home, after the Economic Times' award, marked the beginning of something extraordinary. As we celebrated Freshdesk's milestones and playfully debated competing products, I felt the collective ambition and shared purpose that defined DPC. These were my people—the ones who truly understood the highs and lows of building something from nothing.

Over time, DPC became more than a group; it became a legacy. It shaped not just Freshdesk but the larger SaaS ecosystem in India. The camaraderie, shared knowledge and mutual respect built within this community made the successes sweeter and the struggles more bearable.

And yes, it was also the night I put my wish to meet Rajinikanth into the universe—a wish that would come true sooner than I could have imagined.

—

In December 2015, Chennai was brought to its knees by catastrophic floods. Torrential rains turned roads into rivers, cut off electricity and communication, and brought the city to a standstill. As panic spread and many fled to safer ground, a different kind of energy took hold within the walls of Freshdesk—a spirit called Kudumba, the Tamil word for family.

One of the first to embody this spirit was Body (Vignesh Vijayakumar), a leader in every sense of the word. While others were leaving the city to escape the chaos, Body returned to the Freshdesk office with nothing more than a small bag of clothes and an unwavering resolve to help.

Miraculously, the Freshdesk office was spared the worst of the disaster. It had power, internet and a functioning cafeteria—rare luxuries in a city plunged into darkness. Almost overnight, the office transformed into a refuge and a command centre.

A small group of about fifty–sixty people, including kitchen staff, stayed behind, creating a community within the chaos. Employees who couldn't safely return to their homes found shelter in the office. The cafeteria staff worked tirelessly to cook hot meals and the shower room with hot water became a sanctuary in those days of hardship.

Under Body's leadership, the group quickly mobilized. They began identifying neighbourhoods where people were stranded, assessing needs and coordinating volunteers to deliver supplies. This wasn't just about Freshdesk—it was about the city of Chennai.

Blankets, biscuits, water and other essentials were purchased in bulk and distributed to those in need. The office became a hub for relief coordination, with people stepping up to make a difference wherever they could.

I joined the efforts as well, loading my car with supplies and driving through waterlogged streets to deliver food and essentials to shelters. The roads were treacherous, but the sense of purpose kept us going.

In that moment, it wasn't about Freshdesk or our business. It was about humanity. It was about standing together as a family—kudumba—to help anyone who needed it.

The Chennai floods tested our resilience, but they also revealed the depth of our compassion and camaraderie. What started as an effort to help employees quickly grew into something much bigger: A testament to the power of community.

Chapter 19

WHEN I started Freshdesk, the entrepreneurial journey often felt lonely. In 2012, I attended conferences like NASSCOM Product Conclave and TieCon, hoping to find meaningful connections and actionable insights. While the networking energy was palpable, the content left much to be desired. The sessions often felt diluted, catering to everyone from software entrepreneurs to manufacturing start-ups, and lacked the focus I craved as a SaaS founder.

That's when it became clear: India needed a dedicated space for SaaS entrepreneurs—a place built by founders, for founders.

The first principle of SaaSBoomi was focus. This wouldn't be a general start-up event; it would cater exclusively to SaaS founders, particularly those building global products. This focus gave us clarity: Every session, discussion and interaction would address the unique challenges of SaaS businesses, from growth metrics to scaling beyond $1 million in ARR.

We also segmented the community into cohorts based on the founder's journey—those just starting out, those scaling from $1 million to $5 million and those pushing beyond. Tailoring content to these stages ensured that every founder walked away with actionable insights, no matter where they were in their journey.

—

Traditional conferences often rely on panels, but we found them ineffective—vague advice and feel-good anecdotes left founders frustrated. At SaaSBoomi, we banned panels outright. Instead, we focused on first-hand stories and actionable solutions.

To set the tone, I shared Freshdesk's journey from $0 to $1 million ARR during one of the earliest sessions. I laid everything bare: The decisions we made, the mistakes we regretted, the hacks that worked and those that didn't. The response was overwhelming. Founders valued the vulnerability and the openness, and this ethos became the foundation of SaaSBoomi.

Soon, founders began sharing their own stories—churn rates, conversion struggles and product-market fit challenges. The community became a trusted space where honesty and vulnerability were celebrated, fostering deeper connections and richer learning.

—

To maintain the quality of discussions, we curated the audience. SaaSBoomi was open only to SaaS co-founders. Aspiring entrepreneurs and employees were encouraged to learn elsewhere, ensuring that conversations remained sharp and relevant.

Even sponsors and venture capitalists weren't given automatic speaking slots—a pitfall at many other events. At SaaSBoomi, every speaker earned their place by offering substance. Every session was reviewed in advance to ensure it was anecdotal, actionable and authentic.

One of the biggest hurdles was overcoming the reluctance of founders to share their struggles. In India, it's common for entrepreneurs to guard their challenges closely, fearing judgement or loss of face. But learning can't happen without openness.

To break this barrier, I led by example. I shared Freshdesk's numbers, lessons and even missteps. I wasn't revealing trade secrets; I was showing the terrain we'd crossed to help others navigate the paths. This act of vulnerability inspired others to open up as well. Soon, founders were sharing not just their successes but their struggles, creating a culture of mutual trust and collective learning.

One of SaaSBoomi's most impactful formats was the product teardown. We invited early-stage start-ups to volunteer their websites, pricing pages or sign-up flows for a live critique. A panel of experts—including UI designers, growth marketers and experienced founders—analysed every detail from a customer's perspective.

The feedback was brutal but constructive. We rewrote copy, redesigned interfaces and suggested actionable tweaks on the spot. For the start-ups, it was a crash course in building better products. For the audience, it was a masterclass in practical problem-solving.

—

What started as a small gathering of SaaS founders has grown into a thriving movement. SaaSBoomi isn't just a conference; it's a community built on trust, vulnerability and shared ambition. The sessions are honest, the conversations deep and the learnings invaluable.

Most importantly, SaaSBoomi has become a space where founders learn not just from the successes of others but from their struggles too. It has transformed India's SaaS landscape, proving that collaboration and openness can drive collective growth.

Chapter 20

BY 2017, Freshdesk had grown into something much larger than its name suggested. What started as a customer support product had evolved into a suite of offerings spanning multiple business functions. We were no longer just Freshdesk; we were building an ecosystem of products that touched nearly every part of a business. But as we scaled, it became clear that our brand was falling short of representing who we had become.

The tipping point came at a trade show. A prospect walked up to our Freshservice booth and asked, 'Do you compete with Freshdesk?' It was a moment of clarity—and a little bit of irony. While we laughed it off at the time, it underscored a critical challenge: Our customers didn't see the bigger picture. To them, Freshdesk and Freshservice seemed like disconnected entities rather than part of a cohesive ecosystem. If our brand was causing confusion, it was time to rethink it.

—

Becoming a multi-product company is both an opportunity and a challenge. On the one hand, it gives you the ability to solve a broader range of customer problems. On the other, it demands clarity—both in positioning your products and in explaining your vision to customers.

Imagine a salesperson trying to pitch all our offerings in a single meeting: 'We have products for customer support, IT service management, HR, sales and marketing. They all work together seamlessly!' While it sounds impressive, it often leaves prospects confused. What does each product do? Why do I need them all? And where do I even start?

Clarity doesn't just help customers—it helps your own teams. Without it, sales and marketing teams struggle to align, and product teams lack a unified direction.

To solve this, we took a step back and asked ourselves: What do we really want to be? As we mapped out our products and their use cases, we realized they naturally fell into two distinct categories:

1. Customer experience: Products that help businesses delight their customers, including tools for sales, marketing and support—Freshdesk, Freshchat, Freshsales and Freshmarketer.
2. Employee experience: Products that help businesses empower their teams, including tools for IT service management and HR—Freshservice and Freshteam.

This simple yet powerful framework gave us the clarity we needed. By organizing our products into these two pillars, we created a unified vision that was easy to communicate both internally and externally.

But rebranding wasn't just about product organization, it was about transformation. The name Freshworks represented a broader, bolder vision—to be the alternative to bloated, disconnected enterprise software. Our promise was simple: An integrated, intuitive suite of tools that businesses of all sizes could rely on to deliver seamless experiences, both for their customers and their employees.

Rebranding also positioned us better for the intensifying competition in the SaaS space. By 2017, the industry had become a battleground, with companies racing to expand their offerings and stake their claims.

HubSpot was moving from marketing into CRM. Zendesk, which started in support, was venturing into sales. Atlassian, originally focused on developer tools, was expanding into enterprise service management.

Everyone wanted to be multi-product and the lines between categories were blurring.

Freshworks started in customer support, but we knew we couldn't stop there. The parallels with Atlassian were striking—they started in Sydney and became a global powerhouse. We were following a similar path: Starting in Chennai and aiming to make a global impact. Like Atlassian, we had humble beginnings, fierce competition and the ambition to punch above our weight.

For me, the rebranding to Freshworks was both personal and strategic. It was about giving our company the room to grow while staying true to our roots.

Freshworks was our way of telling the world: We're no longer a single-product company. We're here to help businesses thrive across customer experience and employee experience. The name captured the essence of what we wanted to build—a brand that resonated with start-ups, mid-market companies and enterprises alike.

I'll never forget the day I met Siddharth Malik—or Sid, as we all called him. Our interview was meant to be a quick one-hour chat at the Crowne Plaza hotel in Chennai. Sid had flown in for the meeting and we settled into a quiet corner of the lobby. Strangely, no one came by to take our order, but we didn't notice. We were too immersed in conversation.

What was supposed to be an hour-long meeting stretched into three-and-a-half. Sid didn't just walk me through his résumé—he shared his life story. The choices he made, the challenges he overcame, the lessons that shaped him—it all unfolded with such authenticity that, by the end of our conversation, I didn't just understand his qualifications, I understood the man behind them.

When we finally wrapped up, I didn't need to deliberate. Sid was the one. Typically, for a role as crucial as chief revenue officer, I would interview multiple candidates, weigh every option and agonize over the decision. But with Sid, I felt none of that hesitation. His experience at Akamai was already a standout—Akamai was one of the few companies running a global go-to market operation from India, selling to mid-market and SMB customers worldwide. Sid had been at the helm, leading demand generation, marketing and sales from India for the world. That kind of expertise was a rare find, but it was his presence as a leader that truly set him apart.

Sid had this innate ability to inspire people—a quality that can't be learned or taught. During one of our early conversations, he shared something that stayed with me: 'We lead with heart in the East. In the West, they lead with the mind.' It wasn't just a clever line; it was how he operated. He embodied it. His team didn't just work for him; they believed in him.

I saw it first-hand during those challenging quarters when our targets seemed unattainable. Sid would gather his team, look them square in the eye, and say, 'I don't know how, but I want you to get me this number.' It wasn't a command—it was a statement of trust. His team didn't want to let him down because they knew he had their backs. And time after time, they delivered.

What I admired most about Sid was his unwavering integrity. He never spent company money frivolously, even when he didn't have to think twice. Whether it was team dinners or celebrations, if he felt even a shred of doubt, he'd pull out his own wallet. I remember telling him, 'Sid, this is a company expense!' But he'd just smile and insist.

His generosity extended far beyond expense reports. He'd often surprise his team members with thoughtful and generous gifts. These were quiet acts, done without fanfare, but they spoke volumes about the kind of person he was.

Sid also had a gift for storytelling. He could captivate a room with his words, or connect with sales teams with well-crafted emails, weaving narratives that inspired and energized everyone around him. His energy was infectious and his passion was unmistakable.

Hiring Sid was about bringing in a leader who embodied everything Freshworks stood for: Heart, trust and a relentless commitment to people.

—

In 2017, during one of my trips to Bangalore, Shekhar suggested we meet for dinner. We chose Zen, the Chinese restaurant at the Leela Palace, a place that felt both intimate and grand—perfect for the kind of conversation we didn't yet know we were about to have.

As we settled into the plush chairs, our conversation meandered, touching on business updates, market trends and personal stories. It was the kind of dinner where time slips by unnoticed.

We'd just finished eating when Shekhar leaned in, his tone shifting to something more deliberate.

'Girish,' he began, 'have you thought about what you want to do with Freshworks?'

'What do you mean?' I asked, caught off guard.

'The way I see it, there are two outcomes,' he explained. 'You could sell the company and make a lot of money, or you could take it public and leave a legacy. If you take it public, you'll be the first Indian start-up to go public in the US. So, what do you want—money or legacy?'

—

Legacy. The word echoed in my mind long after the dinner ended.

Something about it stirred something deep within me. Maybe it was my instinct as a trailblazer—after all, my first car was a Pathfinder. The idea of forging a new path, of being first, had always resonated with me. But this was different. This wasn't just about me.

Legacy wasn't about achieving personal greatness; it was about creating something bigger than myself. It meant building a company that could inspire others, that could prove Indian start-ups could compete—and win—on a global stage.

That night, I smiled at Shekhar and gave a noncommittal answer. 'We'll decide in a few years,' I said. But deep down, I already knew.

The seed had been planted and it grew into something unstoppable over the coming months. It wasn't just a personal ambition anymore; it became our collective mission.

At our next all-hands meeting, I stood in front of the team and shared the vision. 'We have the opportunity to be the first Indian start-up to go public in the US. Let's make it happen.'

The room buzzed with energy. For the first time, the dream of a legacy didn't feel like an abstract goal—it felt real.

Over the following months, the idea became a rallying cry. It shaped our decisions, fuelled our ambition and connected us in ways I hadn't anticipated.

Legacy wasn't just about being first; it was about proving what was possible. It was about showing that a company born in Chennai could take on the world, that an Indian start-up could lead not just in revenue but in vision.

That night at Zen, Shekhar's words planted more than a seed—they lit a fire. And as I looked around the room during those all-hands meetings, I knew that the fire wasn't just mine anymore. It burned brightly in everyone at Freshworks.

—

By March 2018, Freshworks crossed $100 million in ARR—a milestone that felt monumental. For most private companies, such achievements are celebrated quietly, shared only with investors or the inner circle. But this time, I wanted to do something different.

Historically, we'd been vague about revenue, even during funding announcements. Reporters would probe and we'd deflect with broad ranges or future projections. But $100 million wasn't just a number—it was a statement. It proved that a global SaaS company could be built from India at scale.

At the time, India's start-up ecosystem was still finding its footing. Big exits were rare and billion-dollar SaaS success stories felt distant. Flipkart's acquisition by Walmart was still a year away. The ecosystem needed proof points and I wanted Freshworks to be one of them.

So, we made a bold decision: To publicly announce our $100 million milestone.

The announcement sent shockwaves through the industry. Friends in the US told me it was being discussed in the boardrooms of enterprise giants. Investors began to see India not just as a cost-effective outsourcing hub but as a breeding ground for global SaaS leaders.

A few months later, I was at Tiger Global's New York office for a board meeting. It was surreal walking their team through Freshworks' story—our challenges, growth and momentum. At the end of the presentation, Scott Shleifer and Chase Coleman pulled me aside.

'Girish,' Scott asked, 'do you see Freshworks as an aberration, or is this the start of a trend? Are there more companies like this coming out of India?'

Without hesitation, I replied, 'This is just the beginning. So many SaaS companies—Chargebee, BrowserStack and others—are on the rise. Freshworks isn't an anomaly. It's the first of many.'

That conversation marked a shift. Investors began to see what I already believed: India wasn't just a back-office destination. It was becoming the birthplace of global SaaS innovation.

The $100 million milestone wasn't just a number; it was a turning point. It forced us to confront hard truths about what it would take to compete on the global stage.

By choosing to announce it publicly, we not only declared Freshworks' ambition but also sent a message: India was no longer just part of the global SaaS conversation—it was leading it.

This milestone set the stage for everything that came next, from opening new doors with investors to navigating the challenges of scaling. And for Freshworks, it was a reminder that the journey wasn't just about revenue. It was about reshaping the narrative about what was possible for SaaS companies from India.

—

If there was one unforgettable Saturday etched in Freshworks' history, it would be 24 March 2018. We had just crossed the $100 million revenue milestone, a landmark achievement for any company, especially one that started in a modest office in Keelkattalai with little more than grit and big dreams.

The idea to celebrate wasn't part of any grand plan; it was entirely spontaneous. That morning, someone messaged me, 'Shouldn't we celebrate $100 million?' At first, I dismissed it as something we could plan later—a proper event, maybe with the entire company involved. But as the day wore on, the thought took hold. Why not celebrate today? After all, this milestone wasn't just about the number—it was about the people who had made it happen.

By late morning, I started texting a few folks, casually asking if they were free to meet up that evening. A small WhatsApp group was created to coordinate, and what began as a plan for ten–fifteen people quickly spiralled into a full-fledged party. Excitement snowballed and, soon, nearly 100 people wanted to be part of the celebration.

We booked the Velveteen Rabbit, a cozy basement bar in Chennai and by evening, the space was buzzing with energy. Drinks flowed freely, music filled the air and, for a few hours, the pressures of start-up life melted away. This wasn't some polished corporate event—it was raw, unfiltered joy shared among people who had been in the trenches together, building Freshworks brick by brick.

—

That night wasn't just about the $100 million milestone; it became a night of stories, connections and memories that underscored why we do what we do.

One moment stands out vividly in my mind: A love story that took a bold leap that very evening. Aditya, a pre-sales team member, had long harboured feelings for Anna, a colleague from another team. Everyone in the company seemed to know they liked each other, but neither had mustered the courage to make the first move.

That night, with the buzz of celebration in the air, I decided to play matchmaker. Between laughs and drinks, I pulled them aside and said to Aditya, 'She's like a daughter to me. Why wouldn't you propose to her?' Perhaps it was the encouragement—or the spirit of the evening—that gave him the courage to finally ask Anna to be his partner. She said yes.

Today, they're happily married and their love story has become part of Freshworks' lore, forever tied to that $100 million celebration.

For me, that night was about more than hitting a revenue milestone. It was a testament to the people behind the achievement—the team that took an audacious idea and transformed it into a global company.

Standing there in that basement bar, enveloped in the laughter, camaraderie and shared pride of colleagues who had become family, I felt the weight of what we had accomplished. That night wasn't about charts or projections—it was about the moments, the people and the relationships that make milestones like $100 million worth celebrating.

—

In September 2019, we announced another milestone: Freshworks had crossed $200 million in ARR. Doubling revenue in such a short span was exhilarating but it also brought new challenges.

Scaling beyond $200 million was uncharted territory. Growing Freshworks from zero to $100 million had been a steep learning curve, but this was different. It required a new level of expertise and an entirely new playbook.

In the US, leadership talent who'd scaled companies from $200 million to $1 billion and beyond existed. But in India, that expertise was scarce.

As Freshworks expanded its product lines, it was only a matter of time before we squared off with Salesforce—the colossus of the CRM world. By 2018, Salesforce's dominance in the CRM market was a challenge we were determined to take on.

—

From the beginning, we knew where our opportunity lay. Salesforce and Zendesk had left SMBs underserved, burdening them with expensive, bloated software designed with larger enterprises in mind. Our strategy was clear: Build intuitive, affordable tools specifically tailored for small and mid-sized businesses.

That year, our instincts were validated by a Forrester Consulting report we had commissioned, which surveyed 300 SMBs across the US, UK and Germany. The results were eye-opening:

- 69 per cent of SMBs were unhappy with their current CRM solutions and were planning to switch.
- Over half described their existing CRMs as bloated, confusing and overburdened with features they didn't need.

These findings became the foundation of our messaging: Freshworks would be the refreshing alternative for SMBs frustrated with complex, overpriced tools.

On 25 September 2018, San Francisco was buzzing with over 100,000 attendees gathered for Dreamforce, Salesforce's flagship conference. The streets were packed, the air was electric and Salesforce was ready to take centre stage.

And then, above the crowd, a massive white blimp appeared, carrying a message that couldn't be ignored: '#Failsforce,' it read on one side. 'Freshworks/Hit Refresh,' read the other.

The stunt was bold, audacious and completely unexpected. Within minutes, social media exploded. Attendees posted pictures and videos of the blimp, and soon, #Failsforce began trending on Twitter.

The impact was immediate and far-reaching. As #Failsforce climbed to the #1 trending spot on Twitter, some enterprising users turned the hashtag into a viral sensation. They designed and sold mugs and T-shirts with the slogan, spreading the message far beyond the Dreamforce crowd.

For hours, speculation swirled about who was behind the blimp. Then, we claimed it. In a blog post, Arvind Parthiban, our marketing director at the time, wrote: 'Salesforce is an amazing company; its story is inspirational. But it's failing customers. Bloated, difficult-to-use cloud CRMs aren't the future. Our message is simple: It's time for a refresh. Hence, #Failsforce.'

The blimp didn't just dominate the skies; it dominated the narrative. It floated above San Francisco for days, capturing attention far beyond the event. More importantly, the campaign resonated with its intended audience: SMBs frustrated by overly complex software.

The campaign worked. Almost overnight, Freshworks became synonymous with being a 'Salesforce rival'. But this wasn't just a clever stunt—it was a strategic move to position ourselves as the next-generation CRM provider.

The parallels to Salesforce's own history weren't lost on us. Just as Salesforce disrupted Oracle and Siebel Systems in the early 2000s with its bold, brash approach, we were positioning ourselves as the refreshing alternative for a new generation of SMBs.

The #Failsforce campaign showed that Freshworks could compete head-on with the biggest names in the industry, not just on product but on messaging and brand.

For SMBs, the message was clear: If Salesforce represented the old guard of bloated, disconnected enterprise software, Freshworks was the future—simple and customer-centric, and built with their needs in mind.

And for us, it was a bold declaration: We were no longer just a challenger from Chennai. We were a global contender, ready to take our place on the world stage.

—

Kiran, Shan and I had always adhered to one guiding principle: Keep It Simple, Stupid (KISS). We didn't chase shiny new tech trends unless they solved an immediate problem. Rails let us move fast, so we stuck with it.

But growth came with complexity. Processes stretched thin, silos emerged and the simplicity that had defined our early days was slipping away.

Scaling meant thinking ahead without overengineering. Kiran, who juggled site reliability engineering (SRE), product engineering and IT, often said, 'Plan for the infrastructure you'll need two years from now.'

This mindset kept us nimble, but, by 2016, the cracks were starting to show. One day, Kiran and Shan came to me, and said, 'We're good coders, but as the organization scales, we need someone who can evangelize engineering culture and inspire engineers. We'd like you to hire a strong engineering leader who can help us scale.'

They were right. Freshworks was at a crossroads. We needed someone who could take our foundation and elevate it—a leader who could not only solve technical challenges but also shape the culture of our engineering team.

That someone was Siripurapu Taraka Subramanya Prasad—STS to everyone who knew him.

STS came to us with a résumé that commanded respect—HCL, Junglee, Amazon, Kosmix, WalmartLabs. Introduced through the Accel network, he was drawn to our vision of bringing enterprise-grade software to small businesses.

When we first met, I sketched a pyramid on a whiteboard, explaining how traditional enterprise software catered to the top—the big companies.

'But the real opportunity,' I told him, 'is at the bottom. SMBs are underserved, but their needs are just as real. SaaS changes the game. With Freshdesk, we can give them tools that were once out of reach.'

STS didn't just see the opportunity—he felt it. 'It was everything I loved about start-ups,' he later said. 'The challenge of scaling something from the ground up with a clear, compelling vision.'

From the moment he joined, STS began transforming our engineering organization. Silos between QA, frontend, backend and release management started to dissolve. He recognized our growing pains for what they were: A company on the verge of losing its rhythm.

STS's solution was Freshwave—our take on Agile development. The philosophy was simple: Break engineering into small, cross-functional teams, each owning their slice of the product end-to-end.

This wasn't Agile for Agile's sake. It was about accountability and adaptability. Freshwave streamlined processes, but more importantly, it reinforced our culture. I'd always envisioned Freshworks as an 'eternal start-up', nimble no matter how big we grew. STS turned that vision into reality. He encouraged engineers to interact directly with customers, broke down barriers between teams and helped create Freddy, our omnibot.

STS also instilled one of the most valuable lessons: Knowing when to say no. It's easy to say yes to every feature request, but that's how products become bloated and lose focus. Under his leadership, we learned the discipline of saying no. We created a technical architect counsel (TAC) which reviewed large complex deals, and would veto deals that had feature requests not readily available in the product and would require heavy customization.

When STS passed away, it left a void—professionally and personally. He was more than a leader; he was a cornerstone of Freshworks. To honour his legacy, we asked ourselves: What would he have wanted?

The answer was clear: Build something that lasts.

The Freshworks STS Software Academy was born with a mission to lift underprivileged youth out of generational poverty by teaching them software engineering.

At Freshworks, we've always valued skill over pedigree. College degrees don't build great software—passion and craftsmanship do. The academy extended this belief beyond our walls. It targeted young adults from low-income families who couldn't afford higher education, offering them the skills to land jobs and transform their lives.

Naming the academy after STS was fitting. His life embodied the values we wanted to pass on: Curiosity, humility and a relentless commitment to excellence. Through the academy, STS continues to shape futures, creating opportunities for those who never imagined they could be part of this world.

STS didn't just help scale Freshworks—he helped us evolve. He bridged the gap between the scrappy start-up we were and the global contender we were becoming. His contributions were as much cultural as they were technical.

He showed us how to grow without losing sight of our core values.

The Freshworks of today, with its global ambitions and expanding product suite, stands on the foundation STS helped lay.

As he used to say, 'Agility isn't about speed. It's about keeping your rhythm, no matter how big you grow.'

Thanks to him, we've never lost ours.

Chapter 21

BY early 2019, Freshworks had reached a significant milestone: $140 million in ARR. Yet, the euphoria of that achievement was tinged with a sobering reality—we were struggling to attract top-tier talent for leadership roles. We needed a CFO, a general counsel and a CMO to prepare for the IPO. But sitting CFOs and CMOs in the US, the hub of global tech leadership, hesitated to even consider us.

The reason was simple, yet unyielding. Freshworks' centre of gravity was halfway across the globe in Chennai. A pre-IPO company with its CEO and core team stationed in India didn't appeal to seasoned leaders who valued proximity to decision-makers. It wasn't a slight against our potential; it was a hard truth of the business ecosystem.

It became clear to me that if Freshworks wanted to play in the big league, I couldn't lead this charge from the sidelines. The Bay Area wasn't just a hub for SaaS innovation—it was the epicentre of talent, expertise and opportunity. I had to be there.

For nearly a decade, Freshworks had crafted its own playbook—rooted in grit, ingenuity and the sheer determination of building a global SaaS business from India. It worked wonders to take us past the $100 million revenue mark. But as we crossed that threshold, the cracks in our approach began to show.

Scaling further would demand more than ingenuity. We needed systems, processes and a culture of scalability—what I had come to think of as the 'science of Silicon Valley'.

This realization hit home during a trip to San Francisco in late 2018. While it wasn't my first visit to the Valley, it was the one that changed everything. Over the course of a few days, I met with CEOs who had scaled start-ups into global powerhouses. Their stories had a common thread: Scaling wasn't just about innovation and hustle—it required precision, discipline and an unrelenting focus on building well-oiled machines.

Before this trip, I had resisted calls from investors to move to the US. I believed that SaaS was borderless—products that were intuitive, powerful and DIY by design didn't need a CEO sitting in the Valley. But as I sat in those meetings, listening to stories of hypergrowth and market domination, I realized our playbook wouldn't take us to the next level.

Freshworks was a $100-million company with ambitions far greater than anything we'd achieved so far. We needed a new approach—one that combined the scrappiness and resourcefulness of Indian entrepreneurship with the precision and discipline of Silicon Valley scaling.

'My mission now is to marry the art of Indian entrepreneurship with the science of Valley scaling,' I later told *Forbes*.

The stakes were clear. If we wanted to reach the next stage of growth, we needed people who had lived through hypergrowth—leaders who understood the challenges of scaling and could build the systems to sustain it.

The trip to the Valley didn't just offer clarity—it made the path forward inevitable. Freshworks couldn't grow into a global SaaS leader with me rooted in Chennai. The US was not only our largest market but also the beating heart of technology and innovation. I had to be there, immersed in the ecosystem, to give Freshworks the best shot at competing with the likes of Salesforce and ServiceNow.

The decision was clear, but it wasn't without its share of resistance. When I shared my thoughts with Suman Gopalan, our CHRO, she was pragmatic. 'Why don't you spend more time there first and see how you feel about it?'

she suggested. It was sound advice, given the challenges of transitioning leadership and the lack of a clear successor for my day-to-day responsibilities in Chennai.

But deep down, I already knew. That second trip to Silicon Valley cemented it. The energy, the ambition, the relentless pace—it was electrifying. I returned to Chennai with a conviction that was impossible to shake.

'I've already bought a house near San Mateo,' I announced to the team. The room went silent. Suman's reaction was a mix of shock and inevitability. 'That's just Girish,' she said with a laugh.

Deciding to move to the US was one thing, leaving Chennai was another. Life in Chennai was more than comfortable—it was home. Our weekends were filled with family gatherings, laughter and a rhythm of togetherness that felt irreplaceable. Our sprawling rented bungalow was a hub of activity, filled with drivers, household help and the effortless support system we'd built over the years.

I still remember the day I broached the topic with Shoba. We were on our way to a birthday party when I laid it all out—the leadership challenges, the IPO plans, and what moving to the US could mean for Freshworks and its people. She listened quietly, her face thoughtful. Finally, she nodded. 'If this is what we need to do, we'll do it.'

Her unwavering support gave me the clarity I needed. This wasn't just a move for us—it was a leap of faith for everyone who believed in Freshworks. It was about creating opportunity, wealth and a future that had once seemed out of reach.

Leaving Chennai wasn't easy, but it was necessary. For Freshworks to soar, I had to make that leap.

When the decision to relocate to the US was announced, it rippled through the Freshworks office like a shockwave. Anxiety found its voice in our all-hands platform, Voxpop. The top question, repeated in variations, was blunt yet understandable: 'G, why are you going to the US? What does this mean for Freshworks, for the India team and for us?'

I knew this was a pivotal moment, one that demanded transparency and purpose. So, I gathered the team. The room was packed, the air thick with uncertainty. Taking a deep breath, I began, my voice steady but resonant with emotion.

'I know many of you are wondering why I'm making this move. Let me explain: I'm doing this for three reasons—for me, for you and for India.'

I paused, allowing the weight of those words to settle. Eyes locked on mine, the room leaned in, waiting.

'This move is about learning,' I began. 'Back in India, I'm celebrated—media interviews, awards, start-ups asking me to mentor them .... It feels great, but let's be honest: We've only crossed $100 million. That's an incredible milestone, but where we want to go—scaling Freshworks to a billion dollars and beyond—is uncharted territory for us.

'The truth is, the people who've done this before, who understand what it takes to scale a company to that level, are not here. They're in the US and I need to learn from them. This is a once-in-a-lifetime opportunity to take Freshworks to heights we've only dreamed of.'

'For you,' I continued, scanning the room, meeting each anxious gaze, 'this move is about creating transformative wealth. Today, Freshworks employees collectively hold stock worth ₹2,500 crore at our current valuation of $1.5 billion. But imagine if we grow this company tenfold. That's ₹25,000 crore.'

I let the number hang in the air before continuing. 'That wealth will change lives. It will create opportunities for you and your families that were once unimaginable. If we don't grow, I'll be fine. Our senior leaders will be fine. But the IC2 engineer who just joined last week, the fresh grad ... They're the ones who will lose out. I'm going to the US to make sure that doesn't happen.'

The anxiety in the room began to shift, softening into something else. Faces that had been tense were now thoughtful, even hopeful.

'And finally,' I said, my voice rising with conviction, 'I'm doing this for India. Imagine what happens when ₹25,000 crore flows into your hands. Some of you will start companies, creating jobs and opportunities. Some of you will support social causes that matter deeply to you. And yes,' I added with a grin, 'some of you will blow it on fancy cars and vacations—but even that helps India's economy grow.

'This wealth will ripple outward, creating an impact far beyond Freshworks. This isn't just about our company. It's about what we can do together, as a team, for a nation.'

The room was silent, the weight of the moment palpable. Then, I stepped back, letting a smile break through the intensity. 'I feel like an Indian athlete who has been given a chance to run in the Olympics. Should I go or not?'

That question, so simple yet so powerful, shifted the mood entirely. The team's collective energy changed. The worry, the doubt—it transformed into something electric. I saw it in their eyes, in the faint smiles, in the subtle nods of agreement. They weren't just accepting my move; they were embracing the journey ahead.

As the meeting drew to a close, I left them with something to ponder. 'In life, we're all playing a game. The question is: What's your game and what's your level? Are you striving for the next level or are you staying where it's comfortable?

'When I began my career, my game was training. I started small, teaching Java to individuals in my home, navigating the distractions of living rooms to get through each lesson.

'Soon, the game levelled up. I moved into corporate training, stepping into the polished offices of companies like Polaris. Here, it wasn't just about teaching—it was about earning the respect of seasoned professionals. That success led me to an even bigger role: Setting up training departments at eForce and AdventNet. My scope widened and so did my confidence. But just when I thought I was finding my rhythm, the game changed entirely.

'At Zoho, I stepped into product management—a game I had no formal qualifications for. It was unfamiliar territory and I had to start from scratch, learning the rules on the fly. There were moments of doubt, even fear, but I leaned into the challenge. Slowly, I mastered the game and, by the time I left, I was a successful product manager who had built global products from Chennai that made their mark in the world.

'Then came the biggest leap yet—starting Freshworks. Suddenly, I wasn't just building products; I was building a company. And I had no idea how. I'd never met a venture capitalist, raised funding or managed critical functions like sales, HR or finance. My game had always been 'product', but now I had to become a venture-backed CEO—a role that required an entirely new skill set.

'Between 2011 and 2018, I immersed myself in mastering this new game. I learned how to pitch to investors, raise funding from the best VCs and build a team capable of exponential growth.

'Now, the game is changing again. Becoming the CEO of a public company is the next level—an arena with its own rules and challenges. The scrutiny, accountability and relentless pace of being the CEO of a publicly traded company demand skills I've yet to fully master.

'Can I handle it? Can I lead Freshworks to thrive on this stage? I believe I can. And that's the challenge I'm embracing next.

'This framework isn't just for me; it's a mindset I encourage everyone at Freshworks—and beyond—to adopt. Whatever your field—business, sports, music—you must ask yourself: What's my game and what's my level?

'It's like cricket. You can play for your street team, your state or the IPL. Or you can aim for the ultimate—representing India on the global stage. The same goes for music. You could be a local singer, a playback artiste in Tamil cinema or someone like A.R. Rahman, whose music transcends borders and unites the world.

'The rules are universal. First, choose your game. Then ask: Am I levelling up? Am I pushing myself towards the global playing field?

'It's not about starting at the top. It's about climbing there, one deliberate step at a time. Every level comes with new challenges, new rules and new rewards. The journey may be daunting, but the view from the top is worth every effort.

'So, what's your game? And what's your level?'

The energy in the room was undeniable now—hopeful, inspired, ready. As the meeting ended, I walked away knowing that they were ready to take on the world together.

The vibe had shifted completely—what began as uncertainty had transformed into a palpable excitement for the future. As the meeting ended, I looked around and saw a collective force brimming with determination and belief. We weren't merely preparing for the journey ahead; we were embracing it with a shared purpose. Walking out of that room, I knew we were ready to carve a path to greatness together.

—

By the summer of 2019, the decision to move to San Francisco had been made. Shoba and I had spent months meticulously planning every detail, from searching for schools for our sons to wrapping up our life in Chennai. The flight was scheduled for the late hours of 10 July and I had deliberately routed us through London. The plan? Spend time with friends and family while also watching the ICC Men's Cricket World Cup final.

As a cricket-obsessed Indian, it seemed inevitable that India would sail through the semi-finals against New Zealand. How could they not? With Virat Kohli at the helm and a rock-solid line-up, the thought of India missing the final never even crossed my mind.

But cricket, as every Indian fan knows, has a knack for breaking your heart.

On 9 July, New Zealand batted first, grinding their way to 211 runs for five wickets before rain paused the match. When play resumed the next day, they added 28 more runs, setting India a modest target of 240. It felt like a straightforward chase.

Until it wasn't.

I sat glued to the screen in the ground floor cafeteria of our Chennai office as India's top order collapsed in a shocking chain of events. Rohit Sharma, K.L. Rahul and even Virat Kohli—gone for just a single run each. By the tenth over, the scoreboard read a crushing 24 for four.

I sank into my chair, resigned to what looked like an inevitable defeat.

But cricket, in its cruel brilliance, always finds a way to toy with hope.

Mahendra Singh Dhoni and Ravindra Jadeja stepped up, turning what seemed like a funeral march into an exhilarating battle. Jadeja, fiery and determined, smashed sixes as if to defy the odds, while Dhoni, ever the composed finisher, anchored the innings with surgical precision. By the final three overs, India needed 37 runs—challenging, but not impossible.

Then it happened.

Dhoni, pushing for a desperate second run, was run out. The bails lit up and, with them, the hopes of 1.35 billion Indians dimmed. Jadeja fell soon after and New Zealand clinched their spot in the final.

The loss felt strangely symbolic—an unexpected shift in plans, a reminder that nothing is guaranteed. The vision of watching the final in London now felt hollow. I picked up the phone, called our travel desk and said, 'Cancel London. Route us directly to San Francisco.'

That night, while the rest of India mourned a heartbreaking loss, I found myself reflecting. Perhaps, this was a sign. India's campaign had ended, but mine was just beginning. Our next innings—Freshworks' most critical one—was waiting.

The World Cup was over for us, but, in that moment, my focus sharpened. It was time to chart a new course, time to face our own global stage.

As I watched our team evolve, I found myself replaying a moment from our flight to California. Descending into San Francisco, the Golden Gate Bridge came into view, its towering cables stretching confidently into the horizon. That image stayed with me.

The bridge wasn't just a marvel of engineering—it was a symbol of connection. It reminded me of what we were building—a bridge between Chennai and Silicon Valley, between possibility and achievement.

This journey wasn't just about Freshworks going public; it was about proving that Indian start-ups could think big, act bold and succeed on a global stage. It was about rewriting the rules and inspiring the next wave of dreamers to follow.

Because making history doesn't happen by playing it safe. It happens when you take the leap, knowing that the landing will change everything.

—

In July 2019, we touched down in the Bay Area—a world that promised high stakes and unparalleled opportunity. The air buzzed with the energy of innovation, where sprawling tech campuses gleamed under the California sun and Teslas hummed silently along endless freeways. But behind the glamour lay an unspoken truth: For all its promise, this was a land of relentless competition. Freshworks had earned its stripes as a SaaS pioneer in India, but here, in the shadow of giants like Salesforce and Zendesk, recognition alone wasn't enough. We had to prove we could scale, and for that, we needed a team ready to take on the impossible.

Yet, building that team felt like scaling a cliff with bare hands.

Back in Chennai, Freshworks was a household name—a place where careers blossomed, where the culture of humility and growth permeated everything we did. But in the US, we were just another start-up. Prospective hires often met us with sceptical smiles or outright amusement. 'An Indian company? Competing with Silicon Valley heavyweights?' Their doubt was palpable. It stung, but it also fuelled a fire within me.

—

December in India always meant homecoming—family, stories, the scent of filter coffee curling through the morning air, the warmth of familiar voices. This time was no different, at least at first. We had flown in as a family, weaving through the bustling chaos of Chennai, catching up with relatives, laughing over childhood memories. But beneath it all, a shadow loomed.

My father was in the hospital. A routine illness, they said at first. Something manageable.

Then I met the doctor.

'Black fungus infection. Multi-organ failure,' he told me.

The words hung in the air, detached and unreal. I nodded, as if understanding, but inside, my mind rejected them. I wasn't ready. I pushed for one of the best hospitals in Chennai—maybe better care, maybe another chance. And, for a while, it seemed to work. He responded. He got stronger.

On 4 January 2020, I was scheduled to fly back to the US, but something held me back. I postponed it to the 7th. He was due to be discharged, after all. Just a few more days, I told myself. Just long enough to make sure he was settled, home, safe.

But hospitals don't operate on sentiment. Paperwork, delays, another day of waiting. That evening, I stood by his bed, held his hand, and said, 'Everything is fine. You're getting better. I'll come back soon.'

He squeezed my hand—hard. His eyes welled up, and for a moment, he just held on.

He had never been like that. He had always been steady, silent, a man of few words. But in that moment, something broke through. Did he know? Did he sense it?

On 8 January, I boarded my flight. That night, jet-lagged, I found myself in a packed theatre watching a Rajinikanth movie with friends. The noise, the energy—it felt like home, a sliver of normalcy after weeks of uncertainty.

Then my phone rang.

My stepmother's voice trembled. My father had collapsed. ICU. Critical.

I needed to get back.

But my passport was in New York, stuck at the French embassy for a visa. Chaos followed—calls, pleading, searching for a way out. My EA, Daniel, pulled every string. An agent raced across the city to retrieve my passport. I caught the first flight from California, met the agent at JFK, grabbed my passport, and within hours, Shoba and I were on a plane to Chennai.

The world, however, had other plans.

Dubai was flooding. Flights were grounded. Airports drowned in delays. I ran from counter to counter, begging, bargaining, but nothing worked.

By the time we landed in Chennai, it was too late.

He was gone.

They had waited. Held him at home. Postponed the last rites. But he wasn't there anymore. I had made it back, but not in time.

Grief didn't come in a single, shattering moment. It seeped in quietly, filling the spaces between breaths, between words. It was in the absence—his empty chair, the silence where his voice should have been, the quiet unravelling of a world I had always known.

My father and I never spoke much, but we never needed to. For years, it had been just the two of us—him in his world, me in mine, bound by something unspoken yet undeniable.

That thread had been cut.

And standing there, in a house that no longer felt like home, I felt something I had never felt before.

Completely, utterly alone.

Finding the right CFO wasn't just a priority—it was an obsession. The stakes were clear: We needed someone who had not only navigated the IPO path but could also see Freshworks' potential through the same lens as we did. The search stretched on for months, each interview blending into the next, each candidate falling short of what we needed. Doubts crept in: Could we find someone with the courage, experience and skill to take on this challenge?

Then we met Tyler Sloat.

At the time, Tyler was CFO of Zuora, a company he had helped scale from $10 million to a $170 million in revenue and a successful IPO. Despite being just next door in San Mateo, he admitted he had never heard of Freshworks. That changed quickly during the interview process.

When Tyler asked for our P&L statement, we handed it over confidently. Numbers don't lie and ours told a story of high gross margins, operational efficiency and disciplined growth. Tyler was impressed. 'These financials are solid,' he said, his curiosity shifting into genuine interest.

Once we agreed on the terms of his employment, I decided to have one last meeting with Tyler at Peet's Coffee in Burlingame. Over steaming cups of coffee, I laid everything on the table. 'Here are all the reasons you should not join Freshworks,' I said, watching the puzzled look on his face. Then I walked him through it: The challenges of working across multiple time zones, the lack of mature 'been-there-done-that' talent for an IPO and the absence of robust processes. I explained the relentless travel demands and the reality of building systems from scratch. 'I want you to walk in with your eyes wide open,' I told him. 'There's a lot to be excited about at Freshworks, but I need you to understand the challenges too. Losing a CFO before the IPO would be a huge setback for the company and I want to be doubly sure this is the right move for you.' Tyler listened intently and, by the end of that meeting, I knew he was the right person. He wasn't fazed by the obstacles. He was energized by them.

When Tyler joined in March 2020, his first words hit like a wake-up call: 'We're not IPO-ready.' He laid it out bluntly—there was no sugarcoating. The public markets demanded a level of precision and rigor we weren't yet operating at. 'You've done well to get here,' he said, 'but scaling to the next level requires systems that are built to last.' Tyler wasted no time. He brought in seasoned leaders to fill critical gaps, including heads of financial planning and analysis (FP&A), SEC reporting, investor relations, global tax and a new general counsel. Together, they set the stage for our IPO readiness. Beyond people, he spearheaded a complete overhaul of our internal systems and processes. We moved to a new accounting system, NetSuite, to modernize our financial infrastructure. Procurement was centralized under a single team to gain better visibility into spending. These changes weren't glamorous, but they were transformative—laying the foundation we needed to meet Wall Street's exacting standards.

With Tyler at the helm of this transformation, the momentum was palpable. Piece by piece, the puzzle came together.

He brought a sense of calm confidence that resonated throughout the organization. The momentum was unmistakable. He wasn't just preparing us for an IPO—he was instilling a culture of discipline and long-term thinking.

—

By 2021, the IPO was no longer a distant dream—it was an imminent reality. Tyler's arrival marked the first major step, but the journey required more than just financial rigor. It demanded a compelling narrative and, for that, we turned to our new chief marketing officer, Stacey Epstein.

Stacey joined as CMO in March 2021, right as we kicked off 'Project Superstar', the codename we gave our IPO push—a nod to my maanaseega guru (mentor in spirit), Rajinikanth. From her first day, Stacey was thrown into the thick of it, leading the effort to craft our S-1. Imagine being dropped into a whirlwind of bankers, lawyers and endless meetings, tasked with distilling over a decade of grit and growth into a single, compelling narrative. That was Stacey's onboarding. The timeline was unforgiving. The target IPO date was 22 September 2022, but the real pressure point was 26 August. That was our 'go/no-go' date. Every system, process and department had to be ready by then.

Tyler, Stacey and the teams in finance, IT, HR and legal poured their hearts into the effort, working tirelessly through long hours, late nights and countless weekends. It was nothing short of a marathon, with each team member pushing themselves to the limit. Yet, despite the gruelling pace, they pushed through the exhaustion, knowing that every ounce of effort brought Freshworks closer to achieving its dream of going public.

There were no shortcuts and no margin for error. We practiced closing our books like we were already public, stress-tested our systems and pushed ourselves harder than ever before. It was a race against time. By the time 26 August arrived, we knew we were ready. The decision was made: We were going public.

Project Superstar became a rallying cry. It embodied everything we stood for, everything we wanted to achieve. And the world noticed. As soon as we flipped the S-1 public, the *Economic Times* ran the headline I had predicted: 'Freshworks Founder Pays Tribute to Superstar Rajinikanth'. That moment, seeing that headline, felt like a victory in itself.

The morning of 13 September 2021 began like a storm brewing on a still lake. The air crackled with anticipation as we launched into the whirlwind of our IPO roadshow. It wasn't the traditional parade of handshakes and conference rooms—this one unfolded entirely on Zoom. Seven days, nearly fifty meetings and countless faces peering at us through pixelated grids—it was a marathon that compressed lifetimes of effort into one relentless week.

By the time the final meeting ended on Tuesday, 21 September, at lunch, the world outside the Morgan Stanley office seemed to sway slightly, like I was still trapped in the motion of the past week. Everything blurred together—questions, presentations, investor expressions—but one thing was crystal clear: The week had stretched far beyond its usual bounds.

That Tuesday afternoon, the air in the pricing meeting was thick with the hum of calculators, whispered figures and the weight of expectation. Our bankers, led by Morgan Stanley, guided us through the labyrinth of the price discovery process. Pages of spreadsheets stared back at us with the cold clarity of decisions yet to be made.

By the end of the day, exhaustion wrapped itself around me like a heavy cloak. I stepped out of the office, the late evening air cool against my face, a small relief after the stifling intensity of the meeting room. It wasn't over—not by a long shot—but I allowed myself a moment to breathe.

That's when Shekhar Kirani and Mohit Bhatnagar of Sequoia called. 'Do you want to grab a drink?' they asked, voices warm with camaraderie. My answer was immediate—yes.

We wandered a few blocks before finding a quiet park, its dimly lit paths lined with low benches and the comforting hum of a live band playing somewhere in the background. The air carried the faint aroma of autumn leaves and the earthy scent of freshly poured beer. Mohit handed me a pint as Shekhar arrived, his familiar presence grounding me further.

'How are you feeling?' Shekhar asked as we settled onto a bench.

I paused, taking a long sip and letting the cool bitterness roll over my tongue. For the first time in days, I allowed myself to exhale.

'Three emotions,' I said finally, my voice calm and steady. 'Pride, fulfilment and responsibility.'

I was super happy and proud of how far we had come with Freshworks—from our humble beginnings in Keelkattalai to a thriving global business.

Fulfilment came from knowing what this milestone meant for everyone who had been a part of the journey: Employees, their families and early investors. This wasn't just about numbers on a screen—it was about lives transformed, dreams realized.

And then there was responsibility. The IPO wasn't the finish line; it was the start of a new chapter. 'Tomorrow, new investors will place their trust in us,' I said, the weight of those words settling around us like the park's evening haze. 'We need to work hard and make sure Freshworks continues to grow and deliver on our promises.'

Shekhar nodded, his expression a mix of pride and nostalgia. He shared a memory from the early days. 'You weren't like other start-ups,' he said. 'Even back in 2011, Freshworks felt different—global, polished, ready.'

The band struck up a new tune as we sat in reflective silence. Around us, life carried on—distant laughter, the rustling of leaves—but, for a moment, time seemed to pause. The roadshow might have blurred into chaos, but this moment of clarity reminded me why we started in the first place.

This wasn't just about Freshworks listing on the Nasdaq. It was about proving that an Indian SaaS company could stand shoulder-to-shoulder with the world's best. It was about rewriting the narrative of what was possible—from a small office in Chennai to the global stage.

Looking back, the moment we rang the bell at Nasdaq was unforgettable. But the real story was in the journey—the grind, the team effort and the shared belief that made it all possible.

—

Nasdaq, New York City: 22 September 2021. The culmination of a journey that began in a small Chennai office with a handful of dreamers daring to think global.

The morning carried a surreal energy—an electric charge that hummed through the streets and into the Nasdaq headquarters at 4 Times Square. Our team of seventy-five, a carefully chosen mix of old-timers from Chennai and key US team members, gathered in quiet anticipation. COVID-19 restrictions kept our numbers lean, but every person present embodied a piece of Freshworks' journey.

Even Neo, our two-year-old Shih Tzu, became part of the story. Originally, he was to stay back at the hotel with my friend Rajavel. But the day felt too significant to leave him out. 'They said family, right?' I asked Stacey. 'Doesn't that include Neo?' A quick check with the Nasdaq team turned into an enthusiastic yes—Neo was in.

The day began ceremoniously with the Nasdaq president presenting us with a plaque. It was more than a token; it was a tangible acknowledgment of the grit, setbacks and victories that defined our journey. As Shekar and I exchanged a glance, no words were needed. This was a dream we had once only whispered to ourselves in a Bangalore restaurant in 2017.

Inside Nasdaq's halls, the energy was palpable. Teams from Morgan Stanley, J.P. Morgan and BofA Securities moved with precision, ensuring every detail was perfect. But the heart of the moment belonged to us. Standing on the Nasdaq podium, I couldn't help but smile—a grin that betrayed my usually calm exterior. In my sharp blue suit and a Freshworks-themed lapel pin, I felt ready for the world's stage.

As the clock ticked closer to the opening bell, I looked out at the crowd—our team, investors, board members, partners—and felt the enormity of what this moment meant. This wasn't just Freshworks' IPO—it was Indian SaaS staking its claim on the global map.

The bell rang and the room erupted. Cheers, laughter and unrestrained joy filled the space. But as I stepped forward to address the crowd, my focus was clear.

'When I moved from India in 2019, I told my team that I felt like an Indian athlete who had gotten the chance to run in the Olympics. Today,' I paused, letting the moment sink in, 'I feel like that Indian athlete has won gold.'

The applause swelled, but I continued, my voice steady but alive with emotion. 'This IPO is our Roger Bannister moment,' I said, and the room quietened down. 'Bannister was the first to run a mile in under four minutes. What's remarkable is what happened after—dozens of others broke that record within a year. Freshworks is IPO-ing first, but this is only the beginning. Our dream of India as a product nation is coming alive. To every start-up scaling towards this journey, I say, "*Apna time aa gaya.*"'

The phrase—'Our time has come'—was more than a declaration. It was a promise, a challenge and a celebration, for every start-up founder hustling and dreaming in Chennai or Bangalore or Delhi.

I took a moment to look out at the crowd, my heart swelling with both pride and purpose. 'While I am happy and proud as a start-up founder who started from humble beginnings in Keelkattalai to see where Freshworks has reached today, I am even more excited about the opportunity ahead of us to scale Freshworks to a billion dollars of revenue and beyond. Today is Day Zero again.'

'Day Zero' was a mindset, a challenge and a reminder of what lay ahead.

By the time I stepped back from the podium, the weight of gratitude and pride pressed against my chest. As I looked out one last time, I knew this was more than an IPO. It was the sound of something far bigger—the arrival of a product nation.

—

'Singa nadai potu sigarathil yeru. Sigarathai adainthal vaanathil eru.'
(Take a lion's walk and climb the peak. Once you reach the peak,
aim for the sky.)

I shared these words from Rajinikanth's *Padayappa* during the media briefing after our listing. At first glance, quoting a Tamil movie dialogue on such a prestigious global stage might have seemed unconventional. After all, an IPO is traditionally about market dynamics, P&L metrics and future growth—not cinematic wisdom. But for me, it felt deeply personal and profoundly fitting.

Rajinikanth isn't just a cinematic icon; he's a maanaseega guru. His dialogues, often rooted in resilience, ambition and self-belief, have a timeless quality that resonates with my journey and the ethos of Freshworks. It's why our IPO was aptly codenamed 'Project Superstar', a tribute to the man whose words have inspired millions, myself included.

The Nasdaq listing was undeniably a peak. It marked the culmination of years of grit, innovation and the shared vision of a team that dared to dream global from a small office in Chennai. But as Rajinikanth reminds us, the journey doesn't end at the summit. *'Sigarathai adainthal vaanathil eru'*—when you've reached the peak, you set your sights on the sky.

That's precisely how I see Freshworks. The IPO wasn't the final destination; it was a significant milestone—a moment to pause, reflect and then push forward with renewed vigour. It wasn't a time to descend. It was our signal to soar higher, to innovate boldly and to dream even bigger.

—

In the days after the IPO, my inbox overflowed with messages. Some were celebratory, others introspective—each carrying the weight of what this moment truly meant.

One message, in particular, stopped me in my tracks.

It was from a longtime employee, someone who had joined Freshworks years ago with just ₹10 lakhs in savings. After the IPO, his net worth had soared past ₹10 crores. But that wasn't what struck me.

'Freshworks gave me more than money. It shaped my thirties. It made me wealthier in ways I never imagined. I learned leadership, strategy and team-building—just by watching you, Satya and Suman up close. The journey was life-changing.'

That's when it hit me.

This wasn't just about a stock listing or a Nasdaq ticker symbol flashing in Times Square. It was about people. The ones who had bet their careers on Freshworks. The ones who worked late nights, took leaps of faith and placed their trust in something that had once been just an idea.

The IPO valued Freshworks at over $10 billion. More than 500 employees became crorepatis (worth over ₹1 crore) overnight. Many made well over ₹5 crores, even ₹10 crores. Nearly 70 per cent of them were under the age of thirty—young professionals whose lives had been transformed in an instant.

For some, the IPO meant finally buying a home. For others, it meant financial security—paying off family loans, funding their children's education or simply breathing a little easier.

Take Srinivasan's story. In 2013, he worked as an apartment complex manager, earning ₹8,500 a month. When he joined Freshworks as an admin staff member, he never imagined the journey ahead. By the time of the IPO, he was leading food and beverage operations for Freshworks. Another facilities team member, who once struggled to make ends meet, found himself building a new home for his mother—an impossible dream just a few years ago.

This wasn't just theoretical wealth. Stock options turned into real, life-changing outcomes—not just for a handful of executives but for hundreds of employees who had believed in Freshworks from the start.

The ripple effects didn't stop at Freshworks. Something shifted across India's start-up ecosystem.

Avinash Raghava, one of the earliest champions of India as a product nation, summed it up best: 'The Freshworks IPO wasn't just a milestone. It was a moment of arrival. It showed the world that Indian SaaS companies could scale globally, compete with the best and win. This wasn't the end of the journey—it was the starting gun for what's next.'

For years, the big question loomed: Could an Indian SaaS company truly go global? Could we build products, not just services?

No one was asking that question anymore.

Standing at Nasdaq, watching the Freshworks logo light up Times Square, my mind wasn't on valuation figures. It was on the next wave of founders—

sitting in Chennai, Bangalore and Pune. The ones pulling all-nighters, chasing their first hundred customers, wondering if success was even possible.

This was proof.

For decades, India's start-up ecosystem had a missing piece. Funding was growing, talent was abundant, but exits were rare. Before Freshworks, the only major liquidity event was Walmart's acquisition of Flipkart—a defining moment, but a consumer-tech story. Indian SaaS was still waiting for its breakthrough.

'Freshworks became a case study,' Avinash said. 'A start-up from India could scale to billions, go public and create generational wealth—just like in Silicon Valley. Investors took notice. Founders started thinking bigger.'

Suddenly, exits weren't theoretical anymore.

Within months, more capital started flowing. Investors weren't just betting on Indian start-ups—they were betting on Indian start-ups going all the way.

McKinsey had already predicted that Indian SaaS could generate $1 trillion in value by 2030. That wasn't a wild guess—it was an inevitability.

SaaS was no longer a niche. It was becoming the backbone of global business. By 2025, SaaS revenues were projected to cross $540 billion, with over half the world's software running on a SaaS model.

The opportunity was massive. And India was ready.

The talent was there—millions of engineers and product managers trained in global tech companies. Capital was flowing. Unicorns were multiplying. But more importantly, the belief had changed.

For decades, India had been the world's tech back office. The Freshworks IPO proved we could be the front office, too.

A few months later, a founder I knew raised a big round of funding. He told me, 'Your IPO helped us. Investors are looking at Indian SaaS differently now. The ceiling has been raised.'

That was it. That was the real impact.

We had taken the first leap. Now, others would follow.

A few weeks before the IPO, someone asked me, 'What's the biggest thing this IPO will change?'

I thought about it for a second: 'Mindset.' Not just for founders, but for the entire Indian SaaS ecosystem.

For the first time, we weren't looking at Silicon Valley for validation. We weren't asking if we could build global product companies—we were doing it.

'This is our Roger Bannister moment,' I had told the team earlier. 'We just ran the four-minute mile. Now, others will follow.' It was Day Zero all over again.

The moment the bell rang at Nasdaq, it felt like flipping a switch. People kept asking me, 'How do you feel?' My answer was simple: Pride and gratitude. I was proud of Freshworks for being the first Indian SaaS company to go public, and grateful to the early investors and employees who believed in us when it was just an ambitious idea.

When I landed in Chennai in October, a few weeks after the IPO, the scene that greeted me was surreal. At 2.30 in the morning, a crowd of forty–fifty Freshworks employees had gathered at the airport. As I stepped out, I saw banners, cheers and faces brimming with pride. They'd even booked a hall at the Westin to cut a cake and mark this milestone—a moment that belonged as much to them as it did to me.

After a quick refresh in my room, I joined the celebrations at 3.30 a.m., surrounded by the warmth and love of the team. It was overwhelming to feel their genuine emotion and see the deep connection they had to Freshworks' journey.

But even amidst the jubilation, I knew we couldn't linger in the moment. I reminded them, 'Let's enjoy this moment and celebrate, but tomorrow, we go back to work. This is not the time to rest.'

The IPO was our gold-medal moment—a crowning achievement built on years of grit, resilience and belief. But for a world-class athlete, winning gold isn't the end. It's the beginning of something far greater. The moment they step off the podium, the expectations rise. They are no longer competing in the shadows; they're on the global stage, expected not just to compete but to win again and again.

With that expectation comes pressure—but pressure, I believe, is a privilege. It's the weight of knowing that what we've achieved inspires others to dream bigger, aim higher and believe that they too can win. Freshworks is now a beacon for Indian start-ups, proof that a company born in Chennai can take on the world. To those watching us, our journey says: Dream big. You belong here.

That's why we can't afford to lose. We owe it to those who believed in us, to the start-ups following in our footsteps and to ourselves. The world is watching and this is our moment to show them what we can do.

So, as I looked around that celebration at the Westin, I felt an unmistakable fire. Tomorrow would be Day Zero again. The race ahead would be tougher, the stakes higher and the competition fiercer. But we were ready.

It's time to go back to work. It's time to train harder, dream bigger and rise higher. The gold medal was just the beginning. Now, we're aiming for the sky.

INTERSTITIAL 3

Lee Fixel on Girish Mathrubootham

by Pankaj Mishra

LEE Fixel isn't just an investor; he's a storyteller in his own right—except he doesn't write with words. He writes with conviction, with the founders he backs, with the companies he helps shape. His fingerprints are all over modern Indian entrepreneurship, from the early days of Flipkart with Sachin and Binny Bansal to CaratLane with Mithun Sacheti.

One of his most defining bets, of course, is Girish Mathrubootham and Freshdesk (now Freshworks).

When I sat down to interview Lee for this book, one thing became abundantly clear: his role in Girish's journey wasn't just financial. It was foundational. He did more than fund a company—he fuelled a vision.

Back in those formative years, when the idea of building a global SaaS company from India seemed far-fetched, Lee saw something others didn't. He saw in Girish not just a capable founder but a missionary—a builder driven by purpose, not profit. And he saw in the Indian market a structural advantage that the world had yet to recognize. His investment in Freshdesk wasn't a mere leap of faith. It was a calculated move, backed by his belief in what Girish could build.

Lee has a way of categorizing entrepreneurs into two types: mercenaries and missionaries. The difference? Mercenaries chase exits. Missionaries chase impact. From the start, Girish fit squarely into the second camp. His obsession wasn't about valuations or funding rounds—it was about solving real problems and doing it better than anyone else. Even when Freshdesk was just a scrappy start-up, he wasn't thinking small. His questions weren't about *if* they could compete with the likes of Zendesk, but *how* they would win.

And through it all, Lee was there—not just as a backer, but as a guide. He helped Girish navigate key inflection points, from the rebranding of Freshdesk to Freshworks to the battles with global competitors. He provided more than capital; he provided clarity.

Their relationship wasn't just transactional. It was built on trust, mutual ambition, and an unspoken agreement: We're building something that will last.

—

Lee recalls his first meeting with Girish in a hotel lobby. What struck him wasn't just Girish's deep knowledge of the space, but his balanced demeanour—calm, insightful, and passionate in a way that wasn't loud.

'He had this rare combination of experience—having run a large P&L at Zoho—while also carrying the hunger of a founder just getting started,' Lee told me. 'It wasn't just about starting a company. It was about solving a real problem, and he understood every nuance of it.'

But if there was one thing missing in those early days, it was the scale of ambition.

Lee remembers telling Girish, bluntly: You're not going to build a massive business on the back of just Freshdesk.

At the time, Girish wasn't entirely sure how far the journey would go. No one was. But what followed was a transformation—not just of the company, but of the founder himself.

With every milestone, Girish's confidence grew. Freshservice was launched. New product lines emerged. Freshdesk evolved into Freshworks, no longer just a single-product company but a full-fledged SaaS platform. And as the vision expanded, so did Girish's conviction in what he was building.

'There's a direct correlation between a founder's confidence and their ambition,' Lee explained. 'As Girish's self-belief grew, so did his appetite for bigger, bolder moves.'

Besides ambition, what defined Girish was people. Even in the early days, he had a magnetic ability to attract talent. Some founders build great products; others build great teams. Girish did both.

Lee had one simple rule when it came to investing: A handshake is a form of due diligence. It tells you everything you need to know about a person.

'Our first deal was done over a handshake,' he said. 'With Girish, there was no hesitation. We trusted each other from the start.'

Looking back, Lee sees three defining traits in Girish's journey:

- Confidence—The self-belief that grew alongside Freshworks' scale.
- Ambition—The drive to expand beyond the initial goals.
- Vision—The ability to see not just what Freshworks was, but what it could be.

'Girish wasn't just building a company,' Lee told me. 'He was building a culture, a movement. And through it all, his growth as a leader mirrored the growth of Freshworks itself.'

—

Ask Lee to describe Freshworks' journey, and he won't talk about dramatic pivots or existential crises. Because, unlike some other start-ups, Freshworks didn't have them.

'Flipkart? That's a different story. That had drama—interpersonal clashes, crises, high-stakes moments,' Lee said. 'But Freshworks was just steady, deliberate, thoughtful progress.'

That doesn't mean it was easy. There were go-to-market strategies that didn't work. Hiring gaps that needed urgent fixing. The daily grind of running a company at scale. But nothing ever felt like a make-or-break moment.

'Some founders get caught up in trying to create big moments. Girish just focused on making progress every single day.'

And that's what makes his journey unique. He wasn't the brash, high-profile founder making headlines. He was the leader quietly building something enduring.

'He's not a "smooth operator" in the traditional sense. That phrase implies slickness. Girish is real—grounded, humble and deeply authentic.'

—

Lee has worked with all kinds of founders—visionaries, empire-builders, and those who start off humble and transform into high-profile moguls.

With Girish, though, the remarkable thing is what didn't change.

'He's confident, but he's stayed the same person throughout. That's rare.'

That's also why Lee says he'd back Girish again, without hesitation.

'If he ever decides to start a new business, I'd give him a blank check—no questions asked.'

But he knows Girish's ambitions have evolved. He's not chasing another unicorn; he's focused on impact. Together Fund, SaaSBoomi, his involvement in sports—everything he does now is about giving back.

That, more than anything, speaks of who Girish is.

'It's never been about empire-building. It's about building communities,' Lee says. 'That's what makes him truly unique.'

—

When Freshworks finally went public on the Nasdaq, Lee stood back and watched.

'It was their moment, not mine,' he says.

But seeing Girish and the team ring the bell, having known them since their $10,000-a-month days, was surreal.

'The shift from Freshdesk to Freshworks wasn't easy,' he reflects. 'But executing that transformation—that's what separates good founders from great ones.'

INTERSTITIAL 4

Thalaivar: The Hero Who Shaped My Dreams

PEOPLE learn life's lessons in different ways—some through books, others through mentors or scriptures. For me, the wisdom that shaped my life came from the silver screen—and no one delivered those lessons quite like Superstar Rajinikanth.

His characters weren't just heroes; they were guideposts: Work hard, dream big, stay humble, treat people with respect and do good with what you have. These weren't just movie themes—they became values I absorbed over the years. Where others saw entertainment, I found a blueprint for life.

But my connection to Superstar went beyond his on-screen persona. It was the man behind the roles—his humility, grounded nature and spiritual depth—that inspired me the most.

—

In 2011, Rajinikanth's hospitalization in Singapore became a global story. Fans prayed for him in temples, lit candles and sent waves of love across continents. It wasn't mere admiration; it was a bond so deep it felt familial.

I began to wonder: How does one man inspire such devotion? What kind of life earns not just respect but unconditional love? The answer wasn't fame or power. It was something intangible—a life lived with humility, generosity and authenticity.

That realization hit me hard: Success might get you to the top, but love and respect must be earned through how you treat people along the way.

—

When Freshworks was preparing for its IPO, I wanted the project name to reflect our aspirations. A colleague suggested 'Falcon', a logical choice because it would be easy for bankers and lawyers juggling multiple IPOs to associate the letter 'F' with Freshworks.

The logic made sense, but the name felt impersonal.

I made a counter-proposal: 'Let's call it Project Superstar.'

'Superstar Rajinikanth is a South Indian icon with global appeal,' I explained. 'Freshworks started in South India, but our ambitions are global. Like him, we aim to achieve success with humility and stay connected to our roots.'

The team embraced the idea and the name became more than a label—it became a philosophy. Rajinikanth's journey mirrored the values we wanted Freshworks to embody: Aspirational yet grounded, ambitious yet humble.

—

In January 2017, I had the privilege of meeting my Thalaivar. Shoba and I arrived at his Chennai home, my heart racing like never before. Despite years of high-stakes meetings, I felt like a nervous teenager once again.

The house was serene, filled with soft 'Om' chants and images of spiritual icons like Mahavatar Babaji and Ramana Maharishi. When Rajinikanth entered, dressed simply in a white shirt and dhoti, his presence was magnetic.

I stumbled through my explanation of Freshdesk, so nervous that I had to apologize. 'I don't usually blabber like this, Rajini sir,' I admitted, half-embarrassed. He laughed warmly, putting me at ease.

'What are your hobbies?' he asked, shifting the conversation to something simple, human. In that moment, he wasn't a superstar. He was someone who genuinely cared, making me feel seen.

When it was time for a photo, I hesitated before asking, 'Can I touch you, sir?' He smiled, placed my hand on his shoulder, and posed for the photo. That gesture will forever remain etched in my memory. For those few moments, I wasn't a CEO or a founder—I was simply a fan standing beside the man who shaped my dreams.

After we left, Shoba and I floated in a haze of awe. It felt like we just had experienced a sacred glimpse of something divine. We replayed every word, smile and gesture for hours, trying to make sense of the surreal experience.

—

When Freshworks went public, one detail made the journey feel complete. Among the IPO's earliest subscribers was Superstar Rajinikanth himself.

For someone who grew up queuing for first-day, first-show tickets to his movies, knowing that he held a 'first-day, first-show' ticket to the Freshworks IPO was surreal. It was a moment that tied my journey back to its roots—a testament to the values that guided me and the man who inspired them.

—

Thalaivar's greatest lesson wasn't in his punchlines or stunts; it was in how he lived. He taught me that success isn't just about reaching the top—it's about staying grounded and earning the love of those who walk beside you.

Rajinikanth's influence extends far beyond the big screen, woven into how I think, lead and aspire to live. For Freshworks, his story serves as a guiding light, a reminder that ambition and humility aren't mutually exclusive.

Because, in the end, success isn't just about what you achieve—it's about how you inspire others along the way.

Epilogue

SOME days, I yearn to step back onto the cool red oxide floors of our Trichy home, to hear my father's steady, calming voice cut through the noise of the world. But life doesn't pause for nostalgia. Those moments feel like relics from another life—one I stepped away from long ago.

Being a founder is like scaling an endless peak. Every step forward comes at a cost. For me, the cost was time—time with my family, moments I'll never get back.

I wasn't there for most PTA meetings. My wife bore that burden alone, sitting quietly in classrooms filled with other parents while I was halfway across the world, consumed by Freshworks' relentless growth. It wasn't something that happened just once or twice; it became our reality. Moving homes, changing schools, uprooting routines—our kids shouldered the consequences of my decisions while I wasn't there to help them make sense of it all.

When we moved to the US, I spent hours meticulously planning their education, trying to soften the blow of yet another transition. The Indian and US schooling systems couldn't be more different. In India, students juggle physics, chemistry and biology every year. In the US, it's one subject per year in high school. To ease the gap, I moved them to an international school with an American curriculum before the move.

But no amount of planning could erase the challenges. I still remember the shift from Montessori—a haven of creativity and freedom—to a very popular and sought-after school in Chennai that thrived on structure and exams. My kids struggled. They didn't fit in. Each move fractured friendships and forced them to start over, again and again.

When we finally settled in the US, my younger son faced a challenge I hadn't foreseen. In those first few weeks, his dark complexion made him a target for teasing. My wife was the one who held him through the hurt, lifting his spirits and giving him the courage to face a new, unfamiliar world. By the end of that first month, his natural charm had won everyone over. He didn't just make friends—he connected with his classmates, coaches and even the groundskeepers.

But I wasn't there. I missed the struggle, the triumph and the quiet moments in between.

One memory still stings. My younger son was born while I was thousands of miles away in Atlanta. I missed the first breath he took, the warmth of his tiny hand, the miracle of his first cry. I wasn't in the hospital. I wasn't there for my wife. I was chasing the dream, and, in that moment, the dream took precedence.

Now, I've made it a point to be more present, to sit with my family at dinner, to be there for the big and small moments. But no matter how hard I try, the truth is this: You can't undo the past. Those missed bedtime stories, the laughter around the table, the hugs when they needed reassurance—they're gone. Success, no matter how grand, can't fill that void.

—

If I could go back and change one thing, it would be this: I wish I had been more present. Founders tell themselves that sacrifices are necessary, that time with loved ones will come later, that success will make it all worth it. But time doesn't wait. Kids don't wait. Life doesn't wait.

Here's what every founder needs to hear: Success isn't just the company you build; it's the life you live while building it. The people who stand by you—through the late nights, the missed dinners and the hard choices—they are the real foundation of your journey.

So take the time. Sit at the table. Be there for the hugs, the bedtime stories and the victories, big and small. Because the climb is only meaningful when you have the right people by your side. They are the true measure of success.

—

One of the biggest myths about success is that wealth is the goal. But the truth is you don't create wealth by chasing it. Wealth is a byproduct of doing what you love and doing it well.

Think of anyone truly successful—Sachin Tendulkar, M.S. Dhoni or a great entrepreneur. Their focus isn't on money but on being world-class in their craft. The endorsements or financial success follow naturally. The moment their passion stops, so do the rewards. Success, in any field, demands focus and passion. Money follows—never the other way around.

Spending money brings happiness and saving money offers security. The art of living well lies in finding the balance between the two.

Early in life, I developed a habit that I've stuck to ever since. Every month, the moment my salary was credited, I'd set aside a portion—15, 20, sometimes even 30 per cent—into investments. The rest, I spent freely.

Saving gave me peace of mind for the future, while spending allowed me to enjoy the present. This small discipline shaped my approach to money. By automating my savings, I never even saw that money in my account—it was gone before I could even think about spending it. And because of that, I could enjoy the remainder guilt-free, knowing I had secured my future.

Over the years, I've seen both extremes: Those who save every rupee obsessively and those who spend recklessly without a thought for tomorrow. Neither finds real happiness. If you save too much, life becomes joyless. If you spend too much, unprepared emergencies can crush you. Balance isn't just ideal—it's essential.

—

Here's another truth about money: It doesn't change people—it amplifies who they already are.

Generous people become even more giving with wealth, while greedy ones become greedier. If someone is arrogant, money magnifies their arrogance. If someone is humble, it deepens their humility.

The real question isn't whether you have money; it's who you become when you do.

For me, wealth has always been a means to enable something bigger. It's a tool—to give back, to build opportunities, to create impact. Success isn't about accumulating wealth but finding purpose in how you use it.

—

At some point, you realize what truly matters. For me, that realization has always been about reputation and purpose.

Reputation is fragile. It isn't something you can buy or find a shortcut to; it's earned through every decision and every interaction. And it can vanish in an instant. It takes a lifetime to be seen as a good person, but one moment of greed—one misstep—and it can all disappear.

This understanding has become my moral compass. Whenever I'm faced with a tempting decision, I ask myself one simple question: Is it worth risking my reputation?

The answer is always no.

—

There's a moment in everyone's life when they ask, 'How much is enough?' That question shaped my values early on.

Yes, money is essential. It buys you a home, a car and the comforts of life. But beyond a point, chasing more becomes meaningless. I've had my indulgences. I love cars and I've picked up a few watches that have caught my eye. But even those desires are finite. They've never overshadowed what I believe money is truly for—serving my family and giving back to society.

For every material possession I've enjoyed, I've made sure to strike a balance. I've never let my wants interfere with my ability to contribute or help others. That's the line I've drawn for myself and it's what keeps me grounded.

In the end, money isn't the goal—it's the enabler. It amplifies your values and your choices. It reflects who you are and what you stand for.

For me, money has always been about creating a life of purpose, not accumulation. It's not just about what you have; it's about what you do with it.

The real wealth isn't in the numbers—it's in the impact you leave behind.

—

The alarm slices through the early morning quiet at exactly 5 a.m. I groggily reach for it, rubbing the sleep from my eyes as I step into the cool tiled floor of my Chennai home. The first order of business? Brushing my teeth and slipping into my tennis gear. But before the game begins, there's a ritual that cannot be skipped—brewing some fresh South Indian filter coffee.

By 5:25 a.m., like clockwork, Ananth bursts through the door with his signature, drawn-out greeting: 'Gooooooooodddd Mooooorrrrrnnnnning Boooooossssss!' His energy is both infectious and unnecessary at this hour, but I wouldn't have it any other way. We settle into our first cups of coffee, catching up on the happenings of the previous day—work, life, the occasional gossip.

By 5:50 a.m., we are out of the door, cruising towards Gandhi Nagar Club in Ananth's car. He heads for the badminton courts, while I step onto the sun-soaked tennis courts for two hours of pure, unfiltered joy of tennis, almost always partnering with my buddy Baskar. But here's the thing—while we all love the sport, it's the camaraderie that keeps us coming back. The friendly banter, the occasional heated debate over a line call, the running jokes that never get old—it's as much about the people as it is about the game. And, of course, the relentless Chennai heat, which drains you faster than any rally ever could. By 8 a.m., I'm exhausted but satisfied, ready to head home, shower, and tackle the workday ahead.

Weekends in Chennai, though, are something else entirely. They are sacred.

The core crew—Ananth, Vignesh (my younger brother from another mother), my ever-reliable physio Aparajith, and my cousin Balu—assemble without fail. Post-tennis, the gang goes for a sumptuous breakfast at Ratna Cafe before converging at my place, indulging in endless chatter and laughter. Then, as always, we head out for the morning show at Satyam Cinemas—a ritual as essential as the game itself. The real treat, though, awaits us at lunch: Shahib's legendary biryani, delivered steaming hot, paired with brinjal curry that is nothing short of divine.

Afternoons are reserved for lazing—sprawled in front of the TV, soaking in the lull of post-lunch satisfaction. By evening, it's time for one last round of rich, frothy filter coffee before we reluctantly part ways, already counting down the days to our next weekend reunion.

Chennai isn't just a city. It's the rhythm of these mornings, the warmth of familiar faces, the taste of a perfect biryani, and the comfort of knowing that no matter how much life changes, some traditions stay the same.

—

In the early days of Freshdesk, hiring for a tech start-up in India felt like climbing a mountain barefoot. In the Bay Area, finding specialists in digital marketing, brand management or DevOps was as simple as posting a job listing. In India? Just finding someone with any software marketing experience was a challenge. It wasn't just marketing—roles like RevOps, pre-sales and customer success barely existed in the local talent market.

The reality was clear: if we wanted a great team, we had to build it ourselves.

India's talent ecosystem had its quirks. Most students pursued engineering not out of passion but because it was expected. Campus interviews were filled with bright, ambitious graduates who didn't know what they truly wanted. A computer science major might hate coding, while a mechanical engineer had never imagined stepping onto a shop floor.

For many, their dreams were tied to the size of their first paycheck. A ₹9 lakh offer was 'a dream job.' And something much less, say, a ₹3 lakh offer? Just a stepping stone until a better one came along. I used to joke with students: 'Don't sell your dreams so cheap.'

But this dynamic also created an opportunity—to rethink how we hired.

From day one, we decided degrees didn't matter. What mattered was raw potential. We built teams around a few experienced 'anchors' and paired them with fresh graduates who had the right attitude and aptitude. A biotech engineer could excel in sales. A computer science graduate might find their calling in customer support. An MBA in operations management? Well, why not channel their creativity into content writing!

I often quoted a principle from *First, Break All the Rules* by Curt Coffman and Marcus Buckingham: 'You can't put in what God intentionally left out.' Instead of focusing on learned skills, we looked for inherent talent. Were they creative? Could they think on their feet? Did they have the patience and the empathy to navigate tough situations? Every role demanded a unique mix, and that's what we prioritized.

Sometimes, the talent we needed didn't fit neatly into traditional job descriptions. Early on, we expected designers to create stunning visuals and code them into HTML and CSS. This rare combination was hard to find, and we realized we were losing brilliant creative folks simply because they couldn't code. So, we split the role—letting designers focus purely on visuals while front-end developers handled the technical side.

One of our best designers at Zoho had come from *Kungumam*, a Tamil magazine. He didn't have web design experience, but his sense of colour and layout was impeccable. Paired with a skilled front-end coder, his designs transformed our product aesthetics. It wasn't an orthodox hire, but it was a brilliant one.

It wasn't just about hiring individuals—it was about building teams that complemented each other. If a sales superstar was terrible at following up on invoices, we didn't let that disqualify them. Instead, we paired them with someone meticulous about collections. By focusing on strengths rather than penalizing weaknesses, we created teams that thrived together.

What started as a necessity became one of Freshworks' greatest strengths. Instead of forcing people into rigid roles, we adapted roles to fit the talent we found.

The lesson is simple: God doesn't make people for job descriptions. If you're willing to look beyond degrees and résumés, to focus on what truly makes someone tick, you'll discover the potential others overlook. It's not the conventional way, but then again, building something extraordinary never is.

—

This isn't a new question. It has lingered in my thoughts for years.

I remember catching up with Gopal Srinivasan of TVS Capital sometime in 2017 or 2018. He looked at me with his characteristic calm yet piercing gaze and asked, 'What is Girish 2.0?'

I laughed, assuming it was a light-hearted jab, but he wasn't joking. 'What's next for you?' he pressed.

I didn't have an answer then. My world revolved around Freshworks—scaling it, solving one challenge after another, expanding into new markets. My mind was a maze of product launches, hiring decisions and funding rounds. The future? There wasn't room to think about it.

But Gopal wasn't asking about metrics or milestones. He wasn't talking about revenue targets or market share. He was asking about purpose. What do you want your life to stand for?

That question lodged itself in my mind, like an ember refusing to extinguish. Over time, it began to shape my thinking in ways I couldn't ignore.

—

India doesn't just need one Freshworks; it needs many.

That belief has been the north star guiding everything I've done—from building Freshworks to sharing our playbooks and helping other founders navigate the chaos of starting up. Success wasn't the goal in itself; it was the proof for something much bigger: That India could be a Product Nation.

When Freshworks grew from zero to $1 million, then $10 million and beyond, I started sharing our journey—not because we had all the answers, but because we had answers that worked for us. I wanted to show founders that building a global product company from India wasn't just a pipe dream. It was possible.

I spoke at events, mentored founders and shared Freshworks' story in its rawest form—the wins, the failures and the lessons we learned the hard way. My message was simple: We hadn't cracked a secret code. What we had done could be replicated, even improved.

But this wasn't just about building Freshworks. The real challenge lay in building the ecosystem around it.

In 2016, I spent months searching for a DevOps leader with SaaS experience. The result? Nothing. That expertise simply didn't exist in India.

And it wasn't just DevOps—it was the same gap in marketing. In the US, SaaS marketing had already evolved into nine distinct specializations—content creation, branding, demand generation, etc. In India, those roles were practically unicorns.

We weren't hiring talent; we were creating it. Product managers? Scarce. UI designers? Rare. Site reliability engineering? Non-existent. Customer success and revenue operations? They weren't even on the radar. Every role was a puzzle we had to solve from scratch.

What felt like challenges, though, turned out to be opportunities. Freshworks became a crucible—a training ground in which young professionals learned to engineer for scale, market for the world and craft products that could compete globally.

And it worked.

By 2018, one of our DevOps leaders—once part of that talent scarcity—was a keynote speaker at a major Bangalore conference. What we couldn't find, we nurtured into existence. Brick by brick, Freshworks built not just a company but a foundation for something far larger.

But this wasn't just about Freshworks. It was about proving that India could shed its image as a 'tech outsourcing nation'.

Sharad Sharma was the first to plant that seed. A relentless provocateur, he'd often say, 'We're not just a back office for the world. We can lead. We can innovate.'

Then came Avinash Raghava, who turned that vision into action. When I met him in our Freshdesk office in 2014, the place was pure chaos—laptops balanced on desks, chairs shoved into corners. Yet, within minutes, it was clear that Avinash wasn't just passionate about Product Nation—he was its heartbeat.

Initiatives like the NASSCOM Product Conclave and later SaaSBoomi emerged as more than just events; they became movements. Through platforms like iSPIRT's Playbook initiatives, founders like Suresh Sambandam, Pallav Nadhani, Krish Subramanian and Manav Garg came together, not as competitors but as collaborators. Together, they laid the groundwork for an ecosystem that lifted everyone higher.

—

At SaaSBoomi 2019, I stood on stage and shared a story that had been on my mind for years. I talked about Roger Bannister, the first person to break the four-minute mile—a feat once considered impossible. Yet, after Bannister did it, dozens of others followed. The barrier wasn't physical; it was psychological.

'Freshworks,' I said, 'is our Roger Bannister.'

It wasn't about Freshworks alone. It was about proving what was possible. If we could do it, anyone could. Freshworks wasn't the finish line—it was the starting gun.

The dream of a Product Nation wasn't born overnight. It was built by countless believers—Sharad, Avinash and so many others—who dared to imagine an India where global products aren't just made but lead the market.

Today, when I see founders scaling SaaS companies from India, I see the dream taking shape. What once felt impossible is now inevitable. And the best part? We're just getting started.

—

In the early days of Freshworks, I began writing small angel cheques. These weren't calculated investments or part of some grand strategy—they were acts of belief, simple gestures of support for founders chasing bold dreams. At the time, I didn't fully grasp the ripple effect those cheques would create.

But over the years, I've come to see that they weren't just about funding start-ups; they were sending signals.

I remember one start-up working on an innovative video platform. When the founders approached me, I initially said no. My plate was full and, frankly, I wasn't sure how much value I could add. But then something unexpected happened. A potential investor threw a curveball: 'Is Girish investing?'

That one question changed everything. The founders returned, their pitch now tinged with urgency. 'They're asking if you're in,' they said. Suddenly, it wasn't about the ₹10 lakh I eventually put in—it was about what that cheque represented. It wasn't just capital; it was a signal. A nod of confidence that said, 'This is worth betting on.' That ₹10 lakh unlocked $600,000 in additional funding. My investment didn't just fund their journey—it lit the path for others to follow.

In another instance, a scrappy founder running an events platform was hanging by a thread. A mutual connection reached out on his behalf, pleading his case. 'This guy is hustling hard,' they said. 'He just needs someone to believe in him.'

I hesitated. The odds didn't look great and I doubted what impact my small cheque could have. But their conviction nudged me forward and I wrote out that ₹10 lakh cheque. What happened next was extraordinary. Just two days later, that tiny act of belief sparked a chain reaction. The founder raised ₹2 crore through a crowdfunding platform.

In both cases, it wasn't the money that mattered—it was the message. Those investments were endorsements. They were a way of saying, 'I see you. I believe in you.' And, sometimes, that's all it takes to turn a flicker of hope into a blazing fire.

These moments taught me a profound lesson: The power of social capital. When a founder with a proven track record backs a start-up, it sends a ripple of legitimacy through the ecosystem. VCs pause. Other investors pay attention. Doors open.

But these experiences also revealed a gap. Writing small, isolated cheques could only go so far. If we wanted to build a true Product Nation, it would take more than scattered acts of belief. We needed a system—a platform where capital, conviction, expertise and operational guidance could converge to empower founders.

That realization planted the seeds for Together Fund.

This wasn't just about pooling money. It was about pooling belief. It was about creating an ecosystem where founders didn't just survive—they thrived.

When Manav Garg floated the idea of starting a fund together, it was the natural next step. Freshworks had shown us what was possible. Together Fund would make it repeatable.

—

Together Fund represents more than just investments—it's a philosophy. It's about leveraging the scars we've earned, the lessons we've learned and the networks we've built. It's about bridging the art of Indian entrepreneurship with the science of Silicon Valley scaling.

Freshworks proved what could be done. Together Fund is the movement that ensures it happens again and again.

When I see founders scaling SaaS companies from India today, I don't just see start-ups—I see a dream coming to life. It's no longer just a vision of a Product Nation. It's a belief that what once seemed impossible is now inevitable.

And, as I look to the future, I know we're only getting started. This isn't just about dreaming anymore. It's about building.

Together.

—

It all began with tiny specks of dust kicked up by tiny tots. Every Saturday, I'd take my younger son, Sanjay, to play football at a local centre in Adyar. The scene was chaotic but electric—eighty kids kicking up clouds of dust as they sprinted, tackled and chased the ball across a makeshift field. Parents perched on rickety benches, some chatting, others buried in their newspapers. The kids, oblivious to the grit in their lungs and the mud on their shoes, played with unrestrained joy.

It was inspiring and frustrating all at once. The raw talent was unmistakable, but so was the lack of infrastructure. It wasn't a pitch; it was a patchy field of mud and grass. Watching them, a single thought gnawed at me: Is this the best we can do?

Occasionally, the centre rented a natural grass field at SSN College. Those weekends felt like stepping into another world. The kids lit up as they darted across the immaculate pitch, their shoes gripping the grass with ease. Parents cheered from proper galleries, their claps ringing louder than usual. For a brief moment, football felt like it could be more than just a game.

On trips to the US, I'd see a stark contrast: Soccer fields at every school—neatly lined, perfectly maintained and, more often than not, empty. There it was: Infrastructure without players. And here we were: Players without infrastructure.

This wasn't just a disparity—it was an injustice. We are a country brimming with talent, but we expect our kids to rise despite the system, not because of it. And somehow, we accept that.

—

The football centre wasn't just a weekend programme. For some kids, it was their lifeline. I'll never forget the story of a boy scouted by a prestigious football academy. When his coaches encouraged him to seize the opportunity, he hesitated. 'This is my club,' he said. 'I'll stay here.'

His loyalty was moving, but it revealed a deeper issue: He didn't understand what he was giving up. The coaches at the centre saw his potential and couldn't let it go to waste. What started as a recreational programme soon evolved into an elite training initiative. They rented an apartment in Thiruvanmiyur, housed a small group of talented boys and began daily training.

—

But growth came with challenges. Competing in the I-League, even at the junior level, required substantial resources. Each match cost around ₹50,000 to cover essentials like ground rentals, feeding players and referee fees. When the coaches called a meeting with parents, hoping for volunteers to help with tasks like arranging sandwiches or transporting referees, the response was silence. Everyone was juggling their own responsibilities and was stretched thin.

Recognizing the need, I immediately transferred the money required for that season to the club's bank account and shared a suggestion with the parents. 'Think of this as a school,' I said. 'Just as we invest in our children's education, we can contribute here to support their growth.' That moment wasn't about finding immediate solutions but about reinforcing a shared belief: If we wanted these kids to thrive, it would take collective support and commitment to the dream.

—

The passion of the coaches was infectious. They weren't just running a football programme—they were nurturing dreams. They arranged housing for players, ensured they were fed and educated, and devoted themselves entirely to training these young athletes. Watching their dedication, I couldn't help but wonder: What if we could do more?

In 2018, we took the next step. A public charitable trust was established and FC Madras was officially launched. We installed turf on a rented plot in Thoraipakkam and entered teams in the U-13 and U-15 I-League junior divisions. That very season, we became Chennai Zone champions.

Then came 2020. The pandemic forced our facilities to shut down, sending the kids home. Those two years became a time for reflection. When the world reopened, it was clear that restarting wasn't enough. We needed to reimagine and rebuild.

—

By 2021, the vision had crystallized. A 23-acre plot in Mahabalipuram became the foundation for something extraordinary. What had been a barren watermelon field was transformed into a world-class, ₹100 crore football academy. It took years of planning, effort and careful investment to bring this vision to life.

Today, FC Madras symbolizes what's possible when bold dreams meet unwavering commitment. The academy now boasts of three FIFAapproved pitches, cutting-edge training and rehab facilities, and a residential programme for sixty-one footballers from fourteen states. Our rigorous selection process is rooted in merit, not privilege, ensuring that opportunity is accessible to all. Every trainee benefits from a scholarship that covers their education, living expenses and football training.

But FC Madras isn't just about football—it's about shaping lives. Trainees follow the NIOS curriculum, balancing education with their passion for the game. Life skills are taught alongside football drills, preparing them to excel both on the field and in life.

—

FC Madras reminds me of Freshworks in its early days. Back then, people doubted us, dismissed us and said building a global SaaS company from Chennai was impossible. But we proved them wrong. FC Madras is on a similar journey—starting with a dream and building something extraordinary, step by step.

To make this vision a reality, I've been fortunate to work with experts like C.K.M. Dhananjai, Abhishek Yadav and Venkatesh Shanmugam. These are people who understand what it takes to create something world-class. My role has been to provide support and ensure they have the resources they need to succeed.

This isn't just a project—it's a mission. India has always had the talent. What's been missing is the infrastructure, belief and systems to nurture it. FC Madras is our answer to that gap.

I often think of Pullela Gopichand, who mortgaged his house to build an academy that produced Olympic medallists. Like him, I believe in dreaming in instalments. If India's football journey begins with breaking into the top five in Asia, that's a worthy start.

Every big dream begins with a single step. For FC Madras, that step has been taken. The road ahead is waiting.

—

Gopal Srinivasan's question—'What is Girish 2.0?'—stayed with me, not because it demanded an immediate answer, but because it invited reflection.

At the time, I didn't have a clear response. I was consumed with Freshworks—its growth, its challenges, its promise. But Gopal's question pierced through the noise, forcing me to look beyond the day-to-day.

'What do you want your life to stand for?'

Years later, I finally have an answer. G2.0 isn't just about scaling companies or building ecosystems. It's about being a catalyst—a spark that helps unlock the immense potential of India's talent. It's about creating opportunities for those who are waiting for their moment to shine.

From SaaSBoomi to Together Fund to FC Madras, every initiative I've been part of connects back to this purpose. They're not isolated efforts—they're chapters in the same story. A story about transforming belief into action, ideas into movements and dreams into realities.

India doesn't just need one Freshworks; it needs many. It doesn't need one Gopichand academy; it needs dozens. The dream of a Product Nation or a world-class football academy isn't built overnight. It takes years of dedication, a community of believers and the courage to push through setbacks.

G2.0 is my way of answering Gopal's question—not with words, but with action. It's about proving that what seems impossible isn't.

Sometimes, all it takes is a dusty field, a coach who believes or a small act of trust. But when those moments align, they can spark something extraordinary.

This isn't the end of the journey—it's just the beginning. We've broken barriers, but the road ahead is long. Together, we can dream bigger, build stronger and create a future where India's talent shines on the world stage.

The best is yet to come.

Acknowledgements

THIS book began long before its first word was written. It started in countless conversations, interviews and observations over the years—of the founders who dared to dream, fought through uncertainty and built something from nothing. Among them, Girish Mathrubootham's journey has been one of the most compelling to follow.

I still remember writing 'The Making of Girish Mathrubootham', a long-form story for FactorDaily. It was an intimate look at a founder who had taken the unconventional path, betting on a SaaS company out of Chennai when few believed it could be done. That story became a launchpad for what you hold in your hands now: This book.

For over two decades, I have tracked and written about founders' journeys, struggles and wins—watching them take crazy risks, push through crushing failures and build companies with sheer grit. But it wasn't until I became an entrepreneur myself that I truly understood what it takes. Reporting on and analysing start-ups is one thing; carrying the burden of each decision every single day and living the entrepreneurial life is an entirely different matter.

Entrepreneurship is often glorified, but the truth is, it's built on the backs of people who rarely get acknowledged: the first employees, the founding team, and the ones who take a leap of faith, work brutal hours and sweat through the chaos of figuring things out. They don't get the spotlight, the big headlines or the valuation hype. But they are the foundation. They are the ones who turn a founder's vision into something real.

And then there are the families and friends of founders—who hold things steady while everything else is uncertain, absorb the stress, pick up the slack at home, and remind the founders that they are more than their companies. These support systems are often overlooked in the noise of start-up culture.

I've also seen a different kind of hustle—the young, first-time founders who land in Bangalore with eyes filled with dreams, much like hopefuls stepping into Mumbai chasing Bollywood stardom. They have the same hunger and relentless drive. Some make it, some don't, but all of them deserve an honest account of what it really takes.

That's what I hope this book contributes to. Not just another success story but an honest, unfiltered look at the journey. Because if we are to enrich India's entrepreneurial literature, we have to stop telling sanitized stories—and start talking about the struggle, the doubt, the unseen sacrifices.

I can still picture Girish in a room full of founders and start-up teams, walking them through his journey from $1 million to $5 million in revenue. There were no filters, no jargon—just real talk. He laid it all out—what worked, what flopped, and what he wished he had known earlier. Those sessions, that openness, shaped the early DNA of Indian SaaS.

By sharing his struggles, failures, and early life, Girish has made this story feel human, not heroic. We need more founders to do the same—to humanize entrepreneurship rather than just celebrate its outcomes.

To Girish for trusting me with his story, the founders who have opened up their lives to me over the years, the first employees, the families and the friends who make these journeys possible—this book is for you.

I'm grateful to the SaaSBoomi community of founders, curated by Avinash Raghava and others, who have helped me see Girish's journey through different lenses over the years—giving me the perspective to make sense of it all. A special thanks to Vignesh 'Body' Vijayakumar, the walking, breathing library of Freshworks and Girish's journey—always ready with the exact anecdote or detail whenever I needed it. This book wouldn't have been possible without the behind-the-scenes contributions of Sanjay Gupta, who helped sharpen the edits, and Abhishek Jha, who meticulously organized conversations and research.

I'd like to thank my literary agent, Anish Chandy of Labyrinth Literary Agency, for his relentless push to chronicle Girish's journey and for believing this story needed to be told. And to the good folks at HarperCollins—Sachin Sharma, Shreya Lall and the entire team—for pulling off what felt like a miracle, turning a manuscript into a book on a timeline that defied all logic.

—Pankaj Mishra

About the Authors

Girish Mathrubootham is the founder and executive chairman of Freshworks, the first Indian SaaS company to be listed on the Nasdaq. A champion of founders and product builders, Girish has invested in over sixty start-ups, co-founded Together Fund, India's first operator-led venture capital firm founded to empower India's SaaS entrepreneurs, and played a key role in shaping India's SaaS ecosystem through SaaSBoomi. Beyond tech, he has founded FC Madras, a grassroots football club nurturing young talent in Chennai.

Pankaj Mishra, journalist and co-founder of FactorDaily, has spent over two decades telling stories that create deep, personal connections. His podcast, *Outliers*, evolved into his bestselling book, *Against the Grain*. Whether it is print, digital or audio communication, or even a random conversation on a train journey, Mishra believes 'even one is an audience', cherishing every reader and listener along the way.

HarperCollins *Publishers* India

At HarperCollins India, we believe in telling the best stories and finding the widest readership for our books in every format possible. We started publishing in 1992; a great deal has changed since then, but what has remained constant is the passion with which our authors write their books, the love with which readers receive them, and the sheer joy and excitement that we as publishers feel in being a part of the publishing process.

Over the years, we've had the pleasure of publishing some of the finest writing from the subcontinent and around the world, including several award-winning titles and some of the biggest bestsellers in India's publishing history. But nothing has meant more to us than the fact that millions of people have read the books we published, and that somewhere, a book of ours might have made a difference.

As we look to the future, we go back to that one word—a word which has been a driving force for us all these years.

Read.

Harper Collins · 4th · HARPER FICTION · HARPER NON-FICTION · HARPER BUSINESS · HCCB HARPERCOLLINS CHILDREN'S BOOKS

HARPER DESIGN · Harper Sport · HARPER PERENNIAL · HARPER VANTAGE · हार्पर हिन्दी